ADOLESCENT SEXUALITY

ADVANCES IN ADOLESCENT DEVELOPMENT:

AN ANNUAL BOOK SERIES

Series Editors
Gerald R. Adams, *University of Guelph, Ontario, Canada*
Raymond Montemayor, *The Ohio State University*
Thomas P. Gullotta, *Child and Family Agency, Connecticut*

Advances in Adolescent Development is an annual book series designed to analyze, integrate, and critique an abundance of new research and literature in the field of adolescent development. Contributors are selected from numerous disciplines based on their creative, analytic, and influential scholarship in order to provide information pertinent to professionals as well as upper-division and graduate students. The Series Editors' goals are to evaluate the current empirical and theoretical knowledge about adolescence, and to encourage the formulation (or expansion) of new directions in research and theory development.

Volumes in This Series

ADOLESCENT SEXUALITY

Edited by
THOMAS P. GULLOTTA
GERALD R. ADAMS
RAYMOND MONTEMAYOR

ADVANCES IN ADOLESCENT DEVELOPMENT
An Annual Book Series Volume 5

SAGE PUBLICATIONS
International Educational and Professional Publisher
Newbury Park London New Delhi

For information address:

 SAGE Publications, Inc.
2455 Teller Road
Newbury Park, California 91320

SAGE Publications Ltd.
6 Bonhill Street
London EC2A 4PU
United Kingdom

SAGE Publications India Pvt. Ltd.
M-32 Market
Greater Kailash I
New Delhi 110 048 India

Printed in the United States of America

Library of Congress: 90-657291

ISSN   1050-8589
ISBN   0-8039-4772-0 (cl.)
ISBN   0-8039-4773-9 (pbk.)

93   94   95   96   10   9   8   7   6   5   4   3   2   1

Sage Production Editor: Tara S. Mead

Contents

Preface

As I write this preface, the United States recorded its two hundred thousandth AIDS sufferer. Other sexually transmitted diseases, such as chlamydia and gonorrhea, continue to spread among adolescents at rates that should generate not merely the expression of concern but action. As in past years, more than 1 million adolescents will become pregnant this year, and roughly 46% of these young women will deliver. Ninety-five percent of those children will continue to live with their child-mother—most in poverty.

I share this sobering information not because I lament for yesteryear, but because as a society we are capable of doing so much more to reduce the incidence of these behaviors and to encourage responsible decision making. As the reader will soon discover from reading the first chapter (on the history of adolescent sexuality), the past was not innocent or devoid of sexually exploited youth. Nor was it any kinder in its understanding of homosexuals or women than it is today. Indeed, if it is possible for a nation to possess collectively a dysfunctional irrational fear, then the United States could be said to suffer from mindless "sexophobia." How else can one explain the barrage of titillation and sexual innuendo available for consumption on television, the radio, and in the print media? How else can we understand a culture that embraces the erotic but rejects responsibility? How else can we understand a culture that is enamored with the body but forgets the meaning? How else can we understand a culture that advertises ecstasy but denies safety?

Humans are sexual beings. Women are sexual beings. Men are sexual beings. Adolescents are sexual beings. Children are sexual beings. These statements cannot be avoided. They cannot be suppressed. They can, however, be ignored, and in this ignorance we entice our youth to repeat the errors of the previous generation.

It was with these thoughts in mind that this volume was organized. It was our intention to provide scholars, practitioners, and

students with a comprehensive overview of adolescent sexuality.
From history (Chapter 1) to anatomy (Chapter 2), statistical data
(Chapter 3) to understanding homosexuality (Chapter 4) and adolescent parenting (Chapter 5) to aberrant sexual experiences (Chapter 6) and sexually transmitted diseases (Chapter 7), this volume
was written to provide the most current information available. It is
my hope that these chapters and the last (Chapter 8), which reviews
previous efforts at promoting sexual responsibility, will be used to
lift the veil of ignorance around this subject matter.

—THOMAS P. GULLOTTA
Child and Family Agency,
New London, Connecticut

1. Historical and Theoretical Perspectives on Adolescent Sexuality: An Overview

A. Chris Downs
Lisa Scarborough Hillje
University of Houston at Clear Lake

Historical and theoretical accounts of adolescent sexuality are both like huge, incomplete jigsaw puzzles. The successful assembly of a jigsaw puzzle is a function of the puzzle itself and of the persons working on it. Factors inherent in the puzzle include the number, shapes, and availability of the pieces and the complexity and coherence of the picture the puzzle represents. The puzzle solver's degree of success is a result of access to the pieces, strategy in linking compatible pieces, availability of a pictorial representation of the entire puzzle, and recognition of the puzzle's delimiters—the edges. In the present analogy the edges represent, for both history and theory, the generally agreed-upon nature of adolescent sexuality.

Historians attempt to assemble a portrait of adolescent sexuality from prehistory to the present. Theorists suggest causal relationships among variables believed to be critical to adolescent sexuality. Neither approach has completed its undertaking. Although both perspectives seem to agree on the *nature* of adolescent sexuality, it is with reference to the *scope* of the phenomenon that the perspectives fail. Indeed, historians and theorists have joined the edge

AUTHORS' NOTE: Book-length expositions could be written on either historical or theoretical perspectives on adolescent sexuality. This overview, of necessity, omits detailed descriptions of large bodies of existing scholarship. To those historians, authors, and theorists whose work or reviews were omitted or mentioned only briefly, we extend our apologies. Our hope is that this overview will stimulate subsequent reviews and more thorough analyses of the perspectives offered here. The authors gratefully acknowledge the comments and advice of Eric S. Hillje in the preparation of this work. The chapter is dedicated to the second author's daughters, Tonya and Melissa Scarborough.

pieces of their puzzles and thereby have demarcated the nature of their respective inquiries. Unfortunately, the interiors of the puzzles, the complex historical and theoretical details of adolescent sexuality, remain in disarray.

THE NATURE AND SCOPE
OF ADOLESCENT SEXUALITY

The *nature* of adolescent sexuality is probably a universal given. Historians, theorists, and researchers—across historical eras, cultures, and interpretive biases—seem to agree on two aspects of the nature of adolescent sexuality. First, adolescents are curious about their own and others' sexual selves (e.g., Chang, 1991; Endleman, 1989; Fowkes, 1991; Hall, 1904). Second, most adolescents experience sexually related physical events such as menarche, spermarche, and hormone changes (e.g., Chang, 1991; Downs, 1990; Hall, 1904; Sorensen, 1973).

It is with the *scope* of adolescent sexuality that both theories and histories are divergent, contradictory, and inconclusive. Indeed, when parsed into specific elements, the scope of adolescent sexuality becomes a vast, multifaceted array of issues for any historian or theorist. A scan of recent adolescent development texts (e.g., Adams & Gullotta, 1989; Dusek, 1991) collectively cite all of the following as part of the scope of adolescent sexuality: dating/puberty rituals; hormone fluctuations; individual differences; masturbation; contraception; sexual decision making; sex roles; desired/undesired pregnancy; abortion; adoption; adolescent parents; sex versus degrees of love; sexual orientation; sexual experimentation; maladaptive reactions to sexual experiences; sexual attractiveness; physical/sexual attributes; sex in relation to marital status; sexual victimization; media- and zeitgeist-driven influences; sexually associated diseases; sex education; the role of socializers in sexual control and expression; and ethnic, socioeconomic status (SES), religious, and demographic factors affecting adolescent sexual activity.

In sum, Confucius (1976), Plato (1956), Hall (1904), Hollingworth (1928), A. Freud (1948), and Dusek (1991) would all agree on the basic nature of adolescent sexuality. Nonetheless, they would define the scope, both historically and theoretically, in different ways.

HISTORICAL PERSPECTIVES

Historical accounts of adolescent sexuality are found in general histories of human sexuality (e.g., Margulis & Sagan, 1991; Symons, 1979) and in reviews of the history of the overall treatment of children and adolescents (e.g., Aries, 1962; Borstelmann, 1983; de Mause, 1974; Demos & Demos, 1969; Elder, 1974; Hall, 1904; Hollingworth, 1928; Kessen, 1965; Kett, 1977; Kiell, 1967). The interface of human sexuality and historical treatment of adolescents includes a sizable number of reports, each varying in eras and topics reviewed (Baizerman, Thompson, & Stafford-White, 1979; Darling, Kallen, & Van Dusen, 1984; Kirkendall, 1965; McCabe, 1984; McKinley, 1980; Smigel & Seiden, 1968; Vincent, 1961; Washington, 1982; Weatherley, 1987).

All historical accounts of adolescents are limited in some respects. Evidence from prehistoric eras is scant (e.g., Wenke, 1990). Once humans began writing, multiple factors obscured the veracity of their reports: The motives, idiosyncracies, and cultures of the authors weighed heavily in descriptions of adolescents; many of the earliest writings were lost or were authored by persons relaying the views of others (e.g., *The Analects of Confucius*); and most of the authors (e.g., Plato) had high or unusual levels of education (e.g., Boswell, 1980). When writing became widespread, religious and sociopolitical climates often obfuscated accounts of adolescents. In the nineteenth and twentieth centuries, authors began systematic efforts to understand the history of adolescent sexuality. Even these, however, contained interpretive and moral biases.

Compounding the difficulties listed above is the fact that most historical information emanates from Greco-Roman, Western, Judeo-Christian, Caucasian, heterosexual, and male sources. Biases from these sources became obvious during the twentieth century when theorists considered the universality, historical continuity, and cross-cultural aspects of adolescent sexuality (e.g., S. Freud, 1965; Hall, 1904). Scrutiny of non-Western, non-Caucasian, and non-Judeo-Christian cultures confirmed the biases extant in Western literature (e.g., Benedict, 1938; Boswell, 1980; Broude, 1976; Duberman, 1991; Eisler, 1987; Endleman, 1989; Fisher, 1979; Kiell, 1967; Luckey & Nass, 1969; Margulis & Sagan, 1991; Mead, 1950, 1953; Morton, 1980; Sansom, 1963; Washington, 1982; Watson, 1989; Wenke, 1990). Consequently, the historical overview of adolescent sexuality presented here will be brief and cautious. It will become apparent rapidly that the only common themes involve the nature, not the scope, of adolescent sexuality.

Prehistory

Healthy, adaptive adolescent sexuality would seem to promote survival during human evolution (e.g., Darwin, 1859; Margulis & Sagan, 1991). Over roughly 5 million years of human prehistory, specific developments pertaining to adolescents seem to have occurred. At puberty, girls began a cycle of menstruation that was, unlike the estrus of other species, relatively independent of sexual activity (Wenke, 1990). Thus adolescents could engage in sex on an as-desired (rather than periodic) basis. Moreover, adolescent girls became the only members of any species whose breasts enlarged during puberty rather than only during pregnancy. Adolescent males' penises grew larger than those of other primates, and both sexes lost most of their body hair compared with other primates (Wenke, 1990); the significance of these two developments is the focus of much scholarly debate (e.g., Margulis & Sagan, 1991).

The human life span was short during prehistory, with few individuals living past age 40 (Wenke, 1990). The brevity of life after puberty very likely had important consequences: Competition among adolescent males for sexual partners was high (Symons, 1979); females' sexual attractiveness became a factor in the number and type of males who approached them (Symons, 1979); many groups, especially in the late Pleistocene epoch, celebrated fertility and pregnancy via art (Wenke, 1990); and cave drawings, which often depicted sexual organs and acts, may have encouraged or recorded sexual activity among postpubertal humans (Fisher, 1979; Wenke, 1990).

Several authors have suggested that prehistoric adolescent males preferred varied sexual partners and practices (e.g., Symons, 1979). Indeed, "human mating patterns have been primarily polygamous for millions of years" (Wenke, 1990, p. 110), especially when cultures were androcentric (Symons, 1979). Eisler (1987) has argued, however, that artifacts recovered from the Paleolithic era indicate that some early religious beliefs emphasized female deities and sex-role parity.

Late in prehistory, increasingly complex chiefdoms, states, and empires emerged, with parallel developments in religions. Apparently, as groups grew more complex, "religious cults that all early states developed . . . [became] a device for social control" (Wenke, 1990, p. 308). Social/religious control very likely affected aspects of adolescent sexuality. Goddess-centered states found in Minoan Crete (c. 6000 B.C.) and in old Europe (c. 5000 B.C.) fostered egalitarian sex-typed roles among adolescents (Eisler, 1987). Early Andean groups (c. 10000-3000 B.C.?) encouraged a variety of sexual practices, including multipartner adolescent sexual expression (Wenke, 1990). In Babylon (c. 5000 B.C.), adolescent fertility was a common art theme, and Sumerian (c. 3000 B.C.) children and adolescents received formal education that included instruction on sexual issues (Wenke, 1990).

In sum, archaeological evidence suggests that concern over adolescent sexuality was prevalent as humans evolved; however, this evidence is almost entirely speculative (e.g., de Lumley, 1991; Wenke, 1990). Speculations about prehistoric adolescent sexuality based on minute data sets are precarious without convergent evidence from other sources. An alternative window for studying prehistoric adolescents could involve ethological research on recent or current "primitive" peoples who have maintained long-term sociocultural continuity (e.g., Endleman, 1989; Wenke, 1990). These peoples would most closely resemble ancestors from the Paleolithic era (Wenke, 1990). Endleman (1989) offers a transcultural point of view wherein developmental patterns of basic sexual characteristics are universal across cultures and epochs. He suggests that "*variable* across cultures are the *details* of how the [sexual] drives . . . are worked out and expressed" (p. 6, emphasis in original). His view is consistent with the notion that prehistoric adolescent sexuality was stable in nature, but not in scope, over human evolution.

A broad sampling of recent and existing primitive peoples underscores both the consistency in nature and inconsistency in scope of transcultural perspectives on adolescent sexual phenomena (e.g., Benedict, 1938, 1950; Endleman, 1989; Ford & Beach, 1951; Gregor, 1985; Hall, 1904; Herdt, 1981; Howitt, 1904; Knauft, 1986; LeVine, 1970; Linden, 1991; Mead, 1950, 1953; Schuster, 1979). In every culture examined, interest in adolescent sexual curiosity and puberty-based physical changes was observed, at least indirectly. In contrast, variability in dealing with *other* elements of adolescent sexuality was dramatic. For instance, though many groups held puberty rituals, these rituals varied in focus (on girls, boys, or both), mood (cruelty to mere acknowledgement), timing (early to late adolescence), and social outcome (e.g., the adolescent becomes an adult or a temporary outcast). Marital arrangements also varied widely, including types (polygyny; polyandry; and lifetime, temporary, or serial monogamy), arrangement (prearrangement, freedom of selection, or no arrangement), and sexual latitude (premarital, nonmarital, extramarital, or strictly marital sex allowed). Furthermore, conceptions of adolescent love, affection, and intimacy shifted dramatically from culture to culture.

On the basis of studies of primitive peoples, coupled with the available archaeological evidence (e.g., Eisler, 1987; Fisher, 1979; Wenke, 1990) and Endleman's (1989) transcultural views of sexuality, we would speculate with caution that prehistoric humans recognized adolescent curiosity and physical/pubertal events. It appears, however, that as each group acquired new skills, belief systems, and knowledge of other groups, their customs concerning collateral elements of adolescent sexuality evolved in ways that probably best served the group.

Ancient History

According to Hall (1904), adolescence "was better understood in Ancient Greece and Rome than now" (Vol. 1, p. xviii). He may have been correct when comparing 1900 with some views from ancient history. Hall offered glowing accounts of Greek philosophers and adolescent males; unfortunately, Hall emphasized *selected* elements of ancient history, probably for moralistic reasons. For instance, he described Spartan adolescent nudity as part of a required health inspection, not as an aspect of sexuality. An in-depth review of ancient views of adolescent sexuality is beyond the limits of this chapter, and interested readers are urged to consider Boswell's (1980) and Gies and Gies's (1989) scholarly analyses.

Hall may have been selective in reviewing ancient writings and cultures for the same reason writers often do so today: Ancient views of adolescent sexuality sometimes shock contemporary readers. Below, we will review briefly the Greco-Roman/male perspectives and then turn to the other ancient perspectives about which knowledge has surfaced during the twentieth century.

Plato (1956) and his educated peers found adolescent *boys'* sexual curiosity, nudity, and experimental affection with both sexes perfectly natural. Scholars of the era openly discussed menstruation, masturbation, and sexual development. As Roman power eclipsed that of the Greeks (c. 150 B.C.), androcentric views of adolescence intensified. Rome was almost entirely male centered, with noble-born adolescent males permitted free sexual expression. In contrast, both adolescent girls and slave boys frequently were forced into prostitution (Gies & Gies, 1989). When Rome fell and predominantly Germanic tribes came into power, sexual victimization of (especially female) adolescents increased, despite the growing influence of the Christian church. As Gies and Gies (1989) report, "Barbarians and Romans gave men sexual freedom; the Church refused it to them. All in unison denied it to women" (p. 42).

Whereas Greek, Roman, and "barbarian" states took an increasingly androcentric approach to adolescent sexuality, numerous other civilizations existed, flourished, and viewed adolescence in their own unique ways. Although Egyptian dynasties existed for centuries (c. 3100-343 B.C.), little is known about Egyptian treatment of adolescent sexuality. Curiously, one of Egypt's most famous pharaohs, Tutankhamen, was an adolescent. Also in the Middle East, ancient Jewish traditions outlined strict laws governing adolescent sexuality and established rigid, male-centered puberty and marriage rites. Moreover, the burning of Alexandria's library—the great storehouse of transcultural knowledge—around A.D. 415 probably destroyed vast numbers of written records on ancient perspectives of adolescents (e.g., Sagan, 1980).

During the first century A.D., both Buddhism and Hinduism flourished in India, and a rigid, four-level caste system had been in place for about 900 years (Watson, 1989). During this time, Vatsyayana wrote the *Kama Sutra*, which portrays "a total absence of guilt" concerning sexual matters (Fowkes, 1991, p. 10). Indeed, with the single restriction of marriage within caste, there was a profound appreciation for adolescent sexual expression. Moreover, "adolescent girls had respected status" during this period; forced child marriages were instituted beginning in the twelfth century A.D. (Watson, 1989, p. 31).

Ancient Chinese views of adolescent sexuality probably underwent significant changes during the period from 570 B.C. to A.D. 850. The Taoism of Lao Tzu, the Mozi of Mo Tzu, and the teachings of Confucius all began in China between 570 B.C. and 391 B.C. Whereas Mozi embraced universal love among persons of all ages, the Tao offered specific sexual instructions for adolescents (Chang, 1991; Morton, 1980; van Gulik, 1974). For instance, Taoism discussed adolescent boys' problems with premature ejaculation, the importance of adolescent girls' orgasms, and variations in the sizes of genitals. Confucianism took a more cautious approach to sex; for example, Confucius (1976) reportedly said that "there are . . . impulses [against] which the nobler sort of man is on guard. In the period of youth . . . he guards against lustfulness" (p. 89). As Buddhism (c. A.D. 150) and Zen Buddhism (c. A.D. 850) blended with the earlier religions, Chinese views of adolescent sexual expression became far more restrictive (Morton, 1980).

Although Native Americans probably lived in the Western Hemisphere for at least 12,000 years, only the encouragement of open adolescent sexual expression among the Andean peoples seems known from this ancient period (Wenke, 1990). Similarly, though there were large, established states in Africa (outside of Egypt) during ancient history, little is known concerning their treatment of adolescent sexuality.

In sum, the nature of adolescent sexuality was observed commonly during ancient history: Adolescents showed curiosity and experienced physical/sexual events. The known cultures took different approaches to the scope of this sexuality, from relative degrees of free adolescent sexual expression (e.g., the Andean and Taoist views) to androcentric approaches (e.g., the Greco-Roman and barbarian views) to varying levels of strictness regarding sexuality (e.g., the Confucian and Jewish traditions). Parenthetically, *early* Christian doctrines were quite liberal concerning (especially male) adolescent sexual behavior and actively promoted conceptions of love. It wasn't until the fourteenth century in Europe that Christianity developed strict regulations governing adolescent sexuality (Boswell, 1980). The attitudes and customs regarding adolescent sexuality among many (if not most) ancient cultures are unknown presently, partly because of the loss of the library at Alexandria. We would conclude that adolescent curiosity and physical/sexual events probably were observed and acknowledged worldwide. Cultural approaches to this sexuality probably varied with the prevailing zeitgeist, traditions, myths, religions, and sociopolitical needs of each culture.

The Dark Ages to the Renaissance

Knowledge of the treatment of adolescent sexuality from about A.D. 500 to A.D. 1600 typically has been dominated by information on Western societies. Recently, attention has been directed toward both Western and a few non-Western societies.

In the early Christian church, few restrictions were placed on adolescent boys' sexual expressions. For instance, Kiell (1967) cites passages from St. Augustine's writings that mirror descriptions of adolescent boys today, including mention of sexual curiosity and body changes. Moreover, although writers differ in their views of the overall treatment of children and adolescents from A.D. 500 to A.D. 1600 (Aries, 1962; de Mause, 1974; Gies & Gies, 1989), there is little question that Christian approaches to adolescent sexuality changed gradually over the centuries toward androcentric, hetero-sexist, and misogynist dogma. Around the sixth century, church "penitentials" were dispersed to govern the sexual conduct of clergy. Parishioners were encouraged to follow these same rules, but probably did not do so (Gies & Gies, 1989). The penitentials specified sex only at certain times of the year and were exclusive to heterosexual marriages. Penalties for other activities, ranging from kissing to oral sex, were severe. Interestingly, prostitution and contraception were not addressed in these guidelines (Gies & Gies, 1989).

Evolving Anglo-Saxon laws probably more closely capture actual adolescent sexual practices before A.D. 1000. Free adolescent males (in contrast with females and slave males) were allowed great latitude in sexual expression, including extramarital sex, homosexual encounters, and having to pay only token monetary or property claims for sexual victimization of others (e.g., rape) (Boswell, 1980; Gies & Gies, 1989). Moreover, adolescent prostitution was common throughout the period, although attempts were made by Charlemagne in A.D. 800 to curb the practice (Boswell, 1980; Gies & Gies, 1989). Even as late as the early 1600s, both the church and the various states solicited funds to maintain, build, and tax brothels and allowed procurers (the forerunners of modern pimps) to seek customers (Otis, 1985). Goodich (1985) notes that the sexual victimization of adolescent girls (typically from the lower classes) was brutal, even in the relatively "enlightened" Renaissance cities of Florence and Venice.

Adolescent girls during the High Middle Ages in Europe had limited sexual freedom and encountered gross sexual victimization. Adolescent boys, especially those from wealthy families, had fewer sexual prohibitions (e.g., Boswell, 1980; Gies & Gies, 1989). For instance, Gies and Gies (1989) note that from A.D. 1000 to A.D. 1300 in Europe, "ordinary sex outside marriage was constrained by rigid but liberal restrictions. For a young bachelor to keep a . . . mistress . . . until he was ready for marriage was not only tolerated but expected" (p. 154). Abortion, infanticide, and (usually ineffective forms of) contraception were also widespread during much of the period. In addition, courtship rites became formal and androcentric. For example, arranged marriages for 14-year-old girls were common, but their husbands were often 10 to 15 years older than they were. Gies and Gies (1989) note that most betrothals among adolescents from wealthier families involved property exchanges. Adolescents from poor families, who could not afford such exchanges, may have been more likely to base their marriages on affection.

During the late Middle Ages, dramatic changes occurred in church and state doctrines governing adolescent sexuality. The Black Death, or plague (beginning c. 1347-1351), led to the lowering of the age when adolescents could marry, with the belief that earlier marriages would produce greater numbers of offspring and thereby replenish the large numbers of plague victims (e.g., Gies & Gies, 1989). The church also sought greater social control over parishioners during this time. These needs led to restrictive measures governing adolescent sexuality, including bans on premarital sex, homosexuality, masturbation, abortion, and contraception (Boswell, 1980). Other evidence reveals the church's role in exerting social control over sexual norms: The first systematic persecution of sexual nonconformists and banning of parishioners from direct access to the Bible occurred contemporaneously with the plague (e.g., Boswell, 1980; Rowse, 1983). Hall (1904) correctly notes that religious-based pubertal ceremonies grew in popularity during this time, but his speculation that chivalry encouraged purer adolescent personal lives is not supported (Boswell, 1980). Generally, the late Middle Ages in Europe were a time of extraordinary sexual victimization of (especially female) adolescents, of war, of religious persecution, and of a plague that reduced the population of some parts of Europe by 65%. Abuse of adolescents was exacerbated by the facts that (a) adolescents had to work alongside adult laborers against whom they had little protection concerning unwanted sexual overtures, and (b) adolescent sexual experimentation with peers of either sex led to severe penalties, including burning at the stake for heresy (e.g., Boswell, 1980). Little else is known about the worldwide treatment of adolescent sexuality during the Dark and Middle Ages. Hall (1904) underscores this point: "No study of adolescence can be complete without some study of nearly one-third of the human race, occupying two-fifths of the land surface of the globe" (Vol. 2, p. 648). We believe Hall's estimates of unknown peoples were extremely conservative. There are some data, however, from other cultures that suggest that as civilizations became more complex, their religious and legal approaches to adolescents became more androcentric, punitive, and restrictive. Islam emerged (c. A.D. 632) and spread widely as a polygamous, androcentric religion. Islamic adolescent girls frequently were subjected to sexual abuse and forced into early marriages and divorces (e.g., Fowkes, 1991; Wenke, 1990). The earlier, relatively enlightened practices of India, China, and Japan also grew androcentric and harsh with respect to adolescent girls (e.g., Chang, 1991; Fowkes, 1991; Morton, 1980; Sansom, 1963). In India, for example, the earlier sexual freedoms were replaced by strict child marriages and prohibitions against many sexual behaviors prior to marriage. In Japan late in the Middle Ages, the sexes were separated at age 7, marriages were arranged, and both younger and female offspring frequently were abandoned or sold into various labors, including prostitution (Sansom, 1963).

A parallel increase in androcentrism has been discovered in the Inca and Aztec civilizations in the Western Hemisphere. Among the Inca (c. A.D. 1476-1526), only in-group marriages were allowed, and "government agents . . . took selected girls of about age ten . . . and . . . apportioned [them] out as wives for the emperor and the nobles" (Wenke, 1990, p. 547). Adolescent life among the Aztecs (c. A.D. 1350-1550) was apparently worse, because human sacrifices were common. As Wenke (1990) reports: "Young men were selected in each year to lead a life of luxury surrounded by complaisant young women and feasting on the best of food, realizing full well that at the end of the year they would be sacrificed" (p. 517).

When viewing the period from A.D. 500 to A.D. 1600 as a whole, the only acceptable conclusion is that, on a worldwide basis, adolescent curiosity and sexual/physical events were recognized. Despite an absence of knowledge about many of the groups that inhabited the planet during this period, it seems appropriate to conjecture that as governments and religions grew, sexual victimization of adolescents, restrictions on adolescent sexual activities, and onerous courtship, dowry, and marriage arrangements all grew as well.

The Renaissance to 1904

As European explorers and settlers circled the globe after A.D. 1492, they brought diseases (including syphilis), warfare, religious persecution, exploitation, and slavery to countless "savage" groups. The decimation was so total that great civilizations and groups that existed between the fifteenth and the nineteenth centuries now cannot be studied except through archival and archaeological analyses (Hall, 1904). Moreover, the impact of European expansionism was so dramatic that most of what was known about adolescent sexuality until Hall's time was viewed through Euro-American, heterosexual, male, and Christian lenses.

Two broad themes characterize the treatment of adolescent sexuality from the Renaissance to 1904. First, the scope of topics believed to be germane to adolescent sexuality slowly increased. Unfortunately, this broadened focus was usually religious and nonscientific rather than objective. Second, the sexual victimization of adolescents that dominated during the Dark and Middle Ages prevailed at least until Hall's time. The brief review presented below provides adequate substantiation of the themes noted above; however, readers are urged to read the original sources for more complete corroboration.

The first theme characterizing the period was a gradual increase in the topics believed to be involved in adolescent sexuality. Kett (1977) claims that with the publication of Rousseau's *Émile* in 1780, a "turning point" (p. 133) in scholarship on adolescence occurred. Rousseau saw puberty as a new birth, and ages 15 through 20 as the time when adolescent sexual drives led to the development of genuine affection. When Rousseau's work is coupled with Tissot's scientific work on adolescent masturbation in 1760 (Hall, 1904) and the demands for cheap adolescent labor brought about by the Industrial Revolution (Demos & Demos, 1969), it would appear that the eighteenth century was a time of renewed interest in adolescents and their sexuality. Whereas earlier interest can be found in occasional prose (e.g., Voltaire's *Candide*, Benjamin Franklin's autobiography, and some of Shakespeare's plays) and educational philosophies (e.g., Comenius, Locke), it was during the eighteenth and nineteenth centuries that educators and philosophers began to widen the scope of their research. The earliest portion of the time between 1500 and 1900 contains very little by way of scientific study of adolescent sexuality. Among the existing anecdotal evidence, however, is a curious reference by Benjamin Franklin in his autobiography. Among a list of virtues he valued, he noted chastity, which he defined by saying, "Rarely use Venery but for Health or Offspring; Never to Dulness, Weakness, or the Injury of your own or another's Peace or Reputation" (Franklin, 1964, p. 150). Franklin's views were probably quite liberal for the era (the late eighteenth and early nineteenth centuries). Indeed, archival data for that period suggests that adolescents were often the victims of sexual abuse. Baizerman, Thompson, and Stafford-White (1979) examined ages at which adolescent prostitution was allowed in England during the 1800s. Before 1814, girls could be forced into prostitution before the age of 12. It was not until 1875 that the age was lifted to 13; in 1885, the age was lifted again, to 16. Hall (1904) supplements these data with observations from Paris in 1832 and Berlin in 1896, wherein rates of adolescent female prostitution were shockingly high.

Prostitution was not the only form of adolescent sexual victimization occurring in the 1800s. Hall (1904) reported data from 1878 Paris in which 68.8% of all reported rape cases for the year involved girls under the age of 13, and an additional 27.5% of rape cases involved girls between ages 13 and 20. Hall (1904) suggested that the age-of-consent laws may have had a great deal to do with sexual victimization of adolescents in both Europe and the United States. In 1863, the age of consent in Paris was 13. In the United States, the situation was worse: In 1881, all of the states had laws with the age of consent set at 10 years or less for girls. In 1900, three states still had such laws, whereas other states had raised the age of consent to ages ranging from 12 to 21 (Hall, 1904).

Kett (1977) discusses the widespread problems that U.S. legal authorities had with adolescent "vice" during the period 1820-1900. Specifically, he notes that adolescent sexual behaviors (including premarital sex) were associated by the experts of the time with large urban areas. Indeed, parents were told to keep their children out of big cities because such cities were conducive to adolescent sexual vices, including both female and male prostitution.

As physiology emerged as a science in the 1800s, physiologically based medical tracts focused on adolescents were circulated (Kett, 1977). Many physiologists and physicians regarded the human biological system as "closed." Consequently, any "draining" of the system led to direct physical or mental harm. Medical literature of the time viewed adolescent masturbation as an act that drained the physiological system and thereby caused physical breakdown or insanity (Kett, 1977). Paradoxically, girls' menstrual cycles were regarded by the medical establishment as part of a normally functioning biological system; physicians' only recommendation for girls' menstrual cycles was rest (Kett, 1977).

In a curious acceptance of physiologists' notions of the closed biological system and a rejection of Darwin's views of evolution, Christian theologians, educators, and psychologists from about 1870 through 1904 began an extraordinary campaign designed to deal with adolescent sexuality. Though this concern may have actually lowered the incidence of sexual victimization, it regrettably placed the study of adolescent sexuality under the direct purview of religion, not science.

The Women's Christian Temperance Union (WCTU) of the 1870s and 1880s attacked all forms of "public indecency," including adolescent vices (Kett, 1977, p. 193). The Young Men's Christian Association complemented the WCTU's activities from the 1870s onward and published scores of pamphlets designed to terrorize adolescents about the evils of sexuality (Kett, 1977). Some religious groups established homes for unwed pregnant adolescents, and Weatherley (1987) reports that in many cases these girls were kept in group homes long after the births of their offspring (who were adopted by others) so as to keep them away from additional exposure to worldly vices. Just prior to Hall's publication, religious leaders and psychologists asserted that the only way to keep adolescents away from sexual activities was religious conversion (e.g., Lancaster, 1897; Starbuck, 1899).

When Hall (1904) published his massive work, he attempted to integrate historic, scientific, Darwinian, and religious perceptions of adolescent sexuality. His task was formidable, and many concluded that he failed (e.g., Hollingworth, 1928). We would argue that Hall provided what he could, given the prevailing social climate of religious fervor, antievolutionary theory, and sexual victimization of adolescents he witnessed. Indeed, we believe that it was Hall's work that set the stage for later researchers' efforts to disconfirm his notions; in that sense, he advanced the study of adolescent sexuality dramatically.

Hall (1904) brought a greater sensibility to the study of adolescent sex. He eschewed some older, invalid ideas and introduced a degree of humanity and scientific precision to the area. He believed that menstruation was a normal biological function and should be approached with "reverence" instead of "shame" (Vol. 1, p. 511). Moreover, Hall joined a growing number of physicians who argued against surgery on women's sexual organs to alleviate "hysteria." He also noted that variations in genital sizes could lead to undue anxiety or modesty, that boys' nocturnal emissions were "probably universal" (Vol. 1, p. 453), and that there were phases in the development of adolescent love. These assertions were scholarly advances for his time.

Unfortunately, Hall (1904) also made moralistic and ethnocentric assertions that are troublesome today. For instance, he argued that with respect to the timing of menarche in Europe, "nearly all agree that blondes precede brunettes" (Vol. 1, p. 475). His views of masturbation, though progressive in 1904 (he did not believe that it caused insanity), were heavily influenced by religious views. He believed masturbation was "evil" (Vol. 1, p. 433) and was caused primarily by laziness, springtime, and erotic pictures. Indeed, Hall felt it led to "lying secretiveness, and hypocrisy" (Vol. 1, p. 443). The cures he suggested included sexual education, a healthy diet, cold baths, swimming and other exercise, circumcision, loose trousers, hard beds, and rising early in the morning. Curiously, Hall either ignored or did not believe that adolescent girls engaged in masturbation. Hall also (courageously, we believe) mentioned "bi-sexual souls" and "homosexuality" (Vol. 2, p. 117). At a time when such phenomena were discussed only in very small medical circles (e.g., S. Freud's), Hall mentioned these sexual orientations openly. Unfortunately, his analyses were hardly favorable; he noted that "these sad phenomena are unquestionably exceptional and degenerate" (Vol. 2, p. 117).

In sum, the period from 1500 to Hall's landmark work in 1904 was characterized by a broadening of the scope of topics included within adolescent sexuality. It was also reminiscent of earlier periods of brutal sexual victimization. During the latter part of this period, the Industrial Revolution, Darwin's evolutionary scientific views, religious concerns, and finally Hall's work all (re)established numerous topics in the scope of adolescent sexuality (e.g., religious values, teenage mothers, masturbation, sexual orientation, sexual victimization).

1904-1992

An incredible number of changes in the treatment of adolescent sexuality have occurred since 1904. Until only recently, however, these changes have been viewed almost entirely from Western perspectives. The changes can be broadly characterized in nine ways, which are detailed below.

Recognition of Adolescence

Few writers before Hall (1904) considered adolescence a unique period. Persons between puberty and young adulthood had been regarded as older children or young adults. Hall's demarcation of adolescence as a special age, replete with unique sexual characteristics, established scientific scholarship on adolescent sexuality.

Scholarly Precision

The advent of more rigorous, reliable, and valid research efforts allowed scholars from diverse disciplines to study adolescent sexuality with greater precision. Knowledge bases grew slowly, but by the 1940s through the 1960s, adolescent sex research was more prevalent. Salient among these efforts was the work at the Kinsey Institute, which revealed the varieties of behaviors in which adolescents engage. Sorensen (1973) and others later substantiated the diversity of adolescent sexual expression. In addition, researchers were able to gauge pubertal changes more accurately and to examine the psychosocial consequences of these changes (e.g., Downs, 1990).

Religious Versus Scientific Views

During Hall's time, religious dogma had nearly overwhelmed scientific approaches to adolescent sexuality (Kett, 1977). Nonetheless, as scientific scholarship grew during the century, hypocritical and false beliefs about adolescent sex were found to be groundless. Today, although religious and scientific views of adolescent sexuality occasionally disagree, scholarly efforts to understand the role of religious beliefs in adolescent sexual decisions have demonstrated the positive influences such belief systems can have (e.g., Thomas & Carver, 1990). In sum, during the twentieth century, the study of adolescent sexuality shifted from the strict purview of religious dogma to a shared hegemony of scientists, educators, and religious leaders.

Zeitgeist and Historical Factors

Zeitgeist and historical events prior to the twentieth century (e.g., the Black Death) had serious consequences for adolescent sexual behavior. Other zeitgeist phenomena (e.g., the burning of Alexandria's library) probably occurred but remain unknown, understudied, or elusive. A long series of twentieth-century events have been shown to have had demonstrable effects on adolescent sexuality. In brief, World War I seems to have led to an increase in premarital sex (Kett, 1977; Smigel & Seidel, 1968) and a decrease (by about 3 years) in the age at which American adolescents began dating (McCabe, 1984). The zeitgeist of the "roaring '20s" in America led to an increased emphasis on adolescent intimacy. This increase was most likely the result of enhanced mobility (cars), greater access to education for both sexes, and a weakening of the chaperon system for dating (Kett, 1977). Though the Great Depression of the 1930s had an impact on adolescent dating patterns (Elder, 1974), the effect of this zeitgeist on other aspects of adolescent sexuality has received little scholarly attention. The aftermath of World War II stimulated a "baby boom," the effects of which were seen in the sexual attitudes of adolescents and young adults in the 1960s and early 1970s. Public concern over "free love" (i.e., sexual experimentation) was voiced among politicians, educators, and psychologists (e.g., Gudridge, 1969). The advent of a highly reliable form of contraception (the pill) may have encouraged adolescents during the 1960s and 1970s to become more sexually adventuresome because the likelihood of undesired pregnancies seemed lower (Grinder, 1973). The *Roe v. Wade* U.S. Supreme Court decision of 1973 may also have allowed adolescent women greater flexibility in issues of pregnancy. Some have reexamined adolescent sexuality data from the 1960s to the 1980s

(Adams & Gullotta, 1989) and have concluded that although there may have been a shift in sexual *attitudes* during this period, radical changes in behavior were unlikely. A century-long zeitgeist effect has been observed in the rapidly developing media industry. Numerous scholars have noted the direct influence of radio, film, magazines, and television on adolescents' sexual attitudes and behaviors (e.g., American Academy of Pediatrics Committee on Adolescence, 1986). The latest, and probably the most ominous, zeitgeist phenomenon of the century was the detection in the early 1980s of the AIDS virus. Indeed, the World Health Organization (Reuters News Service, 1991a) reported that about one third of all 1.5 million AIDS cases worldwide in 1991 involved children. With an average exposure to expression lag time of 10 years, the rates of adolescents with AIDS at the beginning of the twenty-first century could be staggering. Given the apparently high rates of unprotected (i.e., unsafe) sexual behaviors among young adolescents (Melchert & Brunett, 1990) and the high incidence of chemical abuse (which may lower sexual decision-making abilities) (Adams & Gullotta, 1989), the likely impact of AIDS on adolescents is almost unfathomable.

Societal and Demographic Foci

The history of adolescent sexuality has typically been one from the vantage point of Western, Christian, Caucasian, heterosexual, and married males. Further, the focus has traditionally been andro-, hetero-, and ethnocentric. The civil rights movement of the 1950s and 1960s, and the subsequent social movements on behalf of other ethnic groups, women, gay males, and lesbians have all lifted the consciousness of scholars, educators, and historians interested in the history of adolescent phenomena. The results for adolescents have been dramatic: substantial revisions in the definitions of what adolescent sexual behaviors are considered abnormal (American Psychiatric Association, 1987), shifts in perspectives on adolescent sex (and sex-role) differences and similarities (Hare-Mustin & Marecek, 1990), a demand for an accounting of all adolescent SES (socioeconomic status) levels (Hollingshead, 1949), far greater social concern for teenage pregnancies (Riordan, 1991), and intense scholarly interest in the unique histories of adolescent sexuality in non-Caucasian groups (e.g., Washington, 1982) and cultures (e.g., Broude, 1976). In addition, enhanced awareness of adolescent minorities has uncovered previously hidden problems. For instance, although the existence of gay male and lesbian adolescents has been acknowledged for at least a century, increased awareness of the special needs of these youths has led to an identification of extraordinarily high levels of suicides among these teens (Maguen, 1991). Indeed, the chief factor in these suicides appears to be alienation from peers. Social centers have recently been established to assist gay and lesbian adolescents in networking with others to decrease feelings of isolation (Cutbirth, 1991).

Challenging Adolescent Victimization

The history of adolescent sexuality has largely been a history of victimization via rape, forced marriages, and the like. Though this victimization has not been eliminated, heightened social awareness, education programs, and strict laws protecting adolescents emerged during the 1980s (e.g., Dusek, 1991).

The Communication Revolution

Since 1950, communication patterns and knowledge generation have grown exponentially (e.g., Sagan, 1980). Although this has enhanced global exchange of scholarly information on adolescent sexuality, it has also led to the virtual obliteration of smaller, less powerful cultural units (e.g., Linden, 1991). Consequently, the decimation of cultural groups (observed by Hall, 1904) early in the century has grown despite the advantages offered by global communication.

Sex Education

Early in this century, sex education for adolescents typically contained one message: No sex of any sort outside of heterosexual marriage (Kirkendall, 1965). By the late 1920s, more realistic opinions emerged (e.g., Hollingworth, 1928). Most sex education programs in the United States from the 1930s to the 1960s were nonexistent, were offered by religious or civic groups, or (rarely) were taught in schools (e.g., Grinder, 1973). Sex education for adolescents was compulsory in Sweden from 1958 on and was designed to promote responsible sexual attitudes (Grinder, 1973). Progress in the United

States was slower. In the 1960s, sex education books deleted some of the older moral dictums (e.g., sex is wrong), but retained some traditional mythology (e.g., adolescent girls do not experience orgasms, masturbation leads to guilt) (e.g., Southard, 1967). Additional progress came in the 1970s and 1980s and generally reflected the social changes of the period (e.g., Adams & Gullotta, 1989). Currently, while serious debates continue over the "proper" source (e.g., church, family, state) of sexual information, most adults apparently agree that sex education is highly desirable for adolescents (Reuters News Service, 1991b).

Theories of Adolescent Sexuality

The last historical characteristic of the twentieth century was the emergence of a plethora of theories on adolescent sexuality. Although theories had existed prior to this century (e.g., Aristotle), they were typically neither specific nor testable. The twentieth century brought theories that met both criteria.

The outcomes of the changes observed during the twentieth century seem to have led to the current enormous scope of adolescent sexuality. Scholarship on non-Euro-American histories of adolescent sexuality during the twentieth century is noticeably absent. Consequently, the review provided above and the theories discussed below are unavoidably biased and represent Euro-American perspectives.

THEORETICAL PERSPECTIVES

The expansive range of topics germane to the scope of adolescence has led to a legion of theories trying to explain them. Some theories address only specific elements of adolescent sexuality; some purport to explain *all* facets of this sexuality; and still others, though *not* focused on adolescent sexuality, are applicable nonetheless. Generally, the best theories are empirically testable, parsimonious, free of biases, and uninfluenced by zeitgeist effects. Moreover, good theories account for individual differences and offer specific hypotheses that can be refuted. No attempt will be made here to evaluate the worth of theories of adolescent sexuality, nor will the list of theories discussed be exhaustive of all extant perspectives. Rather, we will review briefly pertinent theories in groups based on the areas of emphasis used in the theories' explanations. These groupings include theories stressing emotional constructs, biological processes, cognitive determinants, learning processes, and social factors. Frequently, theories will overlap into more than one grouping. In those instances, they will be mentioned in a final group of combination-construct theories, or, if they place greater emphasis on one construct over others, they will be discussed primarily with reference only to their area of stronger emphasis.

Emotional Constructs

Psychoanalytic theories typically have emphasized emotional constructs in views of adolescent sexuality. Although S. Freud (e.g., 1965) placed little emphasis on adolescence, he did underscore early emotional crises in childhood as factors in later adolescent sexuality. Indeed, it was during adolescence that an individual's sexual object choice became final. Psychoanalysis after S. Freud often placed emphasis on emotional constructs occurring *during* adolescence. A. Freud (e.g., 1948) suggested that emotional crises reminiscent of early childhood conflicts emerged during and after puberty. Adolescents often coped with these crises by using asceticism or intellectualization as defense mechanisms to protect against unconscious sexual urges. Similarly, Rank (1945) emphasized emotional conflicts early in life but indicated that adolescent sexual impulses often were masked by the ego defenses of asceticism or promiscuity. Moreover, Horney (e.g., 1937) agreed that early childhood emotional crises were first manifested during adolescence. For girls, these crises were prominent at menarche, and for both adolescent boys and girls, an emotional need for affection played a pivotal role in eventual sexual orientation. Sullivan (1953) also pointed to a period other than adolescence as important for adolescent sexuality; he argued that during middle childhood, children developed close friendships. The quality of these attachments later influenced adolescents' degrees of success in intimate relations with others of both sexes. Indeed, he suggested that "in my classification of sexual behavior on the basis of the preferred partner, the *homosexual* and the *heterosexual* are obviously related to preadolescent and early adolescent phases of development" (p. 293, emphasis in original). Curiously, Erikson (e.g., 1950, 1968) argued that issues of intimacy tended to be found more often in young adulthood than in adolescence. He noted, however, that adolescents wrestled with the emotion-laden issue of sexual polarization (i.e., heterosexuality, homosexuality, or bisexuality) while forming an identity and as a precursor to intimate relations in adulthood.

Blos (1962) suggested that adolescence was a time of reorganization of emotional constructs. In the process, sexual orientation, love, and earlier psychosexual conflicts were dealt with and concluded in "a phase of consolidation" (p. 129) late in adolescence. It was at this phase that sexual behaviors, object choices, and emotions were concretized.

Deutsch (1944) also emphasized emotional factors in adolescent sexual development. She argued that fantasies were extremely important in adolescent girls' sexual development. More recently, Storms (1980) considered the role of fantasies among early adolescents as determinants of sexual object choice. Storms predicted that adolescents' sexual fantasies were extremely important and suggested that fantasies are typically high or low in same- and/or opposite-sex content. Using a 2 × 2 matrix, he proposed the following classifications of sexual orientation for adolescents: heterosexuality, homosexuality, bisexuality, and asexuality.

Two other theories emphasizing emotional constructs have focused on dating sequences and on how nonsexual needs can become precursors of sexual behaviors. Feinstein and Ardon (1973) proposed a four-stage model of dating based on emotional processes. These stages included sexual awakening (ages 13-15), practice (14-17), establishing sex roles (16-19), and development of final sexual object choice (18-25). Hajcak and Garwood (1988) recently proposed a model of how nonsexual emotional needs lead to sexual behaviors and ultimately to "an artificially high sex drive" (p. 755). Their premise was that adolescents have numerous emotional needs that have little or no sexual basis. If these needs are met in nonsexual ways, the adolescent eventually engages in mature sexual relationships with others. If these needs (e.g., affection, self-esteem) remain unmet, however, they become connected with physiological drives and are directed toward sexual outlets. When this connection persists, the adolescent associates emotional satisfaction only with sexual (rather than nonsexual) outlets and fails to attain more mature levels of emotionality and sexuality.

Biological Processes

Most psychoanalytic theories are premised on biological drives (e.g., libido) that in turn influence the operation of emotional constructs. Numerous nonpsychoanalytic theories have focused directly on the relationship of genetic, physiological, or biological processes to adolescent sexuality. Hall's (1904) recapitulation theory was premised on the idea that "individual growth recapitulates the history of the race" (Vol. 1, p. 1). He argued that during the course of development, humans relive the evolutionary history of the species and that during adolescence the transition from a barbaric to a more civilized human society is reenacted. Important to this transition is the expression of adolescent sexuality in the forms of "a special consciousness of sex" and a contradictory sense of "sex shame" (Vol. 2, p. 97). In Hall's words, "my contention, then, is that young people, especially boys, in their development . . . afford the ontogenetic parallel to . . . phyletic stages" (Vol. 2, p. 101). Most critics dismissed Hall's views as insupportable (e.g., Hollingworth, 1928). Recently, however, Jeter (1983) theorized that "ontogeny recapitulates phylogeny" (p. 141). He suggests that unfolding human sexuality is based on preplanned genetic programming, with adolescence as a time of sexual experimentation.

Some theorists have approached adolescent sexuality from a maturational view. Gesell, Ilg, and Ames (1956) premise their description of the sexual changes observed among adolescents on a maturational sequencing wherein sexual developments are expected at different age periods. For instance, age 15 is viewed as the most critical time during adolescence for the development of sexual maturity.

Other theorists have emphasized the importance of body types and physical appearance in adolescent sexual expression. Sheldon (1940) and Cabot (1938) suggested that muscular boys and thin girls would be more sexually attractive and would engage in more sexual activity than adolescents with other physical characteristics. Zeller (1952) also stressed appearance. He argued that the body gestalt (or wholeness) changed at each phase of development; during adolescence, there was an attempt to integrate one's sexual organs, hormonal changes, and overall physical and psychological functioning. If an event like menarche was viewed as not fitting the adolescent's emerging sense of physical gestalt, she or he could exhibit a dys-functional approach to sexuality.

Other theorists have emphasized hormonal changes as directly affecting adolescent sexuality. For instance, Bernard (1957) argued that eventual sexual orientation was attributable to variations in adolescent endocrine levels. Miller and Fox (1987) described a hor-monal view in which increased testosterone levels in adolescent boys theoretically led to increased levels of sexual activity. Bell, Weinberg, and Hammersmith (1981), after testing and finding no support for a large number of social and learning variables, posited that biological or prenatal factors might be crucial to adolescent sexual orientation.

Cognitive/Attitudinal Determinants

Marcia's (1966, 1967) extension of Erikson's views on adolescent identity development is directly relevant to a cognitive approach to adolescent sexuality. According to Marcia, in the process of morato-rium, the adolescent examined alternatives in numerous personal, social, and sexual domains. The end of this process was a concrete sense of identity that included one's sexual identity and orientation.

Spranger (1955) discussed the development of adolescents' value systems as relevant to sexual and love decisions. In evaluating value systems, adolescents first distinguished between sexuality (as body sensations) and pure love (as spiritually based values toward the self and others). Once these were distinguished and understood, they became integrated into a more mature form of intimacy. Spranger (1955) noted that adolescents in the process of distinguishing be-tween love and sexuality often expressed one (e.g., love) to a partic-ular peer, but the other (e.g., sex) toward another peer. Only after careful evaluation and experience did love and sexuality merge.

Though neither Piaget nor Kohlberg were directly concerned with adolescent sexuality (e.g., Colby & Kohlberg, 1987; Inhelder & Piaget, 1958), the applicability of their theories of cognitive and moral development to adolescent sexuality is obvious. That is, with the onset of formal operational thinking and the prospect of advancing to higher levels of moral reasoning, cognitive and moral judgment-making processes allow adolescents to consider the consequences of their own and others' sexual decisions. Cobliner (1974) has applied Piagetian constructs of concrete and formal operational thinking to adolescents' understanding of pregnancy.

Two other prominent theories have taken cognitive/attitudinal approaches to adolescent sexuality. Davis and Blake (1956) developed a decision-tree analysis concerning pregnancy, contraception, sexual activity, abortion, and adoption options among adolescents. McCreary-Juhasz (1975) also developed a model of adolescents' sexual decision making. In both of these models, current decisions were seen both as the product of earlier decisions and as the precursors to subsequent decisions.

Learning Processes

Numerous behaviorist, learning, and social learning theories are applicable to adolescent sexual behaviors. Among these, Bandura's (1977) theory is one of the most appropriate, although it is not specific to the learning of adolescent sexual behaviors. In an extrapolation from Bandura's theory, adolescents can be viewed as observing the sexual behaviors of others. Subsequent imitation of the model, however, is very much a function of characteristics associated with the model (e.g., similarity to the observer), characteristics of the adolescent observer (e.g., is she or he capable of reproducing the model's sexual behaviors?), and the number, availability, and type of incentives that could reward imitation of the observed behavior. Critically important is the distinction Bandura made between what is *learned* (or acquired by observation) and what is *imitated* (or performed as a function of that observation). He persuasively argued that many behaviors were learned but never performed, because incentives for doing so were absent.

More than 60 years ago, Hollingworth (1928) proposed an alternative learning paradigm of adolescent sexual behavior. She indicated that although sex drives were inborn, they were highly modifiable throughout life. She noted that "adolescent love continues to be one of the most powerful motives of adolescent conduct" (Hollingworth, 1928, p. 105). Indeed, in her view, adolescent sexual behavior was very much a trial-and-error process wherein some sexual behaviors were rewarded and increased in frequency, whereas other behaviors were punished or ignored and thereafter decreased in frequency. In Hollingworth's opinion, although it is true that sex attraction is aroused normally and usually by persons of the opposite sex . . . these are not the only stimuli which can arouse desire. Words, pictures, objects, in fact anything that has once been associated in experience with arousal of the sexual reflexes may achieve the power of a sex stimulus, and may even take the place, through habitual excitations, of the normal stimulus. (p. 115)

Indeed, Hollingworth believed that sexual orientation was learned during adolescence.

Social Factors

One of the earliest theories to emphasize the direct influence of interpersonal and societal factors was Davis's (1944) socialized anxiety view. He argued that each social class and culture exerted its own degree of social control in the form of instilled guilt over emerging adolescent sexual urges. Too little social control or anxiety led to dysfunctional sexual behaviors. An appropriate degree of socialized anxiety, which would vary depending on each culture's values regarding sexuality, led the adolescent to meet external standards for sexual behaviors. A comparable social control theory was offered by Hirschi (1969), who believed that adolescent sexual behaviors increased when agents of social control (e.g., family, schools) failed to convey sociocultural expectations for sexual behaviors. When these social agents conveyed clear expectations via direct teaching, adolescents learned these expectations and exhibited fewer nonapproved sexual behaviors. M. E. Brown's (1979) theory of adolescent prostitution parallels Hirschi's (1969) views. Brown posited that as family background variables (e.g., failure to teach sexual values, presence or absence of sexual abuse in the home) varied, so did adolescent sexual expressions.

Simon and Gagnon (1969) proposed a theory of social scripts wherein adolescents learned the expectations of society, acted in varying degrees of alignment with these expectations, and were rewarded or punished accordingly. Using Simon and Gagnon's views as a springboard, Marsiglio (1988) recently offered a theory of adolescent male sexuality. Marsiglio argued that sociocultural scripts dictated the expected sexual and sex-role behaviors of boys. Although Marsiglio focused only on boys, the theory was noteworthy because it incorporated zeitgeist factors such as AIDS.

Cultural anthropologists (e.g., Benedict, 1938, 1950; Mead, 1950, 1953), though generally not offering specific, testable theories of adolescent sexuality, have underscored the importance of cultural variability in adolescent sexual expression. For instance, Benedict (1950) noted that each culture developed its own set of customs and rituals to assist adolescents in the transition from nonsexual to sexual roles.

Strouse and Fabes (1987) offered an interpersonal theory of the transition that adolescent girls make from virgin to nonvirgin status. They argued that family status, social control, personal preparedness, and the overall social milieu jointly affected girls' decisions to engage in initial sexual relationships. In a similar vein, Strahle (1983) offered an exchange theory on premarital sex and the use of contraceptives among adolescent girls. This two-stage model of causation, complete with 40 testable hypotheses, involved the girls' history, parents, situational factors, physical attractiveness, and educational and occupational aspirations. Allen-Meares and Shore (1986) recently offered a transactional theory based on an "ecological-systems based framework" (p. 75). Taking a social work perspective, they emphasized the adolescent's cognitive, behavioral, and emotional coping patterns; information; skill; coping to survive; affiliation; and achievement; all in interaction with both formal and informal social agencies (e.g., the family).

A host of other theorists have offered "mini-theories" in which one or only a few sociocultural factors are emphasized as having an impact on adolescent sexual expression. Some of these include emphasis on television and the media (e.g., J. D. Brown, Childers, & Waszak, 1990), schools (Berkovitz, 1985), and pediatricians (Greydanus, 1985).

Combination-Construct Theories

Several theories have combined diverse constructs in explanations of adolescent sexuality. For instance, Havighurst (1951) noted nine tasks that are crucial during adolescence. Of these, three were related to sexuality: accepting one's body and sex role, relating to peers of both sexes, and preparation for marriage and parenting. He argued that although all three had biological bases, they were expressed in varying degrees depending on each culture. In contrast, Remplein (1956) argued that sex drives and hormonal changes were linked completely at puberty; during adolescence, sexual experimentation led to emotional development and concrete behavioral expressions toward specific persons. Finally, numerous other theories have used biological changes in combination with learned behaviors, attitudes, and/or emotional constructs as explanations for specific aspects of adolescent sexuality (e.g., Ausubel, 1954; McCabe, 1984; Miller & Fox, 1987; Rowe, Rodgers, & Meseck-Bushey, 1989; Smith, 1989; Udry, Talbert, & Morris, 1986).

CONCLUSIONS

Both historical and theoretical perspectives on adolescent sexuality have linked the edges of their respective puzzles. Indeed, the nature of adolescent sexuality transcends both views: Adolescents are sexually curious and experience physical/sexual changes. Neither perspective, however, has assembled the vast array of pieces that constitute the interiors of their puzzles—the scope of adolescent sexuality. Historians are hampered by destroyed records, biased accounts, and the ongoing extinction of primitive peoples. Theorists must posit causal explanations for the host of factors associated with adolescent sexuality, all the while remaining unbiased, data based, and cognizant of ever-present zeitgeist effects.

Neither a complete history nor an all-encompassing theory of adolescent sexuality seems likely in the twenty-first century. We hope that this assessment is wrong. In fact, we hope that historians and theorists will provide breakthroughs so that these two huge jigsaw puzzles can, at long last, be assembled and reveal the completed pictures of historical and contemporary adolescent sexuality.

REFERENCES

Adams, G. R., & Gullotta, T. (1989). *Adolescent life experiences* (2nd ed.). Pacific Grove, CA: Brooks/Cole.

Allen-Meares, P., & Shore, D. A. (1986). A transactional framework for working with adolescents and their sexualities. *Journal of Social Work & Human Sexuality, 5*(1), 71-80.

American Academy of Pediatrics Committee on Adolescence. (1986). Sexuality, contraception, and the media. *Pediatrics, 78*, 535-536.

American Psychiatric Association. (1987). *Diagnostic and statistical manual of mental disorders* (3rd ed., rev.). Washington, DC: Author.

Aries, P. (1962). *Centuries of childhood.* New York: Knopf.

Ausubel, D. P. (1954). *Theory and problems of adolescent development.* New York: Grune & Stratton.

Baizerman, M., Thompson, J., & Stafford-White, K. (1979). Adolescent prostitution. *Children Today, 8,* 20-24.

Bandura, A. (1977). *Social learning theory.* Englewood Cliffs, NJ: Prentice-Hall.

Bell, A. P., Weinberg, M. S., & Hammersmith, S. K. (1981). *Sexual preference: Its development in men and women.* Bloomington: Indiana University Press.

Benedict, R. (1938). Continuities and discontinuities in cultural conditioning. *Psychiatry, 1,* 161-167.

Benedict, R. (1950). *Patterns of culture.* New York: New American Library.

Berkovitz, I. H. (1985). Healthy development of sexuality in adolescents: The school's contribution. *Medical Aspects of Human Sexuality, 19,* 34-49.

Bernard, H. W. (1957). *Adolescent development in American culture.* New York: World.

Blos, P. (1962). *On adolescence: A psychoanalytic interpretation.* New York: Free Press.

Borstelmann, L. J. (1983). Children before psychology: Ideas about children from antiquity to the late 1800s. In P. H. Mussen (Ed.), *Handbook of child psychology* (Vol. 1, 4th ed., pp. 1-40). New York: Wiley.

Boswell, J. (1980). *Christianity, social tolerance, and homosexuality.* Chicago: University of Chicago Press.

Broude, G. J. (1976). Cross-cultural patterning of some sexual attitudes and practices. *Behavior Sciences Research, 11,* 227-262.

Brown, J. D., Childers, K. W., & Waszak, C. S. (1990). Television and adolescent sexuality. *Journal of Adolescent Health Care, 11,* 62-70.

Brown, M. E. (1979). Teenage prostitution. *Adolescence, 14,* 665-680.

Cabot, P. S. (1938). The relationships between characteristics of personality and physique in adolescents. *Genetic Psychology Monographs, 20,* 3-120.

Chang, J. (1991). *The Tao of love and sex: The ancient Chinese way to ecstasy.* New York: Penguin.

Cobliner, G. (1974). Pregnancy in the single adolescent girl: The role of cognitive functions. *Journal of Youth and Adolescence, 3,* 17-29.

Colby, A., & Kohlberg, L. (1987). *The measurement of moral judgment, Vol. 1: Theoretical foundations and research validation.* New York: Cambridge University Press.

Confucius. (1976). *The analects of Confucius* (L. Giles, Trans.). Norwalk, CT: Easton.

Cutbirth, J. (1991, November 4). Austin group offers supportive climate for homosexual teens. *Houston Chronicle,* p. 12A.

Darling, C. A., Kallen, D. J., & Van Dusen, J. E. (1984). Sex in transition, 1900-1984. *Journal of Youth and Adolescence, 13,* 385-399.

Darwin, C. R. (1859). *The origin of species by means of natural selection.* London: J. Murray.

Davis, A. (1944). Socialization and adolescent personality. *Adolescence: Yearbook of the National Society for the Study of Education, 43,* Part I.

Davis, K., & Blake, J. (1956). Social structure and fertility: An analytic framework. *Economic Development and Cultural Change, 4,* 211.

de Lumley, H. (1991, May 25). Les six etapes de l'aventure humaine. *Le Figaro,* 110-113.

de Mause, L. (1974). The evolution of childhood. *History of Childhood Quarterly, 1,* 503-606.

Demos, J., & Demos, V. (1969). Adolescence in historical perspective. *Journal of Marriage and the Family, 31,* 632-638.

Deutsch, H. (1944). *Psychology of women.* New York: Grune & Stratton.

Downs, A. C. (1990). The social biological constructs of social competency. In T. P. Gullotta, G. R. Adams & R. Montemayor (Eds.), *Developing social competency in adolescence: Advances in adolescent development* (Vol. 3, pp. 43-94). Newbury Park, CA: Sage.

Duberman, M. (1991). *About time: Exploring the gay past.* New York: Meridian.

Dusek, J. B. (1991). *Adolescent development and behavior* (2nd ed.). Englewood Cliffs, NJ: Prentice Hall.

Eisler, R. (1987). *The chalice and the blade: Our history, our future.* San Francisco: HarperCollins.

Elder, G. H., Jr. (1974). *Children of the great depression.* Chicago: University of Chicago Press.

Endleman, R. (1989). Love and sex in twelve cultures. New York: Psyche.

Erikson, E. H. (1950). *Childhood and society.* New York: Norton.

Erikson, E. H. (1968). *Identity: Youth and crisis.* New York: Norton.

Feinstein, S., & Ardon, M. (1973). Trends in dating patterns and adolescent development. *Journal of Youth and Adolescence, 2,* 157-166.

Fisher, E. (1979). *Woman's creation.* New York: McGraw-Hill.

Ford, C. S., & Beach, F. A. (1951). *Patterns of sexual behavior.* New York: Harper-Hoeber.

Fowkes, C. (1991). *The illustrated Kama Sutra.* Rochester, VT: Park Street.

Franklin, B. (1964). *The autobiography of Benjamin Franklin* (L. W. Labaree, R. L. Ketcham, H. C. Boatfield & H. H. Fineman, Eds.). New Haven, CT: Yale University Press.

Freud, A. (1948). *The ego and the mechanism of defense* (C. Bains, Trans.). New York: International Universities Press.

Freud, S. (1965). *New introductory lectures on psychoanalysis* (J. Strachey, Ed. & Trans.). New York: Norton.

Gesell, A., Ilg, F. L., & Ames, L. B. (1956). *Youth: The years from ten to sixteen.* New York: Harper.

Gies, F., & Gies, J. (1989). *Marriage and the family in the Middle Ages.* New York: Harper & Row.

Goodich, M. (1985). Ancilla Dei: The servant as saint in the late Middle Ages. In J. Kirshner & S. F. Wemple (Eds.) *Women of the medieval world* (pp. 119-136). New York: Blackwell.

Gregor, T. (1985). *Anxious pleasures: The sexual lives of an Amazonian people.* Chicago: University of Chicago Press.

Greydanus, D. E. (1985). The teenage girl who is "boy crazy." *Medical Aspects of Human Sexuality, 19,* 120-124.

Grinder, R. E. (1973). *Adolescence.* New York: Wiley.

Gudridge, B. M. (1969). *High school student unrest.* Washington: National School Public Relations Association.

Hajcak, F., & Garwood, P. (1988). Quick-fix sex: Pseudosexuality in adolescents. *Adolescence, 23,* 755-760.

Hall, G. S. (1904). *Adolescence.* New York: Appleton.

Hare-Mustin, R. T., & Marecek, J. (1990). On making a difference. In R. T. Hare-Mustin & J. Marecek (Eds.), *Making a difference: Psychology and the construction of gender* (pp. 1-21) New Haven, CT: Yale University Press.

Havighurst, R. J. (1951). *Developmental tasks and education.* New York: Longman.

Herdt, G. H. (1981). *Guardians of the flutes: Idioms of masculinity.* New York: McGraw-Hill.

Hirschi, T. (1969). *Causes of delinquency.* Berkeley: University of California Press.

Hollingshead, A. B. (1949). *Elmtown's youth: The impact of social classes on adolescence.* New York: Wiley.

Hollingworth, L. S. (1928). *The psychology of the adolescent.* New York: Appleton.

Horney, K. (1937). *The neurotic personality of our time.* New York: Norton.

Howitt, A. W. (1904). *Native tribes of S. E. Australia.* London: Macmillan.

Inhelder, B., & Piaget, J. (1958). *The growth of logical thinking* (A. Parsons & S. Milgram, Trans.). New York: Basic Books.

Jeter, K. (1983). Developmental sexology: Ontogeny recapitulates phylogeny. *Marriage & Family Review, 6*(3-4), 141-151.

Kessen, W. (1965). *The child.* New York: Wiley.

Kett, J. F. (1977). *Rites of passage: Adolescence in America 1790 to the present.* New York: Basic Books.

Kiell, N. (1967). *The universal experience of adolescence.* Boston: Beacon.

Kirkendall, L. A. (1965). Sex education: A reappraisal. *Humanist*, 1-7.

Knauft, B. M. (1986). Text and social practice: Narrative "longing" and bisexuality among the Gebusi of New Guinea. *Ethos, 14,* 252-281.

Lancaster, E. G. (1897). The characteristics of adolescence. *Pedagogical Seminary, 5,* 61-128.

LeVine, R. A. (1970). Cross-cultural study in child psychology. In P. H. Mussen (Ed.), *Carmichael's manual of child psychology* (Vol. 2, 3rd ed., pp. 559-612). New York: Wiley.

Linden, E. (1991, September 23). Lost tribes, lost knowledge. *Time,* pp. 46-56.

Luckey, E., & Nass, G. (1969). A comparison of sexual attitudes and behavior in an international sample. *Journal of Marriage and the Family, 31,* 364-379.

Maguen, S. (1991, September 24). Teen suicide: The government's cover-up and America's lost children. *Advocate,* pp. 40-47.

Marcia, J. E. (1966). Development and validation of ego identity status. *Journal of Personality and Social Psychology, 3,* 551-558.

Marcia, J. E. (1967). Ego identity status: Relationship to change in self-esteem, "general maladjustment," and authoritarianism. *Journal of Personality, 35,* 118-133.

Margulis, L., & Sagan, D. (1991). *Mystery dance: On the evolution of human sexuality.* New York: Summit.

Marsiglio, W. (1988). Adolescent male sexuality and heterosexual masculinity: A conceptual model and review. *Journal of Adolescent Research, 3,* 285-303.

McCabe, M. P. (1984). Toward a theory of adolescent dating. *Adolescence, 19,* 159-170.

McCreary-Juhasz, A. (1975). Sexual decision-making: The crux of the adolescent problem. In R. E. Grinder (Ed.), *Studies in adolescence* (pp. 340-351). New York: Macmillan.

McKinley, E. H. (1980). *Marching to glory: The history of the Salvation Army in the United States of America 1880-1980.* San Francisco: Harper & Row.

Mead, M. (1950). *Coming of age in Samoa*. New York: New American Library.
Mead, M. (1953). *Growing up in New Guinea*. New York: New American Library.
Melchert, T., & Burnett, K. F. (1990). Attitudes, knowledge, and sexual behavior of high-risk adolescents: Implications for counseling and sexuality education. *Journal of Counseling & Development, 68*, 293-298.
Miller, B. C., & Fox, G. L. (1987). Theories of adolescent heterosexual behavior. *Journal of Adolescent Research, 2*, 269-282.
Morton, W. S. (1980). *China: Its history and culture*. New York: McGraw-Hill.
Otis, L. L. (1985). Prostitution and repentance in late medieval Perpignan. In J. Kirshner & S. F. Wemple (Eds.) *Women of the medieval world* (pp. 137-160). New York: Blackwell.
Plato (1956). Symposium. In E. H. Warmington & P. G. Rouse (Eds.), *Great dialogues of Plato* (W. H. D. Rouse, Trans., pp. 69-117) New York: Mentor.
Rank, O. (1945). *Will therapy and truth and reality*. New York: Knopf.
Remplein, H. (1956). *Die seelische entwicklung in der Kindheit und reifezeit*. Munich: Ernst Reinhard.
Reuters News Service. (1991a, October 5). 1.5 million people have AIDS, U.N. world health group says. *Houston Chronicle*, p. 27A.
Reuters News Service. (1991b, November 22). Closer-knit families indicated. *Houston Chronicle*, p. 23A.
Riordan, T. (1991, October 14). Teen woes on the rise, report says. *Houston Chronicle*, p. 4A.
Rowe, D. C., Rodgers, J. L., & Meseck-Bushey, S. (1989). An "epidemic" model of sexual intercourse prevalences for black and white adolescents. *Social Biology, 36*(3/4), 127-145.
Rowse, A. L. (1983). *Homosexuals in history: A study of ambivalence in society, literature and the arts*. New York: Dorset.
Sagan, C. (1980). *Cosmos*. New York: Random House.
Sansom, G. (1963). *The history of Japan 1615-1867*. Stanford, CA: Stanford University Press.
Schuster, I. G. (1979). *New women of Lusaka*. Palo Alto, CA: Mayfield.
Sheldon, W. H. (1940). *The varieties of human physique*. New York: Harper.
Simon, W., & Gagnon, J. (1969). On psychosexual development. In D. Goslin (Ed.), *Handbook of socialization theory and research* (pp. 733-752). Chicago: Rand McNally.
Smigel, E. O., & Seiden, R. (1968). The decline and fall of the double standard. *Annals of the American Academy of Political and Social Science, 376*, 6-17.
Smith, E. A. (1989). A biosocial model of adolescent sexual behavior. In G. R. Adams, R. Montemayor, & T. P. Gullotta (Eds.), *Biology of adolescent behavior and development* (pp. 143-167). Newbury Park, CA: Sage.
Sorensen, R. C. (1973). *Adolescent sexuality in contemporary America*. New York: World.
Southard, H. F. (1967). *Sex before twenty: New answers for youth*. New York: New American Library.
Spranger, E. (1955). *Psychologie des Jugendalters* (24th ed.). Heidelberg: Quelle & Meyer.
Starbuck, E. D. (1899). *The psychology of religion: An empirical study of the growth of religious consciousness*. New York: Scribner.
Storms, M. D. (1980). Theories of sexual orientation. *Journal of Personality and Social Psychology, 38*, 783-792.

Strahle, W. M. (1983). A model of premarital coitus and contraceptive behavior among female adolescents. *Archives of Sexual Behavior, 12,* 67-94.

Strouse, J. S., & Fabes, R. A. (1987). A conceptualization of transition to nonvirginity in adolescent females. *Journal of Adolescent Research, 2,* 331-348.

Sullivan, H. S. (1953). *The interpersonal theory of psychiatry.* New York: Norton.

Symons, D. (1979). *The evolution of human sexuality.* New York: Oxford University Press.

Thomas, D. L., & Carver, C. (1990). Religion and adolescent social competence. In T. P. Gullotta, G. R. Adams & R. Montemayor (Eds.), *Developing social competency in adolescence. Advances in adolescent development* (Vol. 3, pp. 195-219). Newbury Park, CA: Sage.

Udry, J., Talbert, L., & Morris, N. (1986). Biosocial foundations for adolescent female sexuality. *Demography, 23,* 217-230.

van Gulik, R. (1974). Sexual life in ancient China. Atlantic Highlands, NJ: Humanities Press.

Vincent, C. E. (1961). *Unmarried mothers.* New York: Free Press.

Washington, A. C. (1982). A cultural and historical perspective on pregnancy-related activity among U. S. teenagers. *Journal of Black Psychology, 9,* 1-28.

Watson, F. (1989). *A concise history of India.* New York: Thames and Hudson.

Weatherley, R. A. (1987). Teenage pregnancy, professional agendas, and problem definitions. *Journal of Sociology and Social Welfare, 14,* 5-35.

Wenke, R. J. (1990). *Patterns in prehistory: Humankind's first three million years* (3rd ed.). New York: Oxford University Press.

Zeller, W. (1952). *Konstitution und Entwicklung.* Güttingen: Psychologische Rundschau.

2. Anatomy, Physiology, and Gender Issues in Adolescence

Patricia Hyjer Dyk
University of Kentucky

Adolescence is a period of important developmental transitions. Changes occur in cognitive, emotional, and social functioning and, most strikingly, in physical stature and body shape with the onset of puberty in early adolescence. In light of accumulating evidence of the interrelatedness of psychosocial functioning and pubertal changes during early adolescence, researchers studying this period of development increasingly are examining psychosocial processes in relation to the processes of pubertal development. As discussed in a previous volume in the Advances in Adolescent Development series, there is renewed interest in biopsychosocial interactions (Smith, 1989) with regard to adolescent sexuality.

Traditionally, biological and social aspects of adolescent sexuality have been studied separately by medical researchers and social scientists. From a medical perspective, pubertal development is the maturation of adult reproductive capabilities. Unseen changes in hormonal levels trigger visible changes in reproductive organs and secondary sexual characteristics. These changes lead to sperm production and fully mature genital organs in males and to menarche, an ovulatory cycle, and fully mature genital organs in females.

From another perspective, social scientists typically have viewed puberty as the biological, social, and psychological events that interact during early adolescence. They have been interested in hormonal changes primarily as they influence transformations in physical appearance—not as potential direct effects on sexual drives or behavior (Brooks-Gunn & Petersen, 1984).

As Brooks-Gunn and Petersen (1983) note, social scientists have had more difficulty focusing on physical events that occur during adolescence. This has been "in part due to the difficulty in studying physical changes outside a medical setting, their interest in social and psychological processes rather than physical change, and their reluctance to accept a more biologically oriented model of development" (p. xx). They also point to the benefits of dialogue and shared research findings between medical and social science researchers. Increased interest in an interdisciplinary approach to studying adolescent sexuality development is also reflected by the 1986 Kinsey Institute's Symposium on Adolescence and Puberty (see Bancroft & Reinisch, 1990), as well as joint sessions of the Society for Research on Adolescence and the Society of Adolescent Medicine convened in 1989 and 1991.

Thus as we seek to understand the developmental context of adolescent sexuality and the interrelatedness of biological, sociocultural, and psychological processes, it is important to enhance our understanding of biological events (i.e., physical and endocrinological changes) occurring during adolescence to appreciate adolescent sexuality fully. Hence, the focus of this chapter is on the biological factors influencing puberty and gender development: physical changes evidenced by growth and secondary sexual characteristics and endocrine changes. By enhanced understanding of the pubertal process, researchers will be assisted in development of theoretical models and research designs to investigate direct and indirect relations of variables in adolescent sexuality.

PHYSICAL DEVELOPMENT

Puberty is a process that takes place within an existing biological system, not one initiated at puberty. The development of reproductive capacity, both in terms of somatic features and functions, begins at conception. It is during early adolescence, however, that rapid, conspicuous changes in body size and appearance signal the approach of full reproductive capacity. The most visible physical changes include the pubertal growth spurt and the development of secondary sex characteristics.

Growth Spurt

Most early adolescents experience a rapid increase in height and weight that results in the attainment of adult size (Tanner, 1975). From infancy on, the annual rate of growth falls steadily throughout childhood, picks up again rather suddenly at the time of puberty, and ceases in later adolescence when skeletal maturation is completed. Growth in stature has been investigated more rigorously than weight, partly because height is less susceptible to such environmental influences as eating habits and exercise.

There are wide interindividual variations in the age at onset of the pubertal spurt, the slope of the growth curve, and peak growth velocity. Some of the variability is attributable to socioeconomic differences; that is, children and adolescents from families at higher socioeconomic levels generally receive nutritionally balanced meals and grow more rapidly than those at lower socioeconomic levels (Tanner, 1962). Variations are also attributable to genetic determination. Developmental genetic factors have been found to influence height, rate of most rapid developmental growth (peak growth velocity), and age of maximal height gain (Fischbein, 1977).

There are also marked differences both between sexes and within each sex. Although boys and girls are of comparable stature during childhood, their growth curves diverge in puberty. On average, the onset of the growth spurt is about 2 years earlier for girls (9.5 to 14.5 years of age). When boys begin growing faster (10.5 to 16 years of age), they are already taller than girls are when they begin their growth spurt. Also, boys on average have a higher peak growth velocity. Thus in early adolescence, girls in the peak of their growth spurt are taller than their male peers, but when the boys begin their growth spurt, they pass the girls in height and end up with a taller stature.

The growth spurt affects not only body size, but practically all muscular and skeletal components of the body (Tanner, 1975). Bone and muscle diameters increase, with boys showing a considerably greater increase in number and size of muscle cells and in force per gram of muscle than do girls. As a result, physical strength increases rapidly in both sexes, with boys on average surpassing girls. Also, for both males and females, body build is affected by increased width of shoulders and hips. Both of these characteristics increase in males and females, but shoulders grow more in males, and hips grow more in females. Prepubertally, females have a larger shoulder/hip ratio; after puberty, males have a larger ratio (Faust, 1977).

Secondary Sex Characteristics

The major accentuation of the sex differences in external appearance is brought about by the development of secondary sex characteristics. Tanner (1962) has described these changes in terms of a series of pubertal stages based upon genital development (boys), breast development (girls), and pubic hair development (both sexes). For clinical and research purposes, several scales for the normative characterization of pubertal status have been developed. Most widely used are Tanner's photographic and descriptive standards of breast and pubic hair development in girls and genital and pubic hair development in boys (see Tanner, 1975). Although the most accurate estimate of the stages of physical maturity is skeletal age, X-ray determination is often unavailable and impractical. Because research has shown high correlation between Tanner sexual maturity ratings and skeletal age (Harlan, Harlan, & Grillo, 1980), these ratings provide accurate, easily assessable information (e.g., from adolescents or physicians) on pubertal development. The standards comprise five stages: Stage 1 represents prepubertal appearance, and stage 5 indicates attainment of adult secondary sex characteristics. Characteristics of each of the five stages are set forth in Table 2.1.

In girls, the first sign of puberty is usually the appearance of "breast buds" (thelarche). In some girls, the appearance of pubic hair (adrenarche) precedes breast budding, but in the majority it follows. It is important to note that ratings of the breast and pubic hair development may have different ordinal rankings. Use of a mean ranking may mask correlations of some variables with breast or pubic hair ratings. For example, the peak height velocity occurs after the development of pubic hair (stage 2) or breasts (stage 3) (Daniel, 1983).

More or less concurrently with breast development, internal sexual structures, including the uterus and vagina, also grow and mature. Uterine development usually reaches a definitive stage for menarche (the first menstrual period) to occur, usually after the peak of the height spurt has been passed. (Menarche generally occurs several years after thelarche and adrenarche.) Menarche by itself, however, does not signify the attainment of full reproductive capacity. Early menstrual cycles are often anovulatory; that is, they do not produce fertile eggs, and postmenarcheal "adolescent sterility" may last from 1 year to 18 months.

On average, pubertal changes begin in boys only about 6 months later than in girls. The general impression of an overall, considerably earlier maturation of girls largely results from the fact that the

Table 2.1 Pubertal Stages of Sexual Maturity

	Characteristics		
Stage	*Male Genital Development*	*Pubic Hair Development*	*Female Breast Development*
1	Testes, scrotum, and penis about the same size and proportion as early childhood	No pubic hair	Elevation of papilla only
2	Testes, scrotum, enlarge; scrotum reddens and changes texture; little or no enlargement of penis	Sparse growth of slightly pigmented hair along base of penis or along the labia	Breast bud stage; elevation of breast and papilla in small mound; areola diameter increases
3	Penis slightly longer; testes and scrotum continue growing	Darker, coarser, curlier; sparse on the pubes	Breast and areola both enlarged but with no separation of contour
4	Penis larger and broader; testes and scrotum larger; scrotum skin darker	Adult hair; area covered less than adult; no medial thigh hair	Areola and papilla form second mound on breast
5	Adult size and shape	Adult quantity and type; medial thigh hair	Mature stage; only papilla projects; areola recessed to breast contour

growth spurt in girls occurs earlier in the sequence of pubertal changes than in boys. The earliest sign of pubertal changes in boys is a growth acceleration of the testes and scrotum, often accompanied by the thinning and reddening of the scrotal skin. Simultaneously or shortly after, pigmented pubic hairs start to appear. About a year later, spurts in penile growth and height begin. Coinciding with the penile growth spurt, the male internal sexual structures (e.g., the seminal vesicles and the prostate) enlarge and develop. Their maturation is the prerequisite for the first ejaculation of seminal fluid, or thorarche (Levin, 1976), which tends to occur about a year after the beginning of accelerated penile growth (Tanner, 1975).

Tanner (1962) describes aspects of pubertal development in addition to the major characteristics. Axillary hair (i.e., underarm hair) generally develops about two years after pubic hair. Facial hair is usually coincident with axillary hair and develops in a particular sequence: Hair first appears at the corners of the upper lip, then spreads to form the mustache; next, growth occurs at the upper part of the cheeks and at the midline below the lower lip; finally, the beard forms. Facial hair growth in males is seldom completed before stage 5, in which genital and pubic hair development have been attained.

The change in voice pitch is a major pubertal process in males. This is a relatively late occurrence (near the end of puberty) that develops only gradually. The pitch of the female voice also deepens with puberty. In addition, there is a change in quality, or timbre, of the voice in both sexes.

Several changes are also seen in the skin at puberty. The sebaceous and apocrine sweat glands, particularly of the axillary, genital, and anal regions, develop rapidly during puberty. Acne and other skin eruptions resulting from enlarged pores and increased oiliness are also characteristic of puberty. These problems occur more frequently in boys than girls.

Timing of Pubertal Events

In general, the stages of each of these secondary sex characteristics proceed in an invariant sequence. There are wide interindividual variations, however, in the timing of pubertal events. Marshall and Tanner (1969, 1970) have presented data from boys and girls in the Harpenden Growth Study that show the average ages for each pubertal stage. Among girls, for instance, the onset of breast budding varies from age 8 to 13 years, and menarche ranges from age 10 to 16.5 years. In boys, the acceleration of testicular growth may start anywhere from age 9.5 to 13.5 years. The penile growth spurt starts between the ages of 10.5 and 14.5 years, and the penis reaches adult size between the ages of 12.5 and 16.5 years. Nocturnal emissions, another indication of sexual maturity, develop most frequently between the ages of 12 and 16 years.

A particularly interesting phenomenon regarding the onset of puberty, with important implications for the prolonged period of sexual activity prior to adulthood, is the acceleration of puberty. In Western countries, the onset of puberty seems to have dropped gradually in age over the last 150 years (Tanner, 1962, 1975). For example, the average age of menarche has fallen from 17 to 12.8 years

(Zacharias, Rand, & Wurtman, 1976) during this period. This trend is most likely attributable to the complex changes in nutrition, social conditions, and public health brought about by the technological development of the modern industrialized society.

The age at onset of puberty varies because of many factors, genetic as well as environmental (Tanner, 1975). Socioeconomic status also has a strong influence (Tanner, 1966): Menarche occurs several months earlier in girls of a higher social class than in those of a lower social class. Higher social class usually implies better living conditions, including nutrition, sleep, and exercise, and these may be the major factors accounting for class differences in rates of growth in childhood as well as in timing of the growth spurt and menarche.

Increased growth in childhood and early onset of menarche may be tied together by a hypothesis postulating that menarche occurs in females who have reached a "critical weight" (e.g., 47 kg) (Frisch & Revelle, 1970). More recent studies have shown that menarche correlates more closely with body composition than with the critical weight (Frisch, Revelle, & Cook, 1973), which suggests that menarche requires a minimum percentage of body fat (approximately 24%) stored in the body. In girls, athletic training and exercise, in combination with low body weight, can delay breast development and menarche and prevent regular menstrual cycles (Warren, 1980). Lack of nutrition can also delay the onset of sexual maturation in boys (Tanner, 1962).

In addition to the timing of the onset of the pubertal event, the rate of passing through the whole sequence varies considerably between individuals, and some sexual characteristics may mature relatively faster than others. Both adolescent girls (especially between the ages of 11 and 14) and boys (particularly the age group from 13 to 16 years) show a tremendous variation in somatic developmental status, which is one of the important factors explaining the typical problems of adolescent self-image and behavior. The impact of being "early" or "late" is exaggerated, because these changes take place at a time when many adolescents are engaging in social comparisons (Seltzer, 1982) and are very concerned about not being different from their peers. Girls tend to be sensitive about "early" pubertal development. Given that girls enter puberty 12 to 18 months prior to boys, early-maturing girls are the first members of their peer group to show signs of sexual maturation. In comparison, boys tend to be more sensitive about "late" pubertal development. Late-maturing boys may have trouble coping with comparatively smaller physical stature and delayed muscular development, both of which are important factors in athletic activities, an important domain for male adolescent interaction. Perceptions of pubertal timing, however, may be more important for psychological functioning than actual pubertal status (Tobin-Richards, Boxer, & Petersen, 1983).

Pubertal Development and Psychosocial Relations

Recent studies have focused on the interrelationship of pubertal status (based on the development of secondary sex characteristics) and psychosocial adjustment (see, e.g., Lerner & Foch, 1987). Findings indicate that for boys, body image tends to improve with pubertal development (Petersen, Tobin-Richards, & Boxer, 1983); for girls in the later stages of pubertal development (postmenarcheal), self-concept tends to be enhanced (Garwood & Allen, 1979). With regard to interpersonal relations, for both boys and girls, more mature pubertal status is associated with higher levels of heterosocial interactions (Crockett & Dorn, 1987), increased levels of conflict with mothers, although for boys such conflict decreases when they reach the later stages of pubertal development (Steinberg, 1981, 1989).

ENDOCRINOLOGICAL FACTORS

As previously described, changes in adolescent somatic development vary in timing of onset, sequence of events, and rate of passage. Not only are these variables influenced by genetic factors and life events, but pubertal development is regulated by various hormones or endocrine systems. Growth of reproductive organs and functions leading to menarche in females and thorarche (first ejaculation of sperm) in males is controlled by gonadal hormones. Pubic, axillary, body, and facial hair growth (adrenarche) is regulated by adrenal androgen secretions in both sexes. The growth spurt involves growth hormone, adrenal androgen, and (in males) testosterone. In both boys and girls, pubertal hormones seal over the epiphyses (ends of the long bones) and stop statural growth.

Before discussing the influence of hormones on the pubertal process, it is necessary to present some basic endocrine terminology and concepts.

Endocrine Terminology

A *hormone* is a powerful and highly specialized chemical substance that typically travels from its cell of origin to its target cell via the bloodstream. Hormones are produced in glands, but they may also be produced in other body tissues. The circulating active level of a hormone (i.e., unbound or free hormone) is only one component of the process by which a hormone has influence. The receptivity of the target tissue is also an important factor.

The *endocrine system* consists of a collection of glands that produce hormones that regulate the body's rate of metabolism, growth, and sexual development and functioning. The endocrine glands are ductless and release hormones directly into the bloodstream to be transported to organs and tissues throughout the body. In puberty, the glands of central importance are the pituitary gland (which secretes hormones that stimulate the adrenals, gonads, and growth), the adrenal glands (which produce androgens), and the gonads (female ovaries produce estrogens and progesterone; male testes produce androgens).

Normal pubertal development involves two distinct processes, adrenarche and gonadarche. *Adrenarche* is the maturation of adrenal androgen secretion involving the hypothalamic-pituitary-adrenal (HPA) axis and usually occurs between the ages of 6 and 8 years. *Gonadarche* is the reactivation of the hypothalamic-pituitary-gonadal (HPG) axis and maturation of gonadal sex-steroid secretion, which usually occurs between the ages of 9 and 13.

The sex hormones, primarily androgens and estrogens, are not solely produced by the gonads. Although the gonads have sex-specific functions, very few hormones are restricted to one sex. Androgens are thought of as "male" hormones, whereas estrogens frequently are considered "female" hormones. Both types of hormones are produced by both sexes with little difference in levels between prepubertal boys and girls; however, the average mature female produces more estrogens than androgens, and the average mature male produces more androgens than estrogens. The specific hormone(s) causing particular pubertal events cannot yet be determined, except for the well-established fact that testosterone has a major role in the development of male sexual characteristics, and estrogens a major role in female puberty.

Hypothalamic-Pituitary-Gonadal (HPG) Axis

One endocrine system of central interest in puberty is the hypothalamic-pituitary-gonadal axis (HPG) (see Figure 2.1). The HPG, which controls sexual functioning, is understood to have a negative feedback relationship that gradually matures from prenatal life onward. The various components of the system are functional from a very early stage but remain dormant as a result of the inhibitory effect of the hypothalamus, a small area of the forebrain located behind the eyes and above the pituitary gland. Indirectly the hypothalamus affects much of the endocrine system through its direct effect on the pituitary gland. It does this in two ways: through direct nerve connections and through specialized nerve cells that secrete hormones (called releasing factors) into the blood that flow directly to the pituitary. In this way, the hypothalamus can convert nerve signals into hormonal signals.

The level of circulating hormones remains low during childhood, when very small amounts of gonadal hormones inhibit hypothalamic secretion of gonadotropic-releasing hormones. With increasing age and the impact of nutritional health, stress, and other internal regulatory mechanisms, the threshold for the release of hypothalamic secretions gradually is raised. Luteinizing hormone-releasing hormone (LHRH) secretion from the hypothalamus stimulates secretion of the pituitary gonadotropins (hormones that stimulate cell activity in gonads), luteinizing hormone (LH) and follicular-stimulating hormone (FSH), which in turn stimulate gonadal sex-steroid secretion. Thus the ovaries and testes are activated to secrete their own hormones, estrogens, and androgens. As the hypothalamus becomes less sensitive to circulating gonadotropins, the sex-steroid hormone levels increase, which in turn leads to the development of sexual maturity (Hopwood et al., 1990). The increase in gonadal sex steroids estradiol and progesterone in females and testosterone in males induces the secondary sexual changes at puberty. Then the pituitary, through the hypothalamus, senses when an optimum hormone level is attained and responds by maintaining gonadotropin and sex hormone production at this level. In the female,

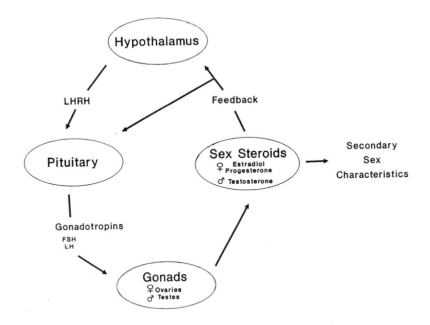

Figure 2.1. Diagram of the Hypothalamic-Pituitary-Gonadal Axis
NOTE: LHRH = luteinizing hormone-releasing hormone; FSH = follicle-stimulating hormone;
LH = luteinizing hormone.

hypothalamic and pituitary secretion are released cyclically to regulate the menstrual cycle. Continuous secretions occur in the male.

Hormone Levels

Endocrinologically, childhood is not a latency period. From about the age of 6 years in both boys and girls, there is an increased production of dehydroepiandrosterone (DHEA), an androgen precursor. Subsequently, from about the age of 8 years onward, there is a rise in androstenedione (an androgen present in large amounts in women's blood and converted to testosterone). These weak androgens are thought to stimulate early pubic hair growth in both sexes.

Between the ages of 6 and 10, there is a gradual rise in FSH and LH; however, increases in gonadal steroids are not yet detected (Bancroft, 1989). Pubertal hormonal maturation begins 6 months to

1 year in advance of the somatic changes that signal sexual development. The increase in FSH stimulates estrogen production and breast budding in girls, whereas in boys an increase in LH induces the production of testicular androgen and growth of the testicles.

When children approach and enter puberty, they consistently show more and more episodes of LH secretory bursts at night as compared to daytime, and the amplitudes of these bursts increase (Boyar et al., 1972). It is not until late in puberty that the daytime secretion also is elevated. Similar findings have been described for FSH (Lee, Plotnick, Migeon, & Kowarski, 1978). Because this phenomenon appears to be independent of gonadal activity, it indicates the active role of the central nervous system in the initiation of the pubertal process.

Interrelations of Hormone Levels and Physical Maturity

Winter and Faiman (1973) found in a cross-sectional study that systematic changes in hormone levels coincided with the first signs of puberty in girls. The first appearance of labial hair or breast budding (thelarche) was accompanied by rises in the levels of FSH, estradiol, and testosterone, whereas levels of LH did not become elevated significantly over prepubertal values before pubertal stage 3. Recent cross-sectional data collected by Nottelmann and her associates (1987) reveal that for girls there is a two- to threefold increase in the gonadotropins FSH and LH from pubertal stage 1 to stage 5. There was also an eightfold increase in estrogen levels, with adult levels not being reached until stage 4. It is not until several months after menarche that adult levels of estradiol appear (as well as its cyclical variation, which is necessary for reproduction).

Analogous data are available for boys. Cross-sectional studies (August, Grumbach, & Kaplan, 1972) show that gonadotropin levels in boys rise gradually between ages 6 and 10, during the prepubertal period, whereas significant rises in testosterone levels tend to occur after this period. These findings have been confirmed in a mixed cross-sectional/longitudinal study by Lee, Jaffe, and Midgley (1974). LH levels rose throughout puberty, the initial rise of LH occurring before testosterone concentrations were significantly increased. Testosterone levels rose progressively from before the appearance of pubic hair until an adult distribution was achieved. Nottelmann et al.

(1987) also report an eighteenfold increase in testosterone levels from stage 1 to stage 5.

An important methodological question for biopsychosocial research is whether hormone measures contribute valuable information above and beyond the assessment of physical development during puberty. The previously mentioned findings that several puberty-related hormones rise before puberty becomes visible suggest that they do. Also, recent studies (Nottelmann, Inoff-Germain, Susman, & Chrousos, 1990; Udry, 1990) point to the probability that there are direct hormonal effects associated with changes in hormone levels that would be undetected if one assessed only pubertal stage of development. Additionally, findings (e.g., Lee et al., 1974) imply that pubertal subjects with similar Tanner ratings may, in fact, show considerable differences in hormone secretion that are likely to be relevant to behavior effects. Nottelmann et al. (1987) report that moderate correlations between hormone levels and physical maturity measures also reflect the range of hormone levels within each pubertal stage. This is a particularly important consideration for the lower ranges of testosterone values characteristic of the early stages of male puberty, in which dose-response relationships between hormones and sexual behavior appear to be more likely than later (Davidson, 1977).

Hormone-Sexual Behavior Relations

The role of pubertal hormones in biopsychosocial interactions has recently become the focus of scientific investigation. It is well-known that hormones influence physical growth and maturation (Nottelmann et al., 1987). Because sexual behavior increases with the onset of puberty, there is interest in the extent to which hormones may influence adolescent sexuality. Yet very little is actually known about hormone-sexual behavior interrelationships in normal adolescents. Most of what we know about hormonal influences on adolescent behavior are based upon extrapolation from studies of animals (primarily rats and monkeys), adults, young children, and clinical or atypical populations. Recent studies have focused on the linkage of androgens (specifically testosterone) and sexual libido in both sexes (for a review, see Smith, 1989); findings suggest that androgens may be a source of sexual motivation in adolescents. Udry, Billy, Morris, Groff, and Raj (1985; Udry, 1990) have been investigating how various hormones and endocrine-related events affect sexual behavior in adolescents. Findings indicate that sexual motivation and sexual behavior are related to testosterone levels in normal male adolescents. For female adolescents, hormone levels (primarily adrenal androgens) were related to sexual motivation and some aspects of sexuality in female adolescents; however, sexual intercourse was found to be influenced primarily by social processes (Udry, Talbert, & Morris, 1986).

In light of differential hormonal development in these endocrinological findings for females and males, it appears that a comprehensive theory of sexual behavior in early adolescence would specify the hormones involved, their behaviorally effective blood levels, sensitive periods of development, differential effects of hormones on the various components of sexual behavior, and the interactions of hormones, pubertal stage, physical appearance, and psychosocial factors by sex.

GENDER IDENTITY

As seen from the previous discussion of pubertal development, biological as well as environmental factors interact in the developing adolescent. The physical changes of adolescence require that one reevaluate oneself as a sexual being. Thus it is important to include a discussion of physiological factors contributing to gender identity development in this chapter on biological factors influencing adolescent sexuality.

In contemporary usage, *sex* refers to biologically based distinctions between males and females, whereas *gender* refers to culturally constructed distinctions. *Gender identity* refers to which sex we believe we are and how we view ourselves as male, female, or ambivalent (Money & Ehrhardt, 1972). This sexual self-concept is the result of seven developmental stages: chromosomes, gonads, hormones, internal sexual organs, external genitalia and secondary sex characteristics, gender assigned at birth (e.g., "it's a girl"), and gender identity (e.g., "I am a girl") (Bancroft, 1989). An eighth stage, sexual differentiation of the brain, develops concurrently with the later stages. Although most research (Ehrhardt & Meyer-Bahlburg, 1981) seems to indicate that prenatal or postnatal hormones or other biological factors are not as important in gender identity development as the way in which we are socialized, biological factors play an important role in early stages of development.

Chromosomes, Gonads, and Hormones

The process of gender identity commences with the sex chromosomes, which are present in every cell of the body. At conception, the X or Y chromosome of the sperm combines with an X chromosome of the ovum. The normal female has an XX chromosomal pattern; the male has an XY chromosomal pattern. The Y chromosome determines maleness. During the initial period of development, the gonads are undifferentiated. About the sixth week of gestation in a normal male, the Y chromosome programs the differentiation of the gonads into testes. In the absence of the male factor, it is not until the twelfth week that the gonads develop into ovaries.

Differentiation is then carried forward by the presence or absence of masculinizing androgenic hormones (e.g., testosterone) secreted by the developing testes from about the eighth week on. (In the absence of the secretions, as noted above, it is not until around the twelfth week that the gonads differentiate into ovaries.) It is important to note that hormones, rather than genetics directly, are responsible for the differentiation of internal and external genitalia into male and female types.

Internal and External Genitalia

Every fetus has the potential for developing both male and female internal sexual organs because of the presence of the Wolffian and Mullerian ducts. Androgen and Mullerian-inhibiting factor (MIF) secreted from the fetal testes ensure that the Wolffian duct develops into the vas deferens, seminal vesicles, and ejaculatory ducts of the male and that the Mullerian ducts atrophy (for diagrams, see Bancroft, 1989). In the absence of MIF and without hormonal stimulation, the Mullerian ducts develop into a uterus, fallopian tubes, and the upper vagina. A characteristic hormonal pattern in these early stages of development is that for male differentiation, the appropriate hormones are required; for female development, hormones may not be required at all.

In contrast with internal genitalia, external genitalia for males and females develop from the same structures. It is not until the eighth week of life that androgen secreted from the testes begins to masculinize the genital area into the penis and scrotum. In the absence of androgen, the female clitoris and labia minora develop. Because of the importance of androgen in sexual differentiation, it is notable that androgen deficiency in males can result in underdeveloped genitalia and (in pubertal development) the lack of muscle development, decreased body hair and beard growth, smooth skin, a high-pitched voice, and reduced sexual drive and performance. Excess androgen in males can stimulate premature sexual development in childhood and initially increase bone growth, but adult height is reduced as a result of long bones ceasing to grow. In females, excess androgen causes virilization (the development of masculine features): increased body hair, deepness of voice, enlargement of the clitoris, and amenorrhea (absence of menstruation). The development of characteristics atypical of one's sex has important implications for development of masculine or feminine gender identity.

Brain

Parallel to genital dimorphism, there is evidence of sexual differentiation in human brains. Testosterone secretion masculinizes and defeminizes various cellular structures throughout the brain. Masculinization is linked to dihydrotestosterone (DHT) and androgen receptors and is the enhancement of male characteristics that would not develop without testosterone secretion (e.g., aggressive behavior). Defeminization is linked to the conversion of testosterone to estradiol and estrogen receptors and is the suppression of female characteristics that would develop without the secretion of testosterone (e.g., cyclic ovulation) (McEwen, 1991). In the brain, testosterone promotes the growth in neurons with estrogen and androgen receptors in certain nerve cells, influencing subtle differences in male and female neural circuitry. Thus boys and girls begin postnatal life with subtle structural and functional brain differences that are thought to influence information processing and erotic responses. Studies of humans exposed to sex-atypical prenatal hormones (anomalies or drugs taken by the mother during pregnancy to prevent miscarriage) have shown effects on the sexual differentiation of the genitalia and brain; hypothalamic regulation of the HPG axis controlling timing of pubertal onset and subsequent fertility;

personality; aggression; and cognitive ability (for a review, see Sanders & Reinisch, 1990).

Gender Assignment at Birth

At birth, the external genitalia initiate the social programming of gender identity as masculine or feminine. The initial observation of anatomical gender—"it's a girl"—acts as a releasing stimulus for behavior culturally and socially defined as appropriate for the female or male infant child. If a child is born with ambiguous-appearing sex organs (indistinguishable as female or male genitalia), sex assignment is made as soon as possible (usually based upon chromosomes), because the concept of being female or male is so important in any society. From the very beginning, parents and others relate differently to their daughters and sons (Notman, 1991; Thorne, 1990).

Gender Identity

The emergence of core gender identity (perceptions of oneself as a girl or a boy) is observable by the time a child begins to speak, at about 18 months (Stoller, 1968). Based upon clinical experience with cases of hermaphrodism (undifferentiated internal genitalia) and ambiguous external genitalia, the belief that "I am a female" or "I am a male" becomes fixed by the age of 3 (Money & Ehrhardt, 1972). Most individuals' gender identity conforms well to their biological sexual development. Some people, however, go through much of their lives feeling uncertain as to which sex they belong, whereas a few (i.e., transsexuals) feel certain that their true gender is the opposite of what their physical appearance indicates. These individuals, feeling trapped inside the body of the wrong sex, may seek medical help and pursue sex-change surgery.

The anatomical differences between girls and boys contribute to their sexual development. The external nature of male genitalia results in a definitive vocabulary about observable organs, curiosity and comparison between peers, masturbation, clear indication of response (erection), and homosexual play between boys. Girls, by contrast, are quite unaware of their genitalia, rarely discuss or explore their clitoris or vagina, and are more likely to discover masturbation by self-exploration or by accident rather than in peer group interaction. There is little information on the incidence or capacity for orgasm in prepubertal children, although both sexes are capable of orgasm before puberty (generally experienced by masturbation).

As the child approaches adolescence, there are important hormonal changes that underlie the development and maturation of secondary sex characteristics. The prepubertal child may have become confident in his or her gender identity, yet changes in physical appearance and sexual response produce uncertainty about the future. Sexuality now becomes an important facet of gender: "Am I sexual in a masculine or feminine way?" For many adolescents, increasing awareness and exploration of sexual feelings and behaviors, as well as attempts at forming sexual relationships, are directed at investigating and reinforcing their more mature gender identity.

Research suggests that androgens (particularly testosterone) appear to be the primary hormone responsible for libido in both sexes and a source of sexual motivation as adolescents mature (Smith, 1989). There is a wide range of individual variation within gender in sexual responsiveness; however, between-gender differences remain apparent. A notable difference between the sexes is the lower threshold for sexual and erotic response to narrative and tactile stimuli in girls and to visual stimuli in boys (Money & Ehrhardt, 1972). A slow, gradual increase in sexual and erotic interests and activities in females from adolescence into adulthood was contrasted with the sudden upsurge in sexual behavior in males at adolescence in the Kinsey studies (Kinsey, Pomeroy, & Martin, 1948; Kinsey, Pomeroy, Martin, & Gebhard, 1953). The extent to which these differing behavioral patterns are regulated biologically or socially is still under investigation. Recent findings (Udry et al., 1985) have revealed that increases in the free testosterone index (FTI) were found to be more important in initiating erotic behavior (number of sexual outlets and frequency of thoughts about sex) than socially mediated factors. In a parallel study of girls around the age of puberty (Udry et al., 1986), the findings suggested that although sexual interest was correlated with androgen levels, the best predictors of whether a girl engaged in sexual activity were not hormonal, but social.

CONCLUSION

This discussion of physiological factors leaves little doubt that anatomy and physiological development influence individual sexual development and gender identity. Current research clearly indicates that puberty is not a sudden development, but part of a gradual process that begins at conception. We might consider puberty as the final, most rapid phase of the development of mature reproductive capability that is activated in early adolescence. Development of anatomically mature genitalia equips adolescents to assume adult sexual roles, whereas Western society still considers them to be children (i.e., minors).

Puberty has different characteristics for males and females because the mature phenotypes differ, but there are also similarities in the process. Among the similarities for both sexes are growth to an adult stature and development of secondary sex characteristics, rapidly increasing levels of gonadotrophic and sex-steroid hormones, and the maturation of the positive feedback systems in the HPG axis. Differences include the onset of puberty 2 years later for boys than for girls. Boys end up taller and heavier than girls, with more facial and body hair and a different basic body shape, and develop a mature penis and testicles with sperm production. Girls develop breasts and a mature vagina-labia region with a menstrual cycle of hormone production, including a menstrual flow of blood.

Critical questions that arise in response to these differences concern to what extent these biological factors determine our gender roles. How different are male and female brains, and how do the subtle differences in neurocircuitry influence our gender identity and sexual behavior? Do high levels of androgens direct males to be the sexual aggressors in relationships? Are structural sexual differences (e.g., muscle mass) determined biologically, or are they encouraged socially by limiting the physical activity of young girls?

It is apparent that we cannot dismiss the dimorphic sexual development of males and females, yet how we weight the level of determinism has great political implications. The role of psychological and sociocultural factors in the development of adolescent sexuality has been addressed only briefly in this chapter. Subsequent articles will focus on these variables. Yet it seems obvious that to understand adolescent sexuality and sexual behavior fully, we will have to include measures of pubertal development and, when financially and methodologically feasible, measures of hormone levels. It is then that we will be able to develop a more complete picture of adolescent sexuality.

REFERENCES

August, G. P., Grumbach, M. M., & Kaplan, S. L. (1972). Hormonal changes in puberty: Correlation of plasma testosterone, LH, FSH, testicular size, and bone age with male pubertal development. *Journal of Clinical Endocrinology and Metabolism, 34*, 319-326.

Bancroft, J. (1989). *Human sexuality and its problems.* New York: Churchill Livingstone.

Bancroft, J., & Reinisch, J. M. (Eds.). (1990). *Adolescence and puberty.* New York: Oxford University Press.

Boyar, R. M., Finkelstein, J., Roffwarg, H., Kapen, S., Weitzman, E., & Hellman, L. (1972). Synchronization of LH secretion with sleep during puberty. *New England Journal of Medicine, 287*, 582-586.

Brooks-Gunn, J., & Petersen, A. C. (Eds.). (1983). *Girls at puberty: Biological and psychosocial perspectives.* New York: Plenum.

Brooks-Gunn, J., & Petersen, A. C. (1984). Problems in studying and defining pubertal events. *Journal of Youth and Adolescence, 13*, 181-196.

Crockett, L. J., & Dorn, L. (1987, April). *Young adolescents' pubertal status and reported heterosocial interaction.* Paper presented at the biennial meeting of the Society for Research in Child Development, Baltimore.

Daniel, W. A. (1983). Pubertal changes in adolescence. In J. Brooks-Gunn & A. C. Petersen (Eds.), *Girls at puberty: Biological and psychosocial perspectives* (pp. 51-72). New York: Plenum.

Davidson, J. M. (1977). Neurohormonal bases of male sexual behavior. In R. O. Greep (Ed.), *International review of physiology, vol. 13: Reproductive physiology II* (pp. 225-254). Baltimore: University Park Press.

Ehrhardt, A., & Meyer-Bahlburg, H. (1981). Effects of prenatal hormones on gender-related behavior. *Science, 211*, 1312-1318.

Faust, M. S. (1977). Somatic development of adolescent girls. *Monographs of the Society for Research in Child Development, 1*(Serial No. 169).

Fischbein, S., (1977). Intra-pair similarity in physical growth of monozygotic and of dizygotic twins during puberty. *Annals of Human Biology, 4*, 417-430.

Frisch, R. E., & Revelle, R. (1970). Height and weight at menarche and a hypothesis of critical body weight and adolescent events. *Science, 169*, 397-398.

Frisch, R. E., Revelle, R., & Cook, S. (1973). Components of weight at menarche and the imitation of the adolescent growth spurt in girls: Estimated total water, lean body weight and fat. *Human Biology, 45*, 469-483.

Garwood, S. G., & Allen, L. (1979) Self-concept and identified problem difference between pre- and postmenarchial adolescents. *Journal of Clinical Psychology, 35*, 528-537.

Harlan, W. R., Harlan, E. A., & Grillo, G. P. (1980). Secondary sex characteristics of girls 12 to 16 years of age: The U.S. health examination survey. *Journal of Pediatrics, 96*(9), 1074-1078.

Hopwood, N. J., Kelch, R. P., Hale, P. M., Mendes, T. M., Foster, C. M., & Beitins, I. Z. (1990). The onset of human puberty: Biological and environmental factors. In J. Bancroft & J. M. Reinisch (Eds.), *Adolescence and puberty* (pp. 29-49). New York: Oxford University Press.

Kinsey, A. C., Pomeroy, W. B., & Martin, C. F. (1948). *Sexual behavior in the human male.* Philadelphia: W. B. Saunders.

Kinsey, A. C., Pomeroy, W. B., Martin, C. F., & Gebhard, P. H. (1953). *Sexual behavior in the human female.* Philadelphia: W. B. Saunders.

Lee, P. A., Jaffe, R. B., & Midgley, A. R. (1974). Serum gonadotropin, testosterone and prolactin concentrations throughout puberty in boys: A longitudinal study. *Journal of Clinical Endocrinology and Metabolism, 39,* 664-672.

Lee, P. A., Plotnick, L. P., Migeon, C. H., & Kowarski, A. A. (1978). Integrated concentrations of follicle stimulating hormone and puberty. *Journal of Clinical Endocrinology and Metabolism, 46,* 488-490.

Lerner, R. M., & Foch, T. I. (Eds.). (1987). *Biological-psychosocial interactions in early adolescence: A life-span perspective.* Hillsdale, NJ: Lawrence Erlbaum.

Levin, R. J. (1976). Thorarche—A seasonal influence but no secular trend. *Journal of Sex Research, 12,* 173-179.

Marshall, W. A., & Tanner, J. M. (1969). Variations in the pattern of pubertal changes in girls. *Archives of Disease in Childhood, 44,* 191-303.

Marshall, W. A., & Tanner, J. M. (1970). Variations in the pattern of pubertal changes in boys. *Archives of Disease in Childhood, 44,* 13-23.

McEwen, B. S. (1991). Sex differences in the brain: What they are and how they arise. In M. T. Notman & C. C. Nadelson (Eds.), *Women and men: New perspectives on gender differences* (pp. 35-41). Washington, DC: American Psychiatric Press.

Money, J., & Ehrhardt, A. A. (1972). *Man and woman, boy and girl: Differentiation and dimorphism of gender identity from conception to maturity.* Baltimore: Johns Hopkins Press.

Notman, M. T. (1991). Gender development. In M. K. Notman & C. C. Nadelson (Eds.), *Women and men: New perspectives on gender differences* (pp. 117-127). Washington, DC: American Psychiatric Press.

Nottelmann, E. D., Inoff-Germain, G., Susman, E. J., & Chrousos, G. P. (1990). Hormones and behavior at puberty. In J. Bancroft & J. M. Reinisch (Eds.), *Adolescence and puberty* (pp. 88-123). New York: Oxford University Press.

Nottelmann, E. D., Susman, E. J., Dorn, L. D., Inoff-German, G., Loriaux, D. L., Cutler, G. B., Jr., & Chrousos, G. P. (1987). Developmental processes in early adolescence: Relations among chronologic age, pubertal stage, height, weight, and serum levels of gonadotropins, sex steroids, and adrenal androgens. *Journal of Adolescent Health Care, 8,* 246-260.

Petersen, A. C., Tobin-Richards, M. H., & Boxer, A. M. (1983). Puberty: Its measurement and its meaning. *Journal of Early Adolescence, 3,* 47-62.

Sanders, S. A., & Reinisch, J. M. (1990). Biological and social influences on the endocrinology of puberty: Some additional considerations. In J. Bancroft & J. M. Reinisch (Eds.), *Adolescence and puberty* (pp. 50-62). New York: Oxford University Press.

Seltzer, V. C. (1982). *Adolescent social development: Dynamic functional interaction.* Lexington, MA: Lexington Books.

Smith, E. A. (1989). A biosocial model of adolescent sexual behavior. In G. R. Adams, R. Montemayor, & T. P. Gullotta (Eds.), *Biology of adolescent behavior and development* (pp. 143-167). Newbury Park, CA: Sage.

Steinberg, L. (1981). Transformations in family relations at puberty. *Developmental Psychology, 17,* 833-840.

Steinberg, L. (1989). Pubertal maturation and parent-adolescent distance: An evolutionary perspective. In G. R. Adams, R. Montemayor, & T. P. Gullotta (Eds.), *Biology of adolescent behavior and development.* Newbury Park, CA: Sage.

Stoller, R. (1968). *Sex and gender: On the development of masculinity and femininity.* London: Hogarth.

Tanner, J. M. (1962). *Growth at adolescence* (2nd ed.). Oxford, England: Blackwell Scientific.

Tanner, J. M. (1966). Growth and physique in different populations of mankind. In P. T. Baker & J. J. Weiner (Eds.), *The biology of human adaptability* (pp. 45-66). Oxford: Clarendon.

Tanner, J. M. (1975). Growth and endocrinology of the adolescent. In L. I. Gardner (Ed.), *Endocrine and genetic diseases of children and adolescence* (2nd ed., pp. 14-61). Philadelphia: W. B. Saunders.

Thorne, B. (1990). Children and gender: Constructions of difference. In D. L. Rhode (Ed.), *Theoretical perspectives on sexual difference* (pp. 100-113). New Haven, CT: Yale University Press.

Tobin-Richards, M. H., Boxer, A. M., & Petersen, A. C. (1983). The psychological significance of pubertal change: Sex differences in perceptions of self during early adolescence. In J. Brooks-Gunn & A. C. Petersen, (Eds.), *Girls at puberty: Biological and psychosocial perspectives* (pp. 127-154). New York: Plenum.

Udry, J. R. (1990). Hormonal and social determinants of adolescent sexual initiation. In J. Bancroft & J. M. Reinisch (Eds.), *Adolescence and puberty* (pp 70-87). New York: Oxford University Press.

Udry, J. R., Billy, J. O., Morris, N. M., Groff, T. R., & Raj, M. H. (1985). Serum androgenic hormones motivate sexual behavior in adolescent boys. *Fertility and Sterility, 43,* 90-94.

Udry, J. R., Talbert, L. M., & Morris, N. M. (1986). Biosocial foundations for adolescent female sexuality. *Demography, 23,* 217-230.

Warren, M. (1980). The effects of exercise on pubertal progression and reproductive function in girls. *Journal of Clinical Endocrinology and Metabolism, 51*(5), 1150-1157.

Winter, J. S. D., & Faiman, C. (1973). The development of cyclical pituitary-gonadal function in adolescent females. *Journal of Clinical Endocrinology & Metabolism, 37,* 714-718.

Zacharias, L., Rand, W. M., & Wurtman, R. J. (1976). A prospective study of sexual development and growth in American girls: The statistics of menarche. *Obstetrics and Gynecology Survey, 31,* 325-337.

3. Sexual Behavior in Adolescence

Brent C. Miller
Cynthia R. Christopherson
Pamela K. King
Utah State University

INTRODUCTION

During the second decade of life, there is a dramatic increase in human sexual interest, arousal, and behavior. Our focus in this chapter is on behavior rather than cognitive variables such as sexual arousal, attitudes, or standards. Sexual behavior during adolescence is of particular interest because of the normative upsurge observed during this time and also because of the potentially negative consequences of sexual intercourse, including the risks of unintended pregnancy (Hayes, 1977; Miller & Moore, 1990), sexually transmitted diseases (Bell & Hein, 1984), and now AIDS (Hein, 1988). In this chapter, we focus on heterosexual behaviors, primarily because adolescent same-sex behavior (i.e, homosexuality) is covered elsewhere in this volume, and because opposite-sex relationships are linked to pair bonding, fertility, and family formation in every human society. We begin with the biological and social contexts of adolescent heterosexual behavior.

BIOSOCIAL ORIGINS

Infants and young children stimulate themselves sexually, and sexual play is common among older children (Martinson, 1980). It is abundantly clear, however, that sexual behaviors become much more

AUTHORS' NOTE: Send correspondence to Professor Brent C. Miller, Department of Family & Human Development, Utah State University, Logan, UT 84322-2905. Cynthia R. Christopherson and Pamela K. King were doctoral and master's candidates, respectively, when this chapter was written.

varied and frequent during adolescence (Constantine & Martinson, 1981; Dreyer, 1982). What accounts for this rapid rise in sexual interest, arousal, and behavior during the second decade of life? And yet why do the timing and type of sexual behaviors exhibited vary considerably across human populations?

Historically, there have been two separate and contrasting explanations for understanding human sexuality in general and adolescent sexual behavior in particular (Miller & Fox, 1987). One paradigm, represented by the work of Sigmund Freud (1933, 1953), explains sexual behavior as largely attributable to the unfolding or emergence of biological urges that begin pressing most urgently for genital expression during adolescence. In contrast with such mostly biological and inner-driven views, a second paradigm explains sexual behavior as the result of socially shaped and learned patterns that are highly variable across cultural space and time. According to this view, cultural elements constrain "the age, gender, legal, and kin relationships between sexual actors, as well as setting limits on the sites of behavior and the connection between sexual organs" (Gagnon & Simon, 1973, p. 4).

Recent views combine elements of both biological and social explanations in understanding the timing and variation of adolescent sexual behavior (Smith, 1989). A biosocial approach argues that hormonal changes early in adolescence have both a direct biological influence on sexual interest and motivation and an indirect influence on sexual involvement by altering the adolescent's physical appearance and heterosexual attractiveness. In addition, social processes are recognized as facilitating or inhibiting sexual involvement, altering the forms of sexual expression, and defining appropriate sexual partners.

Specific Biological Mechanisms

There is little difference in estrogen and androgen hormone levels of prepubertal boys and girls (Smith, 1989). During puberty, however, gradually increasing levels of luteinizing hormone (LH) and follicle-stimulating hormone (FSH) result in the maturation of the gonads. Elevated hormone levels and gonadal development are accompanied by the development of secondary sexual characteristics, such as the deepening of the voice and development of facial hair in males and breast and hip development in females. Pubertal males experience an increase in androgens, and females have an increase in both androgens and estrogens.

Because hormone production is primarily responsible for the timing and pace of individual sexual development, it is not unreasonable to think that some individuals might experience an earlier and perhaps stronger biological push toward sexual interest and behavior than others. There is, in fact, considerable and varied evidence from human and other primate studies that androgens (specifically testosterone) are primarily responsible for sexual arousal (i.e., libido) in both males and females (Smith, 1989).

Links between adolescent testosterone levels, sexual arousal, and sexual behavior have been examined in a series of studies by Richard Udry and his colleagues. Among adolescent males, Udry, Billy, Morris, Groff, and Raj (1985) found that testosterone levels were related to measures of sexual motivation (thinking about sex, sexual arousal), and to sexual behaviors (including masturbation, wet dreams, and frequency of intercourse). Among adolescent girls, an effect of testosterone levels was observed on sexual motivation and masturbation, but not intercourse experience (Udry, Talbert, & Morris, 1986).

In addition to hormones, another biological basis of adolescent sexual behavior appears to be genetic. There is a relationship between mothers' and daughters' ages at menarche, and age at menarche is known to be related to age at first intercourse (Presser, 1978; Udry & Cliquet, 1982). Further, there is evidence that mothers' sexual experience during adolescence has an influence on the sexual experience of their adolescent children, and this relationship appears to operate, at least in part, through their shared biology (Newcomer & Udry, 1984).

Although a biological substrate clearly triggers sexual development and influences sexual arousal among both male and female adolescents, behavioral effects of biological variables appear to differ by gender. Both biological and social explanations appear to be important to understand differences between males and females in adolescent sexual arousal and behavior.

> Girls who progress to more intimate levels of sexual behavior follow a socially learned sequence (kissing, then increasingly intimate petting, then coitus). The degree of involvement in these socially determined patterns is influenced by androgenic hormones, except for coitus. . . .

Differential involvement of girls in coitus is controlled by social processes, not by hormones. Differential involvement of boys in coitus is controlled primarily by hormones, not by social processes. (Udry et al., 1986, p. 226)

Specific Social Mechanisms

In addition to the biological mechanisms referred to above, social processes and cultural contexts also influence the timing and form of adolescent sexual expression. Although physical changes and sexual motivation are propelled most clearly by biological mechanisms, heterosexual behaviors (e.g., kissing, petting, and coitus) are influenced to some extent by social processes, expectations, and social controls (DeLamater, 1981).

Family characteristics and processes are widely regarded as having particularly important influences on the sexual behavior of adolescents (Miller & Jorgensen, 1988). For example, parental values, supervision, and modeling are associated with the sexual behaviors of their children (Hogan & Kitagawa, 1985; Miller, McCoy, Olson, & Wallace, 1986; Thornton & Camburn, 1987). Parents' educational attainment and expectations for their children are related to children's school achievement and educational plans, which are inversely related to adolescent sexual intercourse (Miller & Sneesby, 1988). Other parent-effect mechanisms, such as parent-teen communication, have yielded conflicting results (Kahn, Smith, & Roberts, 1984; Newcomer & Udry, 1985) and might produce interpretable effects only when considered in combination with parental values. For example, Moore, Peterson, and Furstenberg (1986) found no relationship between parent-teen communication and teen sexual intercourse in their total sample, but when the sample was partitioned according to teen gender and parents' values, daughters of traditional parents who had communicated about sex were found to be less likely to have had sex than daughters of more liberal parents or daughters of conservative parents who had not communicated about sex.

Peer influence on adolescent sexual behavior is reflected in a variety of ways. Billy and Udry (1985) found that the sexual behavior of white females was influenced by the behavior of their best male and female friends; that is, those who were virgins at the first round of their longitudinal study were more likely to experience intercourse between survey rounds if they had sexually experienced friends when the study began. Among white male adolescents, however, friends appeared to be chosen on the basis of sexual activity, rather than such activity being influenced by friends' behavior. These relationships were not observed among black adolescents.

Peer influence on adolescent sexual behavior also occurs in other ways. Social pressures were identified in a national poll of adolescents as the main reason why teenagers do not wait to have sexual intercourse until they are older (Harris & Associates, 1986). Both boys and girls named social pressures more than any other influence, but girls (73%) mentioned it more often than boys (50%) did. It is clear that the onset of dating is socially scripted (Dornbusch et al., 1984), and a majority of first sexual intercourse experiences occur in a casual or serious dating relationship (Zelnik & Shah, 1983). Early and steady dating are also related to the timing of first sexual intercourse, frequency of intercourse, and the number of sexual partners (Miller, McCoy, & Olson, 1986; Thornton, 1990).

SEQUENCE OF NORMATIVE HETEROSEXUAL BEHAVIOR

There is substantial research documenting a normative developmental pattern in the sequence of adolescent heterosexual behaviors. Couples generally embrace and kiss first, then fondle and pet, and subsequently engage in more intimate behaviors that include sexual intercourse.

McCabe and Collins (1984) developed a scale of 12 items to measure the depth of desired and experienced sexual involvement among Australian adolescents during various stages of dating. As dating becomes more serious and committed, the level of sexual activity increases. Hand holding and embracing are the most frequently occurring behaviors on first dates, whereas genital masturbation and intercourse are much less common, as shown in Table 3.1 below. Males had more desire for sexual intimacy on a first date than females, but these gender differences decreased with prolonged relationship involvement. Females showed increasing desire toward sexual intimacy with increase in age (McCabe & Collins, 1984).

A longitudinal analysis of the sequence of heterosexual behaviors among younger adolescents in the United States was conducted by Smith and Udry (1985). This analysis used both cross-sectional

Table 3.1 Percentage of Adolescents Engaging in Heterosexual Behaviors at Various Stages of Dating

	Stage of Dating		
Behavior	First Date %	Several Dates %	Going Steady %
Hand holding	90	93	95
Light embrace	93	94	97
Necking	47	82	88
Deep kissing	46	84	90
General body contact	40	79	94
Mutual masturbation	18	45	64
Simulated intercourse	16	44	60

SOURCE: Adapted from McCabe and Collins (1984).

Guttman-scale analysis and longitudinal linking of individual sexual behavior separated by 2 years. At the first round, results for white adolescents aged 12 to 15 showed the expected ordering of heterosexual behavior: Necking occurred most often, then feeling breasts through clothing, feeling breasts directly, feeling sex organs directly, feeling penis directly, and finally intercourse (which occurred least often).

The sequence of behaviors for black adolescents was quite different from the sequence of behaviors among white adolescents. A greater percentage of black teens indicated that they had intercourse than had engaged in the unclothed petting of breasts, sex organs, or the penis. Also, participation in the unclothed petting behaviors among black adolescents did not increase at a regular rate, as shown in Table 3.2 (Smith & Udry, 1985).

Longitudinal data were analyzed in the Smith and Udry (1985) study to determine if the ordering of sexual behaviors for white and black adolescents that was found in the cross-sectional data was predictive of subsequent developmental sequences of behavior. Among white adolescents, the longitudinal results supported the cross-sectional sequence of sexual behaviors. Among black adolescents, there was no apparent predictable progression in precoital sexual activity. Among virgin black males who had not had coitus when the study began, 67.9% experienced intercourse in the 2-year interval, compared to 30.7% of the white virgin males. Only 23.8%

Table 3.2 Percentage of Adolescents Who Have Engaged in Heterosexual Behaviors, by Race and Gender

| | White | | Black | |
| | Male | Female | Male | Female |
	%	%	%	%
Necked	70.1	63.2	83.5	62.9
Feel breasts clothed	66.9	46.7	81.3	48.3
Feel breasts directly	51.6	34.9	67.0	25.9
Feel sex organs directly	47.2	25.8	70.3	26.4
Feel penis directly	34.4	18.4	48.9	20.2
Intercourse	29.3	11.1	75.8	40.5

SOURCE: Adapted from Smith and Udry (1985).

of the white females made the transition to sexual intercourse during the study, as compared to 41.4% of black females (Smith & Udry, 1985).

White and black adolescents in the United States apparently have different sets of normative expectations regarding heterosexual behavior (Furstenberg, Morgan, Moore, & Peterson, 1987). White teens are more likely than black teens to engage in a predictable series of noncoital behaviors for a period of time before their first intercourse. In general, however, an increase in the commitment to their relationship is accompanied by an increasing desire for sexual involvement for both males and females. Females approach males' level of sexual involvement with increasing age and increased commitment to the relationship.

CONTEXTS OF EARLY SEXUAL EXPERIENCE

Heterosexual dating relationships in adolescence progress along a continuum of dyadic commitment, from casual acquaintances to "going steady." The earlier the dating experience begins for an adolescent, the more likely he or she is to become involved in one or more steady, committed relationships, which increase their likelihood of sexual experiences. In one study, among girls whose first date took place at age 14 or younger, two thirds had gone steady before age 16 (Thornton, 1990). Of the girls who began to date between the ages of 16 and 18, however, one third had not gone steady by age 18.

Sexual intercourse is more likely to take place within a committed dating relationship than in one with little or moderate commitment. Adolescents who are steadily dating one person have the highest levels of sexual activity; adolescents dating several individuals generally have moderate levels, and those who are dating only occasionally or are not dating at all have the lowest incidence of sexual activity (Miller, McCoy, & Olson, 1986).

Age at First Sexual Intercourse

Age is strongly related to adolescents' sexual intercourse experience. A clear picture of sexual intercourse experience by age can be seen in graphs that plot the cumulative incidence of intercourse experience by respondent's age. These data have been plotted for whites and blacks, respectively, in different national samples of young women (Hofferth, Kahn, & Baldwin, 1987). The total percentage of young women aged 15 to 19 who reported sexual intercourse experience grew from 47% in 1982 to 53% in 1988. According to the most recent data available, only about 5% of adolescent males have had sexual intercourse by age 13, compared to over 80% of 19-year-old males (Sonenstein, Pleck, & Ku, 1989). Figure 3.1 shows similar data for both males and females, plotted from the National Youth Survey (Elliott & Morse, 1989).

The age of first sexual intercourse is influenced strongly by race, with blacks significantly more likely to report younger ages of first intercourse than whites or Hispanics (Furstenberg et al., 1987; Mott & Haurin, 1988; Zelnik & Shah, 1983). In the recent National Survey of Adolescent Males, 20% of black males said their first intercourse was prior to age 13, compared to only 3% of white and 4% of Hispanic males. Stated differently, black males are about 2 years ahead of white and Hispanic males in the proportion who report having sexual intercourse by a given age. That is, the proportion of black males who had intercourse by their 13th birthday was comparable to the levels for white and Hispanic males who had reached their 15th birthday (Sonenstein, Pleck, & Ku, 1991).

Age is the most important variable distinguishing between adolescents who have and have not had sexual intercourse, but the age of first intercourse itself has consequences. Analyzing longitudinal

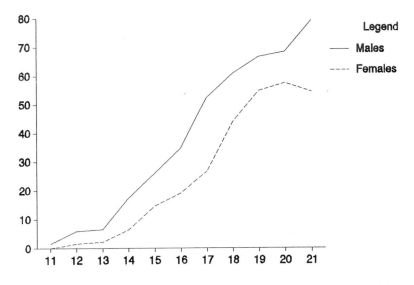

Figure 3.1. Proportion of Youths Who Are Sexually Active, by Race and Sex
SOURCE: Elliott and Morse, 1989
NOTE: Median age-specific annual prevalance rates for study cohorts, 1976-1980.

data over 2 years, Billy, Landale, Grady, and Zimmerle (1988) found that having sexual intercourse between rounds of the study led to having more sexually permissive attitudes and expectations in all race/sex subgroups and, among whites, to selecting friends who were also sexually active. Having intercourse also lowered the importance of going to college among white females and depressed the school grades of white males. Miller and Heaton (1991) analyzed the age of first sexual intercourse in relation to the timing of marriage and childbirth among a large nationally representative sample of young women. Female teens who began sexual intercourse earliest in this sample were most likely to form a family through giving birth rather than through marriage.

Locations of First Intercourse

A home, either one's own or that of a partner, friend, or relative, is the most common site (75%) for adolescents' first sexual intercourse experience. The home as the location for this first encounter is followed by a hotel or motel for blacks and an automobile for whites (Zelnik & Shah, 1983).

Related Deviant Behaviors

There is a positive relationship between the occurrence of adolescent sexual activity, delinquency, and drug use/abuse (Jessor & Jessor, 1977). As age increases, however, sexual intercourse is less likely to be associated with other deviant behaviors, as a result of a normative increase in sexual involvement among older teens (Elliott & Morse, 1989). The typical temporal sequence is usually delinquency followed by drug use and then sexual intercourse, suggesting that sexual involvement usually is not the initial problem behavior but follows experience with other nonnormative behaviors (Elliott & Morse, 1989).

NONNORMATIVE SEXUAL BEHAVIOR

Nonconsensual or coercive sexual acts are perpetrated against the victim's will, without consent, or in an aggressive, exploitative, or threatening manner. Adolescents have been noted to be at risk for sexual victimization (rape or sexual assault) by various predators, including peers (Ageton, 1981), adult acquaintances (Finkelhor, 1979), family members (Lystad, 1982), and strangers (National Crime Survey, 1981).

Since the 1970s, the definition of rape has expanded from vaginal penetration against a female's will to include "statutory and attempted rape as well as completed rape and any other criminal sexual assault, whether homosexual or heterosexual, that involves the use or the threat of force, including coercion and bribery of children" (Burgess, 1985, p. 2). Because of an expanded understanding of the damage caused by all forms of sexual victimization, clinical researchers have broadened the concept of sexual assault to include more subtle forms of sexual pressure and exploitation of either sex. Although in most cases females are victims and males are perpetrators, there are, of course, cases of male victimization.

Acquaintance Rape

Acquaintance rape has been found to occur with disturbing frequency among adolescents. Unlike rape by strangers, acquaintance rape—particularly date rape—takes place in the context of normal adolescent social activities. The full extent of acquaintance rape and sexual exploitation is not known. Adolescents can be taken advantage of because of their fear of getting into trouble, their inexperience and lack of information about sexuality, or their own needs (along with outside pressures) to enter the adult world of love and romance.

The typical adolescent sexual assault is committed during a date by a boyfriend or acquaintance of approximately the same age (Ageton, 1985). Most assaults (55%) occur in the victim's home (Renner & Wackett, 1987). An unstable home environment, involvement in delinquent behavior, and membership in a delinquent network increase the risk of being sexually assaulted; however, adolescents who are involved in delinquent activities are not the only victims of sexual assault.

Culturally transmitted beliefs about the sexes, acceptance of violence, and aggression and rape myths may lead to rape-supportive values in the general population (Burt, 1980). Check and Malamuth (1983) found relationships between sex-role stereotyping and arousal to rape, perceptions of rape victims responding favorably, and men's self-reported likelihood of raping. Furthermore, misunderstandings such as the perception of a woman resisting sexual advances as a part of her femininity (and not as a statement of her displeasure or discomfort), misinterpretation of another's actions (e.g., the woman initiating the date, going to a man's home, or accepting a ride), or the belief that petting means a woman is ready for sexual intercourse may lead to sexual aggression or rape (Check & Malamuth, 1983; Muehlenhard & Linton, 1987).

In one study, high school students (12% of the girls, 39% of the boys) reported that it was acceptable for a boy to pressure a girl for sex if the boy had spent a lot of money on the girl. Likewise, more than one third of the males reported acceptability if the boy was so aroused that he thought he could not stop; 54% found pressure acceptable if the girl changed her mind about having sexual intercourse.

These figures illuminate the dominant sexual and dating values of adolescents (Goodchilds, Zellman, Johnson, & Giarrusso, 1988).

Prevalence

It is difficult to obtain accurate statistics regarding adolescent sexual victimization. Because there are not centralized national or state recording systems, adolescents are often included in adult statistics, and many adolescents are reluctant to report sexual assault. Most studies of date or acquaintance rape have been conducted with college student samples; however, it is clear that sexual aggression occurs at younger ages.

The National Crime Survey (1981), a household survey to identify crimes that are not reported to official agencies, indicated that sexual victimization occurred in 1979 at the rate of 2.5 cases per 1,000 females aged 12 to 15 and at the rate of 5.7 cases per 1,000 females aged 15 to 19. Finkelhor (1979), however, found in his survey of college-age students that 19.2% of the women students reported a childhood sexual encounter with an adult (mean age of exposure 10.2), with 63% not previously having reported the incident. In Finkelhor's study, 8.6% of the male students had experienced a childhood sexual encounter with an older person (mean age 11.2), with 73% not previously reporting the incident. Furthermore, Muehlenhard and Linton (1987) reported that 70.4% of the women and 50% of the men in their college sample experienced some form of sexual aggression while in high school.

More specific data about nonvoluntary sexual intercourse during childhood and adolescence has been reported from the third wave of the National Survey of Children (Moore, Nord, & Peterson, 1989). Seven percent of all sample youths aged 18 to 22 in 1987 responded "yes" to the question, "Was there ever a time when you were forced to have sex (sexual intercourse) against your will, or were raped?" Additionally, it was found that adolescents who have been involved in nonvoluntary sexual behavior have an increased likelihood of participating in voluntary sexual activity at younger ages (Moore, Nord, & Peterson, 1990).

The findings about nonvoluntary intercourse and family characteristics reported above suggest a link between incestuous child sexual abuse and later adolescent sexual behavior and childbearing. Butler and Burton (1990) conducted exploratory interviews of a small nonclinical sample of adolescent mothers and found that more than half had been sexually abused as children. Ten of the 22 sexually abused respondents reported that they had been abused by relatives, and in 3 of these cases the perpetrator was the respondent's father. Most of the cases of sexual abuse involved either verbal threats or physical violence, and in only 3 of the 37 accounts were the police notified. In most cases, disclosure occurred to a close friend or relative some years after the sexual abuse incident(s) occurred. Although the study was based on a very small sample, there was a tendency for self-perceptions among adolescent mothers who were victims of sexual abuse to be more negative than self-perceptions of teen mothers who were not victims of sexual abuse.

SEXUAL INTERCOURSE TRENDS AND CHARACTERISTICS

Frequency of Sexual Intercourse

Sexual intercourse among unmarried adolescents in the more normative population is usually quite sporadic. Zelnik, Kantner, and Ford (1981) concluded that white females (3.0 mean times per month) tended to have sexual intercourse more often than black females (1.7 mean times per month). Vinovskis (1988) found unmarried adolescents to be one fourth less active than their married counterparts. Data from the 1982 National Survey of Family Growth (NSFG) show that 40% of 15- to 19-year-old women who had engaged in sexual intercourse reported having intercourse an average of once a week or more in the preceding 3 months; this percentage had increased to 45% in the 1988 NSFG data.

Number of Partners

The number of years an adolescent has been sexually active accounts for the largest percentage of explained variance in the number of sexual partners (Zelnik et al., 1981). In Zelnik et al.'s 1976 survey, the mean number of partners for sexually active black females was 2.4; white females were slightly higher at 2.8.

That initiation of sexual intercourse early in life is associated with an increased number of sex partners is also borne out in recently collected data ("HIV-Related Knowledge," 1990). In 1988, adolescents who had engaged in sexual intercourse earlier in life reported greater numbers of sex partners. Among 15- to 24-year-olds who initiated sexual intercourse before age 18, 75% reported having had two or more partners, and 45% reported having had four or more partners. Among women aged 15 to 24 who had been sexually active for the same length of time (< 24 months), 45% of 15- to 17-year- olds reported having had two or more partners, compared to 40% of 18- to 19-year-olds and 26% of those older than 29 years of age.

The number of partners reported by sexually active adolescents is particularly important in understanding the risk of sexually transmitted diseases. The percentage of 15- to 19-year-old females who reported two or more sexual partners increased from 38% in 1971 to 51% in 1979 (Moore et al., 1986) and to 59% in 1988 (Pratt & Eglash, 1990).

Male adolescents who have had sexual intercourse reported having an average of 5.1 lifetime heterosexual partners (Sonenstein et al., 1991). Older respondents report significantly more partners than younger respondents, and blacks report more lifetime partners than whites and Hispanics. Sexually experienced 15-year-old Hispanic and white males report an average of only two or three lifetime sexual partners, whereas 19-year-old black males have had an average of just over 11 lifetime sexual partners. Multivariate analyses revealed, however, that most of the racial differences in number of lifetime sexual partners were attributable to the earlier age at which black males began having intercourse (Sonenstein et al., 1991).

Pratt and Eglash (1990) concluded that of females aged 15 to 19, 41.3% had had 1 sexual partner, 28.0% had had 2 or 3 partners, and 6.6% had had 10 or more partners. There is a very strong association between age at first intercourse and number of sexual partners. Among those women who had initiated sexual intercourse before age 18, 20% had engaged in sexual unions with 10 or more men, compared to only 5% of those having first sex at age 20 or older. The association was seen among both black and white women but was weaker among black women.

Trends

There has been an increase in premarital sexual activity since at least the late 1950s (Pratt & Eglash, 1990). Nearly three fourths of women 15 to 55 years of age in 1988 had begun their sexual experience in nonmarital relationships. In 1988, 52.2% of women aged 15 to 19 reported already having premarital sexual intercourse, compared to 44.6% in 1982. Among white females in the same age group, 51.2% had already had sexual intercourse in 1988, compared to 60.0% of black teens.

There was an accelerated increase from 1970 to 1988 in the proportion of women 15 to 19 years of age in the United States who had become sexually active ("HIV-Related Knowledge," 1990). For each year of age, the proportion of adolescent women who reported having had premarital sexual intercourse increased at least 55% between 1970 and 1988. The largest relative increase occurred among those 15 years of age (from 4.6% in 1970 to 25.6% in 1988).

Sonenstein et al. (1989) concluded from the 1988 National Survey of Adolescent Males (NSAM) that 60% of never-married young men aged 15 to 19 were sexually active. Levels of sexual activity increased significantly at each successive year of age. Whereas only one third of the 15-year-old males had experienced sexual intercourse, one half of the 16-year-olds and close to two thirds of 17-year-olds were sexually experienced. At age 19, 86% of the young men in the sample reported that they had engaged in sexual intercourse. Levels of sexual activity also varied significantly by racial and ethnic group. Whereas 81% of black males aged 15 to 19 reported having had sexual intercourse, the proportions were lower among Hispanics (60%) and whites (57%).

Analysis of the NSAM also has provided a more substantial empirical base to evaluate speculations about the extent of promiscuous sexual behavior among adolescent males. Terms such as "sexual adventurers" and "roving inseminators" have been used to describe an indistinct group of promiscuous young males who seek out sexual conquests (Anderson, 1989; Sorenson, 1973). Such promiscuous behavior appears to be quite unusual; on the average, sexually experienced young men reported spending about half of the preceding year with no sexual partner. Further, very few of the sexually active young men had been involved in simultaneous sexual relationships. The investigators concluded that "young men have surprisingly conservative sexual behaviors and relatively few periods of multiple partners; having more than one partner in a year is generally not a sign of being a 'sexual adventurer' but of the instability of adolescent relationships" (Sonenstein et al., 1991, p. 162).

SUMMARY AND CONCLUSIONS

Adolescence often is defined simply as that phase of the life course between childhood and adulthood. Sometimes adolescence is defined more specifically as beginning with pubertal changes, including markers of sexual development, and ending vaguely a decade or more later with the assumption of adult roles.among the other changes and developmental achievements of adolescence, sexual growth and behavior is an important part. Sexual behaviors do not begin with adolescence, and in some respects humans are sexual beings from birth. But the kinds of sexual scripts that are open to adolescents as compared to children, the kinds of sexual behaviors involved, the distribution of these sexual behaviors in the population, and the risks of unwanted fertility and disease all change dramatically during the second decade of life. For the vast majority, adolescence is a time when sexual roles and behaviors take on vastly different meanings and manifestations than before.

Contemporary adolescents typically engage in a series of sequenced heterosexual behaviors that begins with kissing, proceeds to petting, and eventually includes coitus in the midteenage years, on the average. These behaviors tend to be cumulative, especially among whites, and among all races the tendency is for sexual behaviors to be expressed between partners who feel some degree of affection or commitment toward each other. Black adolescents have sexual intercourse sooner than nonblacks, on the average, but by the late teens the large majority of all adolescents have had sexual intercourse. The younger the age of first sexual intercourse, the greater the number of sexual partners, and the greater the risk of negative consequences of adolescent sexual behavior.

Biological changes, such as hormonally linked pubertal changes and heightened sex drive, are among the most common explanations given for the rapid increase observed in normative sexual behavior during the adolescent years. Obvious observable changes in secondary sex characteristics, also under the control of pubertal hormones, serve as signals to individual adolescents (and to others) of the adolescents' sexual readiness and potential. These biologically based explanations seem particularly appropriate for explaining the near-universal sexual distinctions made between children and adolescents. Testosterone levels apparently explain some variation in sexual arousal between males and females and might account for a major portion of the variance in behavior among adolescent males.

In spite of this biological substrate, there are vast differences in the extent of sexual behavior of various adolescent subgroups. Some of these differences in adolescent sexual behavior appear to be accounted for primarily by social and cultural forces such as race, family, and religion. Social forces operate through mechanisms such as modeling, parental control and supervision, social sanctions, and instilling values about acceptable and unacceptable sexual behavior.

Some individuals' involvement in sexual behavior is coerced, abusive, or otherwise nonnormative, often beginning long before adolescence. Among such individuals, adolescent sexual behavior and other aspects of life appear to be strongly and adversely affected by these early involuntary sexual experiences.

Adolescence and sexual behavior seem almost synonymous to the layperson in advanced Western societies. It is true that sexual behaviors become an accepted part of life for most adolescents sometime during the teen years. Yet a significant number of younger children experience nonvoluntary sexual behaviors, a substantial minority of young black males voluntarily begin having sexual intercourse before their teen years, and another minority of older adolescents enter their twenties as virgins. These facts, along with the reality that sexual intercourse poses serious risks of unwanted pregnancy, sexually transmitted disease, and AIDS, make it important to obtain a scientific understanding of adolescent sexual behavior.

REFERENCES

Ageton, S. S. (1981). *Sexual assault among adolescents: A national survey* (NIMH Final Report). Springfield, VA: National Technical Information Service.

Ageton, S. S. (1985). *A research report for adults who work with teenagers: Facts about sexual assault*. Boulder, CO: Behavioral Research Institute.

Anderson, E. (1989). Sex codes and family life among poor inner city youths. *Annals of the American Academy of Political and Social Science, 501*, 59.

Bell, T., & Hein, K. (1984). The adolescent and sexually transmitted diseases. In K. Holmes, P. A. Mardh, P. S. Sparling, & P. J. Wiesner (Eds.) *Sexually transmitted diseases* (pp. 73-84), New York: McGraw-Hill.

Billy, J. O. G., & Udry, J. R. (1985). Patterns of adolescent friendship and effects on sexual behavior. *Social Psychology Quarterly, 48*, 27-41.

Billy, J. O., Landale, N. S., Grady, W. R., & Zimmerle, D. M. (1988). Effect of sexual activity on adolescent social and psychological development. *Social Psychology Quarterly, 51,* 190-212.

Burgess, A. W. (1985). *The sexual victimization of adolescents.* Rockville, MD: National Institute of Mental Health.

Burt, M. R. (1980). Cultural myths and supports for rape. *Journal of Personality and Social Psychology, 38,* 217-230.

Butler, J. R., & Burton, L. M. (1990). Rethinking teenage childbearing: Is sexual abuse a missing link? *Family Relations, 39* 73-80.

Check, J. V. P., & Malamuth, N. M. (1983). Sex role stereotyping and reactions to depictions of stranger versus acquaintance rape. *Journal of Personality and Social Psychology, 45*(2), 344-356.

Constantine, L. L., & Martinson, F. M. (Eds). (1981). *Children and sex: New findings, new perspectives.* Boston: Little, Brown.

DeLamater, J. (1981). The social control of sexuality. *Annual Review of Sociology, 7,* 263-290.

Dornbusch, S. M., Carlsmith, J. M., Gross, R.T., Martin, J. A., Jennings, D., Rosenberg, A., & Duke, P. (1981). Sexual development, age and dating: A comparison of biological and social influences upon one set of behaviors. *Child Development, 52,* 179-185.

Dreyer, P. (1982). Sexuality during adolescence. In B. Wolman (Ed.), *Handbook of developmental psychology* (pp. 559-601). Englewood Cliffs N.J.: Prentice-Hall.

Elliot, D. S., & Morse, B. J. (1989). Delinquency and drug use as risk factors in teenage sexual activity. *Youth and Society, 21,* 32-60.

Finkelhor, D. (1979). *Sexually victimized children.* New York: Free Press.

Freud, S. (1933). *New introductory lectures on psychoanalysis.* London: Hogarth.

Freud, S. (1953). *A general introduction to psychoanalysis.* New York: Permabooks.

Furstenberg, F. F., Morgan, S. P., Moore, K. A., & Peterson, J. L. (1987). Race differences in the timing of adolescent intercourse. *American Sociological Review, 52,* 511-518.

Gagnon, J. H., & Simon, W. (1973). *Sexual conduct: The social sources of human sexuality.* Chicago: Aldine.

Goodchilds, J., Zellman, G. L., Johnson, P. B., & Giarrusso, R. (1988). Adolescents and their perception of sexual interaction. In A. W. Burgess (Ed.), *Rape and sexual assault, Volume 2* (pp. 245-270). New York: Garland.

Harris, L., & Associates, Inc. (1986). *American teens speak: Sex, myths, TV, and birth control* (Planned Parenthood poll). New York: Author.

Hayes, C. O. (Ed). (1987). *Risking the future: Adolescent sexuality, pregnancy and childbearing, Vol 1.* Washington, DC: National Academy Press.

Hein, K. (1988). *AIDS in adolescence: A rationale for concern* (Working paper). New York: Carnegie Council on Adolescent Development.

HIV-related knowledge and behaviors among high school students—selected U.S. sites, 1989. (1990, June). *Morbidity and Mortality Weekly Report, 39,* 384-397.

Hofferth, S. L., Kahn, J. R., & Baldwin, W. (1987). Premarital sexual activity among U.S. teenage women over the past three decades. *Family Planning Perspectives, 19*(2), 46-53.

Hogan, D. P., & Kitagawa, E. M. (1985). The impact of social status, family structure, and neighborhood on the fertility of black adolescents. *American Journal of Sociology, 90*(4), 825-855.

Jessor, S. L., & Jessor, R. (1977). *Problem behavior and psychological development: A longitudinal study of youth.* New York: Academic Press.

Kahn, J. R., Smith, K. W., & Roberts, E. J. (1984). *Family communication and adolescent sexual behavior.* Unpublished manuscript, American Institutes for Research, Cambridge, MA.

Lystad, M. (1982). Sexual abuse in the home: A review of literature. *International Journal of Family Psychiatry, 3*(1), 13-31.

Martinson, F. M. (1980). Childhood sexuality. In B. B. Wolman and J. Money (Eds.), *Handbook of human sexuality* (pp. 29-59). Englewood Cliffs, NJ: Prentice-Hall.

McCabe, M. P., & Collins, J. K. (1984). Measurement of depth of desired and experienced sexual involvement at different stages of dating. *Journal of Sex Research, 20,* 377-390.

Miller, B. C., & Fox, G. L. (1987). Theories of adolescent heterosexual behavior. *Journal of Adolescent Research, 2,* 269-282.

Miller, B. C., & Heaton, T. B. (1991). Age at first sexual intercourse and the timing of marriage and childbirth. *Journal of Marriage and the Family, 53,* 719-732.

Miller, B. C., & Jorgensen, S. R. (1988). Adolescent fertility-related behavior and its family linkages. In D. Klein & J. Aldous (Eds.), *Social stress and family development* (pp. 210-233). New York: Guilford.

Miller, B. C., McCoy, J. K., & Olson, T. D. (1986). Dating age and stage as correlates of adolescent sexual attitudes and behavior. *Journal of Adolescent Research, 1,* 361-371.

Miller, B. C., McCoy, J. K., Olson, T. D., & Wallace, C. M. (1986). Parental discipline and control attempts in relation to adolescent sexual attitudes and behavior. *Journal of Marriage and the Family, 48,* 503-512.

Miller, B. C., & Moore, K. A. (1990). Adolescent sexual behavior, pregnancy, and parenting: Research through the 1980s. *Journal of Marriage and the Family, 52,* 1025-1044.

Miller, B. C., & Sneesby, K. (1989). Educational correlates of adolescent sexual attitudes and behavior. *Journal of Youth and Adolescence, 17,* 521-530.

Moore, K. A., Nord, C. W., & Peterson, J. L. (1989). Nonvoluntary sexual activity among adolescents. *Family Planning Perspectives, 21,* 110-114.

Moore, K. A., Peterson, J. L., & Furstenberg, F. F. (1986). Parental attitudes and the occurrence of early sexual activity. *Journal of Marriage and the Family, 48,* 777-782.

Mott, F. L., & Haurin, R. J. (1988). Linkages between sexual activity and alcohol and drug use among American adolescents. *Family Planning Perspectives, 20*(3), 128-136.

Muehlenhard, C. L., & Linton, M. A. (1987). Date rape and sexual aggression in dating situations: Incident and risk factors. *Journal of Counseling Psychology, 34*(2), 186-196.

National Crime Survey. (1981). *Criminal victimization in the United States, 1979.* Washington, DC: U.S. Department of Justice.

Newcomer, S. J., & Udry, J. R. (1984). Mothers' influence on the sexual behavior of their teenage children. *Journal of Marriage and the Family, 46,* 477-485.

Pratt, W. F., & Eglash, S. (1990). *Premarital sexual behavior, multiple partners, and marital experience.* Paper presented at the annual meeting of the Population Association of America, Toronto.

Presser, H. B. (1978). Age at menarche, socio-sexual behavior, and fertility. *Social Biology, 25,* 94-101.

Renner, K. E., & Wackett, C. (1987). Sexual assault: Social and stranger rape. *Canadian Journal of Community Mental Health, 6*(1), 49-56.

Smith, E. A. (1989). A biosocial model of adolescent sexual behavior. In G. R. Adams, R. Montemayor, & T. P. Gullotta (Eds.), *Biology of adolescent behavior and development.* Newbury Park, CA: Sage.

Smith, E. A ., & Udry, J. R. (1985). Coital and non-coital sexual behaviors of white and black adolescents. *American Journal of Public Health, 75,* 1200-1203.

Sonenstein, F. L., Pleck, J. H., & Ku, L. C. (1989). Sexual activity, condom use, and AIDS awareness among adolescent males. *Family Planning Perspectives, 21,* 152-158.

Sonenstein, F. L., Pleck, J. H., & Ku, L. C. (1991). Levels of sexual activity among adolescent males in the United States. *Family Planning Perspectives, 23*(4), 162-167.

Sorenson, R. (1973). *Adolescent sexuality in contemporary America.* New York: World.

Thornton, A. (1990). The courtship process and adolescent sexuality. *Journal of Family Issues, 11,* 239-273.

Thornton, A., & Camburn, D. (1987). The influence of the family on premarital sexual attitudes and behavior. *Demography, 24,* 323-340.

Udry, J. R., Billy, J. O. G., Morris, N. M., Groff, T. R., & Raj, M. H. (1985). Serum androgenic hormones motivate sexual behavior in adolescent human males. *Fertility and Sterility, 43,* 90-94.

Udry, J. R., & Cliquet, R. L. (1982). A cross-cultural examination of the relationship between ages at menarche, marriage, and first birth. *Demography, 19*(1), 53-63.

Udry, J. R., Talbert, L., & Morris, N. M. (1986). Biosocial foundations for adolescent female sexuality. *Demography, 23,* 217-230.

Vinovskis, M. A. (1988). *An epidemic of teenage pregnancy?* New York: Oxford University Press.

Zelnik, M., & Shah, F. K. (1983). First intercourse among young Americans. *Family Planning Perspectives, 15,* 64-70.

Zelnik, M., Kantner, J. F., & Ford, K. (1981). *Sex and pregnancy in adolescence.* Beverly Hills, CA: Sage.

4. A Developmental, Clinical Perspective on Lesbian, Gay Male, and Bisexual Youths

Ritch C. Savin-Williams
Cornell University

Richard G. Rodriguez
University of Massachusetts

INTRODUCTION

Our primary purpose in writing this chapter is to increase the visibility of lesbian, gay male, and bisexual adolescents for the readers of this volume. The invisibility of such youths is increasingly becoming a part of our past as gay youths express their courage in refusing to be silent and neglected. Their presence and life-styles must especially become known to those who frequently would rather be blind. We hope that you, the reader, want to acknowledge and understand the lives of gay youths. For our part, we will review in this chapter what we consider to be some of the fundamental issues that bisexual, gay male, and lesbian youths face as they confront the unique tasks involved in being a "sexual outlaw" in a society that assumes heterosexuality of all its members and institutions.

This heterosexism most likely includes audiences who will be reading this volume: social science researchers, educators, policymakers, health care providers, social workers, and clinicians. These are the same individuals who must be responsive to the needs of gay adolescents but who continue to write, publish, teach, and establish public policy as if such youths not only were invisible but also did not deserve to exist.

The invisibility of these youths is all around us and was aptly illustrated at the 1990 meetings of the interdisciplinary and international Society for Research in Adolescence. Not a single presentation among literally hundreds of posters, symposiums, and invited addresses focused on lesbian, bisexual, or gay male youths. When textbooks on adolescence discuss "homosexuality," it is separated in a special, usually short (1 to 2 pages is the norm) section located in the latter half of the adolescent sexuality chapter, near the end of the book and sandwiched around such topics as self-stimulation, contraceptive use, sex education, and sexually transmitted diseases. The discussion is devoted primarily to the "it's-normal-nothing-to-worry-about" approach to adolescent homosexual behavior, the prevalence and causes of homosexuality, societal attitudes toward homosexuality, and the pain of being gay (e.g., high rates of suicide attempts, substance abuse, peer harassment). The reality of gay teen life is barely audible; the reader will discover absolutely nothing regarding how an average gay youth lives her or his life. The reader is left to assume that the homosexual adolescent is just like all other youths in pubertal maturation, cognitions and emotions, family relations, social relationships, culture, identity, moral development, careers, and all of the other topics outlined in most textbooks.

Another example of the invisibility of gay youth is illustrated by a recent article submitted for review in the mainstream and influential journal *Developmental Psychology*. In this paper, there is an assumption that the only kind of sexual activity that adolescents engage in is heterosexual by nature. Apparently, according to the measure used, an adolescent only dates, kisses, holds hands, makes out, pets heavily, and goes all the way with those of the opposite sex. Interpretations of the results by the authors assumed that none of the randomly sampled adolescents were homosexual or bisexual or had experienced same-sex sexual behavior. In addition, the authors stated that one effect of puberty was to make "females sexually attractive to males." It was not mentioned that it might also make them attractive to other females!

From our perspective, the coverage given by social scientists is devoted more to homosexual behavior during adolescence than to gay youths as unique and complex beings. It enhances the invisibility of bisexual, gay male, and lesbian youths to researchers, public policymakers, educators, and health care professionals. We believe this state of events in the field of adolescent development is short-sighted and ignorant. By our silence, we commit a great disservice to such youths and to our own integrity as professionals.

It is usually assumed that those who write about homosexuality must be of that "affliction" as well. We proudly confirm that suspicion; the succeeding pages of this chapter are influenced heavily by that fact and affirmation.

In this chapter, we highlight information and perspectives about gay youths that we feel are necessary for our audience. We cannot cover all aspects of the lives of such youths in these pages. Thus we have decided to focus on issues of the recognition, establishment, and expression of sexual identity; the stigmatization and self-devaluation of being gay; sexual identity and psychological health; and the diversity of a gay life based on race and ethnicity. But first, we discuss problems inherent in defining a gay adolescent, and thus the importance of distinguishing between sexual behavior and sexual identity.

SEXUAL BEHAVIOR AND SEXUAL IDENTITY

All youths are considered innocent and straight until proven guilty and gay. This is a pervasive assumption in our culture. The difficulty, in part, for health care professionals may be simply attributable to uncertainty and confusion regarding what homosexuality is and how it manifests itself in youths under the age of 21 years.

It is generally conceded that youths are not likely to identify themselves as lesbian, gay, or bisexual, primarily because of cultural stigma attached to such labels (Boxer, Cook, & Herdt, 1991; Coles & Stokes, 1985; Remafedi, Resnick, Blum, & Harris, in press; Savin-Williams, 1990). Few gay scholars accept the low percentages (1% to 3%) reported by surveys as an accurate reflection of the number of youths who really are gay or who will come to define themselves as gay at a later age. Such individuals may retrospectively view this time in their lives as, "Well, I was really gay back then, but I couldn't really say that to myself or others." Because nearly all extant research is cross-sectional in design, relatively little is known concerning the developmental processes, events, or experiences that are critical in allowing a youth to say to herself or himself, "I'm lesbian" or "I'm gay." In this chapter, we add relatively little new knowledge to these issues.

Our stance in regard to the number of gay youths is of a different, and perhaps unpopular, perspective, but we believe that it has direct bearing on clinical and research efforts directed at bisexual, gay male, and lesbian youths. It is becoming increasingly easier for youths to identify themselves as gay, because of the striking visibility of homosexuality in our culture. AIDS has done this, but so has the media with television shows (e.g., "Our Sons," "What If I'm Gay?"), movies (e.g., *Poison, Paris Is Burning, Longtime Companion*), books (enter any gay/lesbian bookstore and note the avalanche of recent publications on almost any topic), numerous newspaper and magazine articles and lead stories (including teen magazines such as *Sassy*), and celebrities (Madonna talks about it and celebrates it in videos and media interviews). Six states have gay rights bills, and others will follow. Many universities, cities, towns, and counties have enacted ordinances protecting and hence publicizing and legitimatizing homosexuality. A few high schools have gay student groups, and some cities, including several that are not large urban areas, have gay youth services and organizations. All of this has occurred within a relatively brief span of time.

What this means for youths is relatively simple and yet profound: It is more difficult for a homoerotically inclined youth to ignore the reality of her or his attractions, impulses, and desires than in previous generations. It still happens, all too frequently, but efforts to repress, suppress, avoid, project, or deny these feelings are considerably more problematic. The result, we believe, is striking. It is our impression, buttressed by the impression of others (Boxer et al., 1991), that the age of coming out to oneself and others is dramatically falling, although good empirical evidence that directly addresses this issue is not available. Most studies conducted in the 1970s and early 1980s report that the age of coming out to nongays is in one's early to mid-20s (Dank, 1971; Harry & DeVall, 1978; Koodin et al., 1979; McDonald, 1982; Riddle & Morin, 1978; Troiden, 1979). Current research, which has a less retrospective bias, places the age in the late teenage years (Boxer, 1988; Remafedi, 1987a, 1987b; Savin-Williams, 1990; Troiden, 1989). The match during pubescence among sexual libido, cognitive abilities, and sexual behavior is increasing such that a pubescent youth is better able to realize that her or his sexual desires, attractions, and behavior fit the category or definition of a particular sexual identity.

By *sexual identity*, we imply an enduring sense of oneself as a sexual being fitting into a culturally prescribed category. The self-recognition need not be static nor declared publicly, but one's sexual impulses, attractions, and behavior must make cognitive and affective sense to oneself. There need not be total consistency among these; for example, one can have a gay identity but engage in heterosexual behavior and feel attracted to both males and females in differential ways (e.g., lust toward females, emotional love for males). With advancing age through adolescence and young adulthood, however, there is likely to be an increasingly high correlation among one's sexual impulses, attractions, behaviors, and identity.

The positive but probably low correlations among these at the onset of adolescence may reflect the sexual hesitancy and experimentation of many early adolescents. Remafedi et al. (in press) reported that the percentage of adolescents who marked "unsure" as to their sexual orientation decreased from 26% among 12-year-olds to 9% among 18-year-olds. Perhaps somewhat tellingly, "unsure" youths were more likely than others to have homosexually oriented attractions and fantasies and less likely to have engaged in heterosexual sex. Various forms of sexual activity may be played out regardless of one's attractions or impulses, perhaps out of curiosity, peer or familial pressure, opportunities that emerge, or lustful desire. For example, the majority of lesbians and gay men have engaged in heterosexual sex, usually during their adolescence (Bell & Weinberg, 1978; Saghir, Robins, & Walbran, 1969; Savin-Williams, 1990). Remafedi et al. (in press) noted in their study that 54% of the gay males and 81% of the lesbians between the ages of 14 and 23 years reported engaging in heterosexual sex. The percentages of heterosexually and homosexually identified adolescents who engaged in heterosexual sexual behavior was nearly identical, at approximately 65%.

It is also apparent that some lesbian and gay male youths come to the realization of a homosexual sexual identity without the benefit of same-sex sexual activity (Boxer, 1988; Hedblom, 1973; Manosevitz, 1970; Remafedi, 1987a; Roesler & Deisher, 1972; Sanders, 1980; Savin-Williams, 1990). The timing of this realization is difficult to determine, because little is known about the sequence of events in terms of sexual behavior and identity development. That is, it is not obvious from the cross-sectional data available at what point virginity ended relative to the classification or labeling of one's sexual identity. All that we can be assured of in this matter is that some youths come to the realization of a gay identity without the benefit of homosexual sex (or, for that matter, any sex, or having had exclusively heterosexual sex).

One of the most comprehensive surveys of adolescent sexual orientation is a 1986-87 representative sample of nearly 35,000 junior and senior high school students in Minnesota (Remafedi et al., in press). Less than 1% of those who were sure about their sexual orientation identified themselves as bisexual (.9%) or gay/lesbian (.4%). One percent of the total sample and 2.8% of the 18-year-old boys reported at least one homosexual sexual encounter, although this was the one question most frequently skipped by the teenagers. Far more, however, reported predominantly homosexual attractions (4.5% of total sample, but 6.4% of the 18-year-olds) and bisexual or homosexual fantasies (2.6% of total sample). Thus relatively few of the adolescents who had homosexual attractions, fantasies, or behavior reported a gay or lesbian sexual orientation. Homosexual identities, attractions, and behaviors increased with age. "Taken together, these data suggest that uncertainty about sexual orientation and perceptions of bisexuality gradually give way to heterosexual or homosexual identification with the passage of time and/or with increasing sexual experience" (Remafedi et al., in press). Remafedi et al. concluded that adolescents may not conform with adult classification schemes: "Ultimately, the findings illustrate the complexities and difficulties in assigning sexual orientation labels to adolescents."

Even though few youths identify as bisexual, gay, or lesbian by the end of adolescence, more, especially males, are willing to admit to engaging in homosexual sex (Fay, Turner, Klassen, & Gagnon, 1989; Manosevitz, 1970; Remafedi et al., in press; Saghir & Robins, 1973; Savin-Williams, 1990; Sorensen, 1973). How many of such youths later "become" gay is not known, but it is clear that homosexual sex is not solely the province of gay men, lesbians, and bisexuals. Less than 30% of students with homosexual experiences identified themselves as gay, bisexual, or lesbian (Remafedi et al., in press). Ross-Reynolds (1982) concluded, "The majority of adolescents who engage in homosexual behavior do not continue this practice into adulthood" (p. 70). These youths are not the concern of this chapter. We note this only as a further example of the discrepancy between sexual identity and behavior during adolescence for many youths. Although we as bisexuals, lesbians, and gay men do not have ex- clusive rights to homosexual behavior during adolescence, we tend to have more of it (probably because we like it more), and at a higher percentage relative to heterosexual sex, than do straight youths (Bell, Weinberg, & Hammersmith, 1981; Manosevitz, 1970; Saghir & Robins, 1969; Saghir et al., 1969).

We fully recognize the difficulties inherent in identifying gay male, lesbian, and bisexual youths to themselves and to others during their adolescence. Yet it is abundantly clear that we exist during our childhood and adolescence, sometimes with heterosexual sex, sometimes with homosexual sex, sometimes with both heterosexual and homosexual sex, and sometimes without sex. Our sexual identity may be clear, ambivalent, or confused, but eventually most of us emerge as healthy adults. How this comes about is a mystery to clinicians and researchers, and even sometimes to ourselves. We turn now to a more elaborate consideration of these issues regarding identity development among gay youths that are contained in "coming out" models.

COMING OUT TO SELF

Overview

As clinicians and scientists, we know relatively little about one of the most important developments in the lives of lesbian, gay male, and bisexual youths: how they come to the point of identifying themselves as gay persons. At what age did this occur? What were the important events or processes that led to this conclusion? Was the sexual identity there before the sexual behavior? Were there profound fears, self-devaluation, and anxieties associated with this realization? These are difficult questions, and at this point we can provide relatively few answers, although both of us are engaged currently in research projects that address these blind spots in our knowledge (Rodriguez, 1991; Savin-Williams, 1991).

Considerably more attention has been devoted to the process of disclosing and concealing sexual identity to others than has been explored concerning self-disclosure. There is an abundance of coming-out models, based on a variety of theoretical writings (e.g., Erikson, Piaget, Freud), that describe the various stages that an individual undergoes in her or his movement from first realization to being "out" publicly. These models provide a sketch of the feelings and thoughts that a "pregay" child or adolescent might have regarding the intrusion of homoerotic attractions into consciousness and the ways in which she or he might protect the self from this unwelcomed information. Yet the process of identity formation is probably a lifelong process that can begin as early as first thoughts or feelings or as late as one's deathbed. Some doubt that the process is ever concluded; as the personal and cultural constructions of sexuality evolve, so too do their significance and meaning for one's sense of self, self-image, and self-worth.

Research Dilemmas

One primary impediment to understanding, at least from a scientific point of view, how coming to terms with sexual identity influences a youth's sense of self is designing research that adequately addresses the issues. For example, such a study would need to begin data collection with a very large, representative sample of preadolescents, because relatively few (estimates range from 4% to 15%) ultimately would self-identify as bisexual, gay, or lesbian. When to begin data collection is also problematic; the youths should be as young as the research instruments reliably can assess aspects of the self and sexual identity. This age may be as young as 5 or 6 years, although there is debate concerning when the cognitive abilities of a child are developed sufficiently to have a global sense of the self-concept (Harter, 1983). Very little is known concerning when the notion of sexual identity becomes accessible to the individual, although the generally accepted assumption appears to be that by late adolescence, the young adolescent's sexual experimentation should be completed.

In terms of measures, the researcher has a plethora of self instruments to choose among, some of which are applicable for children, but there is almost an absolute dearth of acceptable measures of sexual identity that are applicable for children and adolescents. Within the last few years, alternatives to the Kinsey Scale have been published (Coleman, 1990; Klein, 1990; Shively & DeCecco, 1977), and although some could be modified for adolescents, few if any could be given to children. These are primarily self-report measures rather than behavioral or physiological instruments. Self-concept and sexual identity need to be measured every 6 months to maximize assessing the relationship between the two. One possible result might be that those with a low or high level of self-integration would be less or more likely to self-disclose their sexual identity at an early or late age. Perhaps the relationship is not linear; there may exist a "critical age" (i.e., the onset of puberty) or "lag time" (i.e., the change in one may not have an immediate effect on the other) when self-concept and sexual identity become most intimately related to each other. It is also critical to assess the cause-and-effect relationship between the two (i.e., which comes first). Unaddressed is the ethical dilemma facing the researcher of justifying to human subject committees the means of assessing the sexual identity of minors.

Initial Awareness

One common experience reported by lesbians, bisexuals, and gay men is that from an early age, usually before adolescence, they felt different: "They saw themselves as more sensitive than other boys; they cried more easily, had their feelings more readily hurt, had more aesthetic interests, enjoyed nature, art, and music, and were drawn to other 'sensitive' boys, girls, and adults" (Isay, 1989, p. 23). They avoided aggressive situations and other competitive opportunities. They were outsiders, wanting but fearing to be let in.

In research with adults, 75% to 85% of gay men and lesbians but only 10% of straight men and women felt this way (Bell et al., 1981; Troiden, 1979). The origins and meanings of this sensation, which at times become almost overwhelming, are seldom clear to the prepubescent child. But what is clear (and becomes increasingly so with age) is that this "apartness" or "isolation" is indeed very important (Martin, 1982; Robertson, 1981). Adult explanations include possessing what society defines as inappropriate interest in activities, behaviors, and characteristics of the other sex, and not fitting in with one's own sex. One adolescent reflected, "I never felt as if I fit in. I don't know why for sure. I felt different. I thought it was because I was more sensitive" (Troiden, 1979, p. 363).

These early feelings frequently become translated or are given meaning during adolescence. This can be a bolt of lightning or, more likely, a series of small realizations sandwiched around efforts to deny or conceal them from one's consciousness. Malyon (1981) noted the importance of biology in the realization process: "With the maturation of erotic and intimate capacities, homosexual preferences first became perceptible" (p. 323). It is biology with an existential meaning, because it frequently feels as if one is within an uncharted, uninhabited country.

The "feeling different" is recognized by some as a lack of erotic, intimate interest in persons of the other sex. These interests seldom are labeled as homosexual attractions by the youth; she or he may be some distance away from applying the term *homosexual* to the self. As novelist and Brown University professor Edmund White (1982) wrote in his autobiographical *A Boy's Own Story*, "I guess now that what I wanted was to be loved by men and to love them back but not to be a homosexual. . . . It was men, not women, who struck me as foreign and desirable" (p. 169). The societal and familial pressures to reject and deny the definition of these feelings and of oneself as homosexual are legendary, recounted in coming-out stories of adolescents (Heron, 1983) and adults (Curtis, 1988; Eichberg, 1990; Penelope & Wolfe, 1989). Many fears emerge, most prominent of which are fears of being rejected and isolated both emotionally and socially. A youth begins to doubt her or his ability to meet heterosexual obligations; not having the sexual interest, motivation, and activity of peers can become a source of great anxiety, perhaps in large part because the youth does not understand what is "going wrong." "Perhaps I'm a late bloomer?" "Perhaps I just have higher morals?" "Perhaps my sex drive is lower?" The questions can become devastating if the answers confirm one's worst fears and thus become more than the adolescent can cope with by herself or himself.

Coming to Terms With Self-Recognition

Most identity or coming-out models propose that after the early feelings of alienation, confusion, and uneasiness comes the battle set by puberty: the growing realization that these feelings have a sexual component. From that point through the course of adolescence, it becomes increasingly more difficult to deny the sexual attractions. For example, among Rodriguez's (1988) Utah gay men, the average ages of the following were reported:

awareness of same-sex attractions	11.1 years
same-sex erotic fantasies	13.9 years
label feelings as homosexual	16.2 years
first consensual homosexual orgasm	16.9 years
label self as homosexual	20.6 years
label self as gay (includes life-style)	22.9 years

Few investigators have probed adequately the issue of whether the sequence of events, such as that shown above, is the same for all persons regardless of sex, social class, race, and generation. There may also be much variation in the age of achievement of milestones across samples and time, based in part on the sex of the youth, community size and location, religiosity, social class, racial and ethnic characteristics, level of sex education, and strength of homosexual impulses. A rural, religious, white female may be quite late in self-recognition, but if her homosexual impulses are strong and she has a lesbian aunt who serves as a model, then self-recognition may be advanced; an urban male from an openly sexualized family may be expected to be early, unless his Jewish family stresses the absolute necessity for their only son to carry on their religious tradition.

Reactions to the homosexual realization range from, "Oh good, now I understand" to "I've got to kill myself." A number of defenses against self-recognition and labeling have been described. These serve to delay, perhaps necessarily so, self-acceptance of oneself as bisexual, lesbian, or gay. Among the classic defenses are the following:

"I was drunk."
"It's just a phase."
"I've heard all guys do it once."
"I just love her and not all girls."
"He gave me head; I didn't touch him."
"I was lonely."
"I only did it as a favor for my best friend."
"Hey, I got $20 for it."
"I was just curious."

These defenses may be temporary or lifelong; they may be useful (e.g., motivating one to redirect sexual energies into academic pursuits) or destructive (e.g., marrying someone who is not erotically or emotionally attractive to the individual).

SELF-DEVALUATION AND
STIGMATIZATION OF HOMOSEXUALITY

It is reasonable to argue that the societal and cultural ideas and beliefs that we share influence, regulate, and even exert control over the meanings and perceptions that we have about our sexuality, as well as about the sexuality of others. It is thus also reasonable to infer that these same cultural and societal sources of power influence the beliefs, attitudes, and prejudices that are ascribed to lesbians, bisexuals, and gay men. What is not clear, however, is the effect that discrimination, societal prejudices, and the social stigma attached to being a gay male, lesbian, or bisexual have on the psychological adjustment and well-being of a gay adolescent. This is because, as a society, we do not care enough to be concerned. What happens to our youth because of homophobia that is expressed continually in daily life is a low cultural priority, as low as issues of sexism, racism, and classism.

Such devaluing processes have been suggested elsewhere among groups that have been the object of oppression, including women, blacks, Jews, and clinical populations (Allport, 1954; Goffman, 1963; Lewin, 1941; Tajfel, 1981). The psychological impact of incorporating negative and devaluing beliefs about one's gay identity may be just as devastating as being discriminated against because one is a female or African-American, Latino, or Asian-American. The process of victimization caused by one's homosexuality or bisexuality is critical to understanding the development of a sexual identity and, consequently, the psychological adjustment and self-evaluation of gay youth.

Self-devaluation and *self-derogation* refer to a process of incorporating and internalizing negative feelings of self-worth and negative self-evaluations. For lesbian, gay male, and bisexual youths, self-devaluation can occur through the internalization of negative beliefs and feelings about homosexuality and being gay. The devaluing content includes the homophobic attitudes and beliefs concerning one's sexual identity manifested in statements such as, "I am not going to tell people that I'm gay because it's only one part of my true personality, not all of it." Self-devaluation among gay youths can also be expressed in such less obvious, indirect forms as laughing at gay jokes, putting down effeminacy in boys or masculinity in girls, or ego defenses (e.g., reaction formation, projection, minimalization, exaggeration, and compartmentalization) (Allport, 1954; Malyon, 1981-1982). For example, such projective statements as "Everyone who knows I'm gay hates me because of it" may reflect a negative belief about oneself for being gay. Statements such as "I could never have a real family now that I'm a lesbian" might also suggest self-devaluing material directed toward one's sexual identity.

These self-devaluation expressions often are expressed toward other known gay individuals or toward a gay community (Nungessor, 1983). If directed toward other gay individuals, these statements may serve to help the youth feel identified with her or his straight peers and less like the outsider one usually experiences oneself to be. By directing hostility and anger toward other gays, the adolescent protects and distances herself or himself from negative feelings about her or his own homosexuality. These attitudes and thoughts are reinforced continually and colluded with through social contacts, societal prejudices, and the heterosexual assumptions that surround a youth in our culture.

Perhaps the most prevalent and ultimately damaging way for a gay youth to express her or his own feelings of self-devaluation is through the means of "passing." *Passing* refers to the hiding of "information about one's real social identity, receiving and accepting treatment based on false suppositions concerning the self" (Goffman, 1963, p. 42). Passing strategies include supplying information that conceals one's homosexuality or bisexuality and using avoidance or role-playing behaviors to divert attention from one's true sexual identity. Passing behavior is used as a way to manage the social tensions that are attached to being gay, as well as a means to cope with the feelings of distress and uncomfortableness about being gay. Passing behaviors include lying to others or stating that one is straight or that one is attracted to the "appropriate" sex. Avoiding being seen with known gay others, suppressing overt stereotypical feminine or masculine mannerisms and behavioral expressions, and using generic pronoun expressions instead of the terms *she* or *he* are all forms of passing strategies. Passing behaviors can also be more subtle, such as not supplying information that would suggest that in fact one is gay or not correcting societal assumptions that one is heterosexual.

These self-devaluing processes among gay male, lesbian, and bisexual youths are primary developmental struggles of the adolescent that, most likely and unfortunately, will continue into young adulthood. Self-devaluation is, we believe, the construction that arises from the institutional, interpersonal, and psychological processes attached to being a member of a socially stigmatized or oppressed group. Such groups, because of how they have been defined socially, receive negative values and beliefs that have been displaced onto them, resulting in discriminatory and hostile acts and outcomes directed toward its group members relative to members of the society at large (Crocker & Major, 1989). We need to know far more about the net outcome of such self-devaluation. Evidence suggests it may result in gay youths being at increased risk for drug abuse, suicide, pregnancy, and HIV infection (Gibson, 1989; Remafedi, Farrow, & Deisher, 1991). How can we as clinicians, health care professionals, youth workers, educators, and parents give up on our youths and allow them to destroy themselves? The answer is both political and personal and must be addressed at both levels.

SEXUAL IDENTITY AND PSYCHOLOGICAL HEALTH

Clinical Perspective

From a clinical perspective, the development of an identity evolves "in an interpersonal context and serves as the basis for all subsequent object relations" (Malyon, 1981, p. 326). One might not want to push a young adolescent too hard to "make sense" of her or his growing awareness of attractions to members of the same sex (Dank, 1971). Because the primary developmental task of adolescence is the consolidation of one's identity, initial awareness of homoerotic impulses and attractions that are known by the adolescent to be highly condemned in Western culture may result in considerable anxiety and consternation with the expected social disapproval and intrapsychic conflict (Malyon, 1981).

Malyon (1981) believes that to disclose the information to others is also destructive to a healthy outcome. Too often the self-acknowledged lesbian, bisexual, or gay male adolescent is alienated, ridiculed verbally, abused physically, and disowned by family and peers. Physical, personal, social, and institutional supports are seldom available. Malyon believes the psychological consequences of these conditions are "morbid." If a gay youth seeks to pursue the development of an identity in the hostile heterosexual community, then estrangement and confusion are likely; in the adult-oriented homosexual community, identity development may lead to alienation from peers and a premature assumption of adult responsibilities. The former can result in identity confusion; the latter, identity foreclosure.

One adaptation is a compartmentalization of sexual desire, resulting in fragmentation of identity: "Homophobic content becomes internalized and often causes protracted dysphoria and feelings of self-contempt. The juxtaposition of homosexual desire and acculturated self-criticism is inimical to healthy psychological development" (Malyon, 1981, p. 324). Repression of sexual desire is likely to lead to later panic or major disruption of coping styles and life patterns.

Another perspective is taken by writers (Coleman, 1982; Kimmel, 1978) who suggest that the psychologically healthiest approach is coming out to oneself at an early age, during early adolescence when the "feeling different" sensations begin to be interpreted as homoerotic attractions, but revealing that orientation only to absolutely safe others until after emotional and financial independence have been established (usually after high school). A youth thus avoids the pitfalls of experiencing a discrepancy between inner feelings and self-identity and the negative consequences of being known as homosexual in the usually homophobic world of junior and senior high school. Destructive defenses such as denial, repression, and compartmentalization are reduced. The adolescent can disclose only to those who will provide support, understanding, and growth. The youth has an opportunity to learn crisis management and an internal sense of self-respect and ego integrity that will prove beneficial in the adult homophobic world that most will soon be entering.

Malyon (1981) appears to favor a third approach—the suppression of homosexual impulses during adolescence. He acknowledges some negative consequences: a temporary developmental moratorium; a truncated identity-formation process that is completed in a second phase of adolescence during the third or fourth decade of life; career over- or underachievement as an attempt to compensate for or to give in to feelings of alienation and inadequacy; a chronic state of psychological unrest and disequilibrium; and a lack of personal integrity and self-acceptance when significant aspects of one's identity are not expressed because they are considered to be unnatural or worthy of condemnation.

All argue that the best solution is to change cultural attitudes and policies, develop psychological and social support systems for gay adolescents, and provide psychotherapeutic intervention for individual youths. Few of us are very optimistic that these will occur any time soon for most gay adolescents.

Empirical Evidence

There is empirical evidence, primarily from retrospective research, suggesting a positive association between coming out to oneself and feelings of self-worth. The psychologically well-adjusted bisexual, lesbian, or gay male individual is most out to herself or himself; such individuals have the highest levels of identity congruence, because they have integrated and managed elements of their personal identity (see reviews in Savin-Williams, 1990; Troiden, 1989). Because self-recognition of one's sexual identity and self-worth are both self-attitudes, it makes some sense that they would be highly related to each other. On the other hand, disclosing this information to others evokes other concerns that are external to one's self-attitudes, such as physical safety, living conditions, need for parental financial support, career choice, and geography.

The same reviews reported that gay male youths tend to disclose to others considerably earlier on average than do lesbians. Lesbians may be more circumspect in whom they disclose to, and such behavior may be relatively independent of how they feel about themselves. That is, they may not disclose to others simply because they feel good about themselves, nor may such disclosure cause them to feel better about themselves. Gay men, however, may base their disclosure on how they feel about themselves, and such disclosure in turn may increase further their sense of self-worth.

In Harry and DeVall's (1978) study of 238 Detroit gay men ranging in age from 18 to 50 years, self-esteem level was not related to current age, but those who defined themselves as gay prior to the age of 17 years tended to have higher adult levels of self-esteem than those who defined themselves as gay after age 17. In a study of 317 youths between the ages of 14 and 23 years, males who were aware of homosexual attractions at an early age (a different variable than Harry and DeVall's self-definition as gay) did not differ from those who became aware of such feelings at later ages in terms of present self-esteem level (Savin-Williams, 1990). On the other hand, one of the best predictors of current self-esteem level among lesbian youths was an early recognition of homosexual attractions; the lesbians who knew that they were lesbian at an early age appeared to be a special group with particularly high self-esteem. Unanswered, however, is whether the high self-esteem or the recognition of homosexuality came first. Those with a solid sense of self might have been equipped better to recognize this aspect of their personality; such women may be generally more insightful and self-accepting than those who are unaware of their homosexuality until late adolescence or young adulthood. Or perhaps the longer developmental period that these women had to come to terms with this difficult recognition meant that by late adolescence they had integrated this aspect of their life sufficiently into their personality. They were thus able to seek psychological and social resources and services that further enhanced their sense of self at the time that data were collected.

Similar dynamics may not operate with bisexual and gay males. Perhaps recognition of "deviant" homoerotic attractions at an early age is developmentally too early for the psychological skills and maturity that many early adolescents possess. Or perhaps such males were "brought to awareness" by peers because of their gender-atypical behaviors and mannerisms. Dank (1971) noted that because the male adolescent is particularly sensitive to how he is perceived by peers, the terms peers use to label a nonheterosexual orientation become especially destructive for a healthy sense of self. To preserve a sense of self-worth, a male adolescent is not likely to put himself into such categories. Indeed, research has demonstrated that "feminine" gays tend to have lower self-esteem levels than more androgynous and masculine gays (Carlson & Steuer, 1985; Green, 1987; Harry, 1984; Hooberman, 1979). Such behavior may have elicited peer and familial ridicule, resulting in low self-esteem. The prohibition for females to behave in a gender-atypical manner is less severe and may even be rewarded, thus having relatively little effect on their self-esteem level.

In all areas of concern, too little research has addressed our understanding of gay youths. It is an open field with far more gaps than substance. Several researchers, such as Boxer, Herdt, Remafedi, and Savin-Williams, are beginning the process of studying garden-variety gay youths, but much more is needed.

MULTICULTURALISM AND GAY YOUTHS

Lesbian, gay male, and bisexual youths encounter many of the same maturational tasks that other adolescents experience during the process of identity formation. A major difference in development among gay youths, as suggested in this chapter, is the formation of a homosexual or bisexual identity and the host of problematic issues that encompass this "afflicted" identity. For the gay youth struggling with a new, stigmatizing identity, this time can be psychologically conflictual, often distressing, and possibly damaging. Coupled with outside pressures from family, peers, and others to be heterosexual, gay youths struggle to form a healthy sense of self.

The gay youth of color also experiences the development of a gay identity and the problems that come with being gay. But she or he faces a further formidable task in the development of a mature identity: forming a multiple identity consisting of an ethnic, cultural, or racial identity within the context of also being a lesbian, a gay male, or bisexual. It may be possible that the racial or ethnic background of a gay youth presents not an impediment but an advantage in developing a positive identity, high self-esteem, and a healthy sense of self-worth. For this to occur, three concerns that we believe face the gay youth of color are (a) developing and defining both a strong gay identity and a strong ethnic identity; (b) potential conflicts in allegiance, such as reference group identity within one's gay and ethnic community; and (c) experiencing both homophobia and racism.

The bisexual, lesbian, or gay male youth of color, identifying with both an ethnic and a gay community, is in a perplexing position. The adolescent can gain, from two different and rich sources, a wide array of knowledge and social support. The individual is likely to gain support from the gay community that her or his cultural community is not able to give, including supporting and affirming one's sexuality and gay identity, providing a place in which to feel relaxed and open about same-sex relationships, and identifying social structures that cater to other gay individuals, including homophile organizations and gay networks. Similarly, familial, racial, ethnic, and cultural ties often give a youth a cultural identification, a strong sense of heritage and values, and a sense of self (Morales, 1983). At the same time that the adolescent closely identifies with both communities, she or he may also experience a conflict in allegiance because of her or his dual role and identity. Two communities may in fact present the youth with conflictual information, including ideas about "appropriate" gay or ethnic behavior in different community situations, ideas about the importance of choosing one identity over the other, and ideas about being gay or being an ethnic minority.

Among many ethnic minority groups, for example, great importance is placed on the family and the interconnections among family members. Attitudes generally include marriage and the assumption of the traditional roles of husband, wife, and children. Family is defined biologically, and unique and important roles usually are given to extended family members, including grandparents, aunts, uncles, and cousins.

Beliefs and attitudes held by the homophile community are far more diverse, however, and are at times in direct contrast to these traditional beliefs of ethnic communities. Family may be defined only weakly as biological and frequently also might include people meaningfully significant to the person, such as lovers and friends. Family, for a gay youth, is often an uncertain construct marked with unresolved emotional attachments to people who typically would be designated, accepted, or excluded as family members.

Youths, regardless of color, experience major life changes during the period of adolescence, including the formation and development of various reference group identities. For some adolescents, developing a gay identity complicates other reference group identifications, especially when one's gay identity comes into conflict with another group identity. The adjustment to a healthy and positive gay identity is no easy transition for ethnic minority youths. One's ethnic identity and one's gay identity may at times be incongruent with each other. For example, it is a hallmark of machismo among Latino males to be a defiantly heterosexual-appearing male. This belief is common in the Latin community because of its prevalence as a traditional virtue within the Latino heritage (Carrier, 1989; Parker, 1989). It includes assumptions and expectations that Latinos hold to traditional male sex roles, such as overt male-defined appearances, traditional interactions and relations with females and males, and a strong sense of pride. The net result is an incorporation of information that is internalized in developing a sense of the self as a Latino male. A bisexual male Latino, especially during the formation of a sexual identity, may thus experience a need for a different perspective of masculinity and machismo, one that includes nontraditional male roles and unconventional expectations in relationships with females and males. For a youth who is bisexual and Latino, the definition and actions of being male and having masculine-defined behaviors and relationships with others are derived from a Latin and bisexual identification and from the adaptation required of conflictual reference group identities.

Many of the difficulties experienced by lesbian, gay male, and bisexual youths of color also come from the social prejudice and institutional discrimination that are inherent in this society. Homophobic and racist attitudes and beliefs continue to be rampant and to permeate the youth's social settings, including her and his school and family settings. It is not difficult to understand how many of these youths never come to develop a healthy integration of their identity and positive feelings of self-worth. Morales and Eversley (1980) found in a survey of Third World gays and lesbians that 85% of the sample perceived themselves as having been discriminated against by both the straight and the gay communities for being ethnic and/or gay. They found that ethnic gays and lesbians as a group ranked discrimination to be the second most important problem in the gay and lesbian communities, following the AIDS crisis.

A difficult issue that must be addressed is how we as clinicians and researchers can recognize and meet the needs of gay youths of color. We stress the importance of understanding the dual identities, multiple roles, emotional conflicts, and psychological adjustment that result from the complex situations in which gay youths of color find themselves. For mental health professionals, Gock (1986) emphasizes that factors that must be considered include the appropriateness of the therapeutic orientation, definitions of adjustment applied to gay youths of color because of their dual identity, an integrated treatment approach, and therapeutic factors that facilitate change. Developing a healthy perspective that integrates multiple self-identifications, such as an ethnic/racial identity and a gay identity, is a continual process in human development. Learning the skills to acquire adaptive responses during adolescence may help with facilitating the adaptation of interpsychic conflicts in adulthood. We must help gay youths of color develop a healthy perspective with a positive integration of these multiple identities.

PARTING THOUGHTS

Defenses against self-recognition may be so entrenched, the stigmatization of homosexuality so severe, and the adolescent's ego so fragile and diffuse that it may be exceptionally difficult to offer any assistance that will be useful. How can one be helped for a problem that "does not exist?" An adult or another youth can be the perfect role model and be patient, open, sensitive, and understanding—but it may not be the right time for the adolescent. The adolescent may resist the undesired attractions and lead a straight life or present a socially acceptable heterosexuality while maintaining the secrecy of her or his inner homosexual life (i.e., passing). A few may try to blend their emerging gay identity with a life in the straight culture of high school and the trade-off of accepting social ostracism in turn for feeling true to oneself. Colgan (1987) believes that passing is the worse strategy, resulting in youths with low self-regard, inner turmoil, acting-out behavior, and low levels of interpersonal intimacy. Others have noted the dire consequences of being untrue to oneself. Healthy personality development is thought to require validation of the self through self-disclosure to significant others in the environment. Personal authenticity needs self-validation if a person is to develop a sense of self-worth; passing as something one is not is hypocritical and alienating (Jourard, 1971; Lee, 1977; Martin, 1982; Maslow, 1954).

These issues may very well be compounded for the adolescent of color who perceives that she or he may be feeling yet a second stigma—the first being her or his race or ethnicity, and the second that of being bisexual, gay, or lesbian. The double stigmatization frequently exists in the straight, white adolescent world, but the adolescent of color may also encounter racism in the gay community and homophobia in her or his cultural community. We would prefer to hope that the gay youth of color would find sources of support and encouragement from these nonwhite, nonstraight communities, and many do. But it is a risky venture, with profound repercussions for the integration of the youth's sense of self. Such a youth may be able to pass as straight, but not as white.

What happens when a youth decides not to pass and to come out? It can be a physical and psychological nightmare. A youth can suffer verbal and physical abuse, and all of her or his stereotypes and fears about being gay can come crashing in as true. What are not readily apparent to most gay male, bisexual, and lesbian youths are positive alternatives to a straight existence. Even the meaning of being gay is mysterious: How will I lead my life? How can I meet others like me? Can I still marry, have kids, and find a good job? There are few models and even fewer avenues of assistance. Where are the adult gay male, lesbian, and bisexual relatives, teachers, rabbis, athletes, actors, and singers? Where are the social agencies, the youth groups, the social clubs, and the counseling centers? With these not visible and not available, many lesbian and gay male youths return to the closet to reemerge in safer times, frequently college.

REFERENCES

Allport, G. W. (1954). *The nature of prejudice.* Cambridge, MA: Addison-Wesley.
Bell, A. P., & Weinberg, M. S. (1978). *Homosexualities: A study of diversity among men and women.* New York: Simon and Schuster.
Bell, A. P., Weinberg, M. S., & Hammersmith, S. K. (1981). *Sexual preference: Its development in men and women.* Bloomington: Indiana University Press.
Boxer, A. M. (1988, March). *Betwixt and between: Developmental discontinuities of gay and lesbian youth.* Paper presented at the Society for Research on Adolescence, Alexandria, VA.
Boxer, A. M., Cook, J. A., & Herdt, G. (1991). Double jeopardy: Identity transitions and parent-child relations among gay and lesbian youth. In K. Pillemer & K. McCartney (Eds.), *Parent-child relations throughout life* (pp. 59-92). Hillsdale, NJ: Lawrence Erlbaum.
Carlson, H. M., & Steuer, J. (1985). Age, sex-role categorization, and psychological health in American homosexual and heterosexual men and women. *Journal of Social Psychology, 125,* 203-211.
Carrier, J. M. (1989). Gay liberation and coming out in Mexico. *Journal of Homosexuality, 17,* 225-252.
Coleman, E. (1982). Developmental states of the coming out process. *Journal of Homosexuality, 7,* 31-43.
Coleman, E. (1990). Toward a synthetic understanding of sexual orientation. In D. P. McWhirter, S. A. Sanders, & J. M. Reinisch (Eds.), *Homosexuality/heterosexuality: Concepts of sexual orientation* (pp. 267-276). New York: Oxford University Press.
Coles, R., & Stokes, G. (1985). *Sex and the American teenager.* New York: Harper & Row.
Colgan, P. (1987). Treatment of identity and intimacy issues in gay males. *Journal of Homosexuality, 14,* 101-123.
Crocker, J., & Major, B. (1989). Social stigma and self-esteem: The self-protective properties of stigma. *Psychological Review, 96,* 1-23.
Curtis, W. (Ed.). (1988). *Revelations: A collection of gay male coming out stories.* Boston: Alyson.
Dank, B. M. (1971). Coming out in the gay world. *Psychiatry, 34,* 180-197.
Eichberg, R. (1990). *Coming out: An act of love.* New York: Dutton.

Fay, R. E., Turner, C. F., Klassen, A. D., & Gagnon, J. H. (1989). Prevalence and patterns of same-gender sexual contact among men. *Science, 243*, 338-348.

Gibson, P. (1989). Gay male and lesbian youth suicide. In *Report of the secretary's task force in youth suicide* (pp. 3-110–3-142). Rockville, MD: U.S. Department of Health and Human Services.

Gock, T. (1986, August). *Issues in gay affirmative psychotherapy with ethnically/culturally diverse populations.* Paper presented at the 94th Annual American Psychological Association.

Goffman, I. (1963). *Stigma.* Englewood Cliffs, NJ: Prentice-Hall.

Green, R. (1987). *The "sissy boy syndrome" and the development of homosexuality.* New Haven, CT: Yale University Press.

Harry, J. (1984). *Gay couples.* New York: Praeger.

Harry, J., & DeVall, W. B. (1978). *The social organization of gay males.* New York: Praeger.

Harter, S. (1983). Developmental perspectives on the self-system. In P. H. Mussen (Ed.), *Socialization, personality, and social development, vol. 4: Handbook of child psychology* (4th ed., pp. 275-385). New York: John Wiley.

Hedblom, J. H. (1973). Dimensions of lesbian sexual experience. *Archives of Sexual Behavior, 2*, 329-341.

Heron, A. (Ed.). (1983). *One teenager in ten.* Boston: Alyson.

Hooberman, R. E. (1979). Psychological androgyny, feminine gender identity and self-esteem in homosexual and heterosexual males. *Journal of Sex Research, 15*, 306-315.

Isay, R. A. (1989). *Being homosexual: Gay men and their development.* New York: Farrar-Straus-Giroux.

Jourard, S. M. (1971). *The transparent self* (2nd ed.). New York: Van Nostrand.

Kimmel, D. (1978). Adult development and aging: A gay perspective. *Journal of Social Issues, 34*, 113-130.

Klein, F. (1990). The need to view sexual orientation as a multivariable dynamic process: A theoretical perspective. In D. P. McWhirter, S. A. Sanders, & J. M. Reinisch (Eds.), *Homosexuality/heterosexuality: Concepts of sexual orientation* (pp. 277-282). New York: Oxford University Press.

Koodin, H., Morin, S., Riddle, D., Rogers, M., Sang, B., & Strassburger, F. (1979). *Removing the stigma: Final report, task force on the status of lesbian and gay male psychologists.* Washington, DC: American Psychiatric Association.

Lee, J. A. (1977). Going public: A study in the sociology of homosexual liberation. *Journal of Homosexuality, 3*, 47-78.

Lewin, K. (1941). Self-hatred among Jews. *Contemporary Jewish Record, 4*, 219-232.

Malyon, A. K. (1981). The homosexual adolescent: Developmental issues and social bias. *Child Welfare, 60*, 321-330.

Malyon, A. K. (1981-1982). Psychotherapeutic implications of internalized homophobia in gay men. *Journal of Homosexuality, 7*, 59-69.

Manosevitz, M. (1970). Early sexual behavior in adult homosexual and heterosexual males. *Journal of Abnormal Psychology, 76*, 396-402.

Martin, A. D. (1982). Learning to hide: The socialization of the gay adolescent. *Adolescent Psychiatry, 10*, 52-65.

Maslow, A. H. (1954). *Motivation and personality.* New York: Harper.

McDonald, G. J. (1982). Individual differences in the coming out process for gay men: Implications for theoretical models. *Journal of Homosexuality, 8,* 47-60.

Morales, E. S. (1983, August). *Third World gays and lesbians: A process of multiple identities.* Paper presented at the 91st annual convention of the American Psychological Association, Anaheim, CA.

Morales, E. S., & Eversley, R. (1980). *A survey of ethnic gay men and lesbians in San Francisco.* Unpublished report.

Nungessor, L. G. (1983). *Homosexual acts, actors, and identities.* New York: Praeger.

Parker, R. (1989). Youth, identity, and homosexuality: The changing shape of sexual life in contemporary Brazil. *Journal of Homosexuality, 17,* 269-289.

Penelope, J., & Wolfe, S. J. (Eds.). (1989). *The original coming out stories.* Freedom, CA: Crossing.

Remafedi, G. (1987a). Male homosexuality: The adolescent's perspective. *Pediatrics, 79,* 326-330.

Remafedi, G. (1987b). Adolescent homosexuality: Psychosocial and medical implications. *Pediatrics, 79,* 331-337.

Remafedi, G., Farrow, J. A., & Deisher, R. W. (1991). Risk factors for attempted suicide in gay and bisexual youth. *Pediatrics, 87,* 869-875.

Remafedi, G., Resnick, M., Blum, R., & Harris, L. (in press). The demography of sexual orientation in adolescents. *Pediatrics.*

Riddle, D. I., & Morin, S. F. (Eds.). (1978). Psychology and the gay community. *Journal of Social Issues, 34,* 1-138.

Robertson, R. (1981). Young gays. In J. Hart & D. Richardson (Eds.), *The theory and practice of homosexuality* (pp. 170-176). London: Routledge & Kegan Paul.

Rodriguez, R. A. (1988, June). *Significant events in gay identity development: Gay men in Utah.* Paper presented at the 96th Annual Convention of the American Psychological Association, Atlanta.

Rodriguez, R. G. (1991, June). *Self-devaluation in gay-identified men.* Paper presented at the American Association of Applied and Preventive Psychology, Washington, DC.

Roesler, T., & Deisher, R. (1972). Youthful male homosexuality. *Journal of the American Medical Association, 219,* 1018-1023.

Ross-Reynolds, G. (1982). Issues in counseling the "homosexual" adolescent. In J. Grimes (Ed.), *Psychological approaches to problems of children and adolescents* (pp. 55-88). Des Moines: Iowa State Department of Education.

Saghir, M. T., & Robins, E. (1969). Homosexuality I: Sexual behavior of the female homosexual. *Archives of General Psychiatry, 20,* 192-201.

Saghir, M. T., & Robins, E. (1973). *Male and female homosexuality.* Baltimore: Williams & Wilkins.

Saghir, M. T., Robins, E., & Walbran, B. (1969). Homosexuality II: Sexual behavior of the male homosexual. *Archives of General Psychiatry, 21,* 219-229.

Sanders, G. (1980). Homosexualities in the Netherlands. *Alternative Lifestyles, 3,* 278-311.

Savin-Williams, R. C. (1990). *Gay and lesbian youth: Expressions of identity.* Washington, DC: Hemisphere.

Savin-Williams, R. C. (1991, June). *Patterns of child and adolescent sexual activity and the development of identity among gay youth.* Paper presented at the American Association of Applied and Preventive Psychology, Washington, DC.

Shively, M. G., & DeCecco, J. P. (1977). Components of sexual identity. *Journal of Homosexuality, 3,* 41-48.

Sorensen, R. (1973). *Adolescent sexuality in contemporary society.* New York: World Book.

Tajfel, H. (1981). *Human groups and social categories: Studies in social psychology.* New York: Cambridge University Press.

Troiden, R. R. (1979). Becoming homosexual: A model of gay identity acquisition. *Psychiatry, 42,* 362-373.

Troiden, R. R. (1989). The formation of homosexual identities. *Journal of Homosexuality, 17,* 43-73.

White, E. (1982). *A boy's own story.* New York: E. P. Dutton.

5. Adolescent Pregnancy and Parenting

Stephen R. Jorgensen
Texas Tech University

At various times during the past two decades, both the rate and number of pregnancies experienced by adolescents in American society have been described as an "epidemic" (Alan Guttmacher Institute, 1976, 1981) and as "placing our future at risk" (Hayes, 1987; Hofferth & Hayes, 1987). The basis for concern is that adolescent pregnancy and parenting have well-documented costs and negative consequences that are serious enough to categorize them as a significant social problem (Furstenberg, 1991; Hayes, 1987).

Millions of dollars in federal, state, and private resources have been dedicated to the study of the adolescent pregnancy phenomenon since the early to mid-1970s in the search for ways to understand better the dynamics underlying its causes and consequences. Our knowledge has grown exponentially as a result of innumerable empirical investigations of adolescent pregnancy and parenting. In contrast to two decades ago, when the study of teenage pregnancy and childbearing represented a quite limited focus of adolescent and family researchers, we now know substantially more about the antecedents of adolescent sexual activity and contraceptive use; the demographic, social, and psychological correlates of teen pregnancy and childbearing; pregnancy-resolution decision making (keeping the baby, relinquishing the baby for adoption, or abortion); and the developmental consequences of teen pregnancy for the mother, father, child, family members, and society (Miller & Moore, 1990).

Despite these significant gains in knowledge, however, we have been unable to translate this understanding into effective policies and programs for significantly reducing the number and rate of adolescent pregnancies in American society. The United States continues to have among the highest, if not *the* highest, adolescent pregnancy rate in the developed world (Jones et al., 1986). The lack of a coherent plan to bring about a substantial reduction in adolescent pregnancy is a direct result of the sensitive, and thereby controversial, issues involved: sex education, sexual behavior, contraception, abortion, welfare support for pregnant and parenting teens, and parental involvement in adolescent decisions regarding sexuality, contraception, and abortion. Debate over these issues has involved clashes of liberal and conservative political agendas, divergent religious doctrines, and competing moral philosophies. The result has been a patchwork of relatively uncoordinated policies and intervention programs that, collectively, have had only a modest impact on the problem.

It is the purpose of this chapter to review the current status of adolescent pregnancy and parenting research. Pregnancy rates and their sociodemographic correlates will be reviewed along with trends in pregnancy-resolution decisions. The concept of pregnancy risk will be defined and discussed in the context of contraceptive behavior among adolescents. The chapter will conclude with a selective review of the consequences of teen pregnancy and childbearing and a discussion of the policy implications of the current situation.

ADOLESCENT PREGNANCY AND PARENTING: THE SCOPE OF THE PROBLEM

Does the adolescent pregnancy situation truly constitute an epidemic or a problem of crisis proportions? This question has been the source of some controversy and appears to depend upon how one chooses to define the terms *epidemic* and *crisis*. According to Vinovskis (1988), who conducted a historical analysis of adolescent fertility rates from the colonial days of early America through the twentieth century, adolescent pregnancy during the 1970s and 1980s was incorrectly labeled as an "epidemic" by politicians and family planning advocates. This was done, according to Vinovskis, as a basis for enacting federal legislation to provide increased family planning services and welfare programs to those trapped in the "cultures of adolescent childbearing and poverty." In showing that the rate of adolescent childbearing actually began a long-term decline after 1960 and through the 1980s, and that the rate in the 1920s was actually comparable to that in the late 1980s, Vinovskis concluded that use of the term *epidemic* to describe the current adolescent pregnancy and childbearing phenomenon was alarmist and thereby misleading. The result of the "epidemic" claim was federal legislation to address the problem (the Adolescent Health, Services, and Pregnancy Prevention Act of 1978) that was "hastily conceived and poorly drafted" (Vinovskis, 1988, p. 24) and missed the mark by almost exclusively providing funding to provide support services to pregnant teenagers rather than focusing on prevention strategies. According to Vinovskis (1988):

> By failing to see the issue from a broader, long-term perspective, the general public and many policymakers . . . thought that their legislation had addressed the problem of adolescent pregnancy. In reality, it only provided very limited services for a small percentage of pregnant teenagers. . . . Most witnesses and almost all of the decision makers simply accepted the myth of an "epidemic" of adolescent pregnancy as a growing and unprecedented problem that necessitated immediate action. (pp. 36-37)

In responding to Vinovskis's conclusion that the adolescent pregnancy phenomenon was elevated falsely to an epidemic or crisis level in order "to suit the political agenda of certain moral entrepreneurs" (p. 128), Furstenberg (1991) agreed that teenage fertility rates had been declining for nearly a decade prior to its emergence as a major public issue and its being labeled an epidemic. Furstenberg's analysis, however, led to his conclusion that the adolescent childbearing situation, though not truly an epidemic in the sense that pregnancy and fertility rates were sharply higher in the 1970s and 1980s relative to prior decades, was "legitimately propelled into public visibility" (p. 130). It was not a problem that was invented to satisfy the political agendas of welfare and family planning advocates, who were accused of misrepresenting the facts "to make it appear like teenage childbearing was growing when, in fact, it was not" (p. 130).

Furstenberg noted that a number of conditions prevailed in the 1970s that fueled the concern over adolescent pregnancy and provided a legitimate basis for its emergence as a major social problem. First, the large cohort of baby-boom children were entering middle to late adolescence at this time. This expanding number of teenagers caused the pregnancy and fertility rates per 1,000 population to fall, but kept the absolute number of births to teens at a high level. According to Furstenberg (1991), "demographers saw a declining rate of teenage fertility; but, service providers saw their case loads of pregnant teens and young mothers grow by leaps and bounds" (p. 129).

A second basis for genuine concern about the adolescent pregnancy problem was that a rapidly growing number of pregnant teenagers in the 1970s were choosing not to marry before delivering their babies, particularly among low-income black teenagers, and more were opting to remain in school. This situation produced an expanding group of economically disadvantaged, single-parent mothers dependent upon welfare support and other costly government-subsidized programs. During the 1980s, moreover, the gap between blacks and whites narrowed in regard to fertility rates and the number of childbearing teens choosing not to marry. The rate of non-marital childbearing among white adolescents more than doubled between 1975 and 1988. No longer viewed as primarily a problem of the black population, the concern about adolescent pregnancy expanded to all corners of society. Exacerbating the problem were the increasing rates of adolescent sexual intercourse, the associated rise in rates of sexually transmitted diseases, a continuing lag in the willingness of sexually active adolescents to employ effective contraception, and the relative reliance by teenagers on abortion to terminate unwanted pregnancies.

In sum, the question of whether or not the adolescent pregnancy and childbearing phenomenon constitutes an epidemic or a major social crisis as it has evolved over the past two to three decades is probably moot. Although the proportion of all births in the United States that are to teenagers has declined since 1975, when the number and rate were at their peak, every year approximately 1 million females age 19 and younger experience a pregnancy. The pregnancy rate among American teenagers continues to be among the highest relative to other countries in the developed world. As will be documented in the next section, nearly half of these pregnancies result in live births. The human, economic, and societal costs continue to be staggering, and the search for solutions to this problem continues to be warranted, if not yet successful. Although a sudden "epidemic" or "crisis" may not be the best way to describe this situation, few would dispute seriously its status as a social problem of the highest order.

ADOLESCENT PREGNANCY AND CHILDBEARING IN THE UNITED STATES

A number of scholars have published recent reviews of adolescent pregnancy and fertility rates that are more comprehensive than space limitations will allow here (see Furstenberg, 1991; Henshaw & Van Vort, 1989; Voydanoff & Donnelly, 1990). In 1985, 1,031,000 teenagers (ages 19 and younger) experienced a pregnancy, and it is estimated that 31,000 of these were adolescents under the age of 15 (Henshaw & Van Vort, 1989). Not counted, however, were many more adolescent pregnancies that occurred to 19-year-olds, because these births did not actually occur until the mothers were 20 years old.

Adolescent Pregnancy Outcomes

Approximately 46% of the adolescent pregnancies in 1985 (477,710) resulted in live births, whereas more than 40% (416,170) were terminated by induced abortion. The balance of adolescent pregnancies (14%) resulted in miscarriages or stillbirths. As would be expected, older teenagers experienced higher pregnancy rates (16.6% of those aged 18-19, 7.1% of those aged 15-17, and 1.7% of those under 15 became pregnant in 1985), and sought more abortions (233,570 18- or 19-year-olds versus 165,630 15- to 17-year-olds obtained an abortion in 1985). A slightly higher percentage of pregnancies to young adolescents, however, were terminated by induced abortion in 1985 (45.6% for those under 15, versus 41% for those aged 18-19). Females below the age of 20 accounted for 26% of all abortions and 13% of all births. Basing their estimates on these 1985 data, Henshaw and Van Vort (1989) estimated that 9% of this cohort of adolescents would have had at least one abortion by age 18, and 9% would have had at least one live birth. By age 20, it was estimated that 18% would have had an abortion, and 20% at least one child.

Among teenagers who actually carry their pregnancies to term, the vast majority keep their babies rather than relinquishing them through adoption proceedings. Approximately 5% of all unmarried childbearing adolescents relinquish their babies for adoption, with the probability being higher that whites will relinquish for adoption than will blacks (Bachrach, 1986). In 1982, slightly more than 7% of babies born to unmarried white teenagers were relinquished (down from 18% in 1971), compared to less than 1% born to unmarried black teens (down from 2% in 1971). In conjunction with the legalized availability of abortion since 1973, these trends in adoption decisions among teenagers have contributed to a reduction in the number of babies available for adoption since the early 1970s.

Trends Over Time

Table 5.1 shows the trends in pregnancy rates, birthrates, and abortion rates for 15- to 19-year-old females over the 9-year period from 1977 through 1985. Representing the number of each outcome per 1,000 population in this age group, these figures show only gradual fluctuations over the years. In 1985, for example, there were 109.8 pregnancies per 1,000 females aged 15-19, meaning that nearly 11% of all adolescent women in that age group experienced a pregnancy. This is virtually the same as the 11.1% figure for 1980, and only slightly higher than the 10.5% pregnancy rate for 1977. Actual birthrates also remained rather consistent over the years, as 5.1% of all 15- to 19-year-old females experienced a live birth in 1985, compared to 5.3% in both 1977 and 1980. The abortion rate shows the greatest change over the years, although the increases are still only modest. In 1985, 4.4% of all 15- to 19-year-old females experienced an abortion, compared to 3.8% in 1977.

Racial Differences in Pregnancy,
Fertility, and Abortion

In regard to racial differences in pregnancy, fertility, and abortion rates, Table 5.1 shows that nonwhite (primarily black) adolescents in 1985 had significantly higher pregnancy rates, birthrates, and abortion rates per 1,000 population than did their white counterparts. In 1985, the nonwhite pregnancy rate was exactly twice as high as the white rate (185.8 vs. 92.9), whereas the nonwhite birthrate was more than double the white rate. The racial differences are magnified among early adolescents under age 15: The nonwhite abortion rate in 1985 was more than five times that of the white rate, and the birthrate was more than six times higher (Henshaw & Van Vort, 1989). The nonwhite fertility rate, however, declined somewhat more between 1980 and 1985 than did the white birthrate (5.3% vs. 4.9%). Also, among pregnant adolescents aged 15-19, the percentages of nonwhites and whites choosing abortion to terminate the pregnancy are about the same (42% in 1985). Hispanic adolescents, who constitute a growing proportion of the American adolescent population, have birthrates and abortion rates that are lower than blacks but higher than non-Hispanic whites (Hayes, 1987; Henshaw & Van Vort, 1989; Moore, Simms, & Betsey, 1986).

Table 5.1 Pregnancy, Birth, and Abortion Rates per 1,000 15- to 19-Year-Olds, by Race, 1977-1985

Variable	1977	1978	1979	1980	1981	1982	1983	1984	1985
All Races									
Pregnancy rate[a]	104.6	105.4	109.4	111.2	110.8	110.3	109.9	108.6	109.8
Birth rate	52.8	51.5	52.3	53.3	52.7	52.6	51.7	50.9	51.3
Abortion rate	37.5	39.7	42.4	42.9	43.3	42.9	43.5	43.2	43.8
White									
Pregnancy rate[a]	NA	89.9	94.6	96.1	96.0	95.2	94.3	92.7	92.9
Birth rate	44.1	42.9	43.7	45.0	44.7	44.5	43.6	42.5	42.8
Abortion rate	NA	34.9	38.3	38.3	38.5	38.1	38.2	37.9	37.8
Nonwhite									
Pregnancy rate[a]	NA	186.3	185.2	186.3	182.3	180.9	181.9	180.6	185.8
Birth rate	99.5	96.0	96.5	94.7	91.3	90.7	89.3	89.0	89.7
Abortion rate	NA	64.7	63.1	66.0	66.1	65.5	67.9	67.1	71.1

SOURCE: Adapted from Henshaw and Van Vort (1989, p. 86). Reprinted with permission of The Alan Guttmacher Institute from S. K. Henshaw and J. VanVort, "Teenage Abortion, Birth and Pregnancy Statistics: An Update," *Family Planning Perspectives, 21,* 2, March/April 1989.
NOTE: NA = data not available.
a. Rate by age at outcome of pregnancy.

These racial differences in pregnancy and fertility can be explained, in large measure, by the fact that large black-white differences exist in the age at which sexual activity is initiated in adolescence, the frequency of intercourse, the tolerance of attitudes toward sexual activity outside of marriage, and the perceived tolerance in the community for nonmarital births (Furstenberg, Morgan, Moore, & Peterson, 1987; Miller & Moore, 1990; Moore et al., 1986). In analyzing data gathered from more than 13,000 female high school sophomores in 1980 who were again studied in 1982 (the High School and Beyond panel study), Abrahamse, Morrison, and Waite (1988) reported that 41% of black respondents stated that they either would or might consider having a child outside of marriage. This compared to 29% of the Hispanic respondents and only 23% of the non-Hispanic whites. Indeed, actual nonmarital childbearing was more frequent over the 2-year period of the study among those who, at baseline, stated that they were willing to consider single parenthood as a viable option for them.

Moreover, racial differences in adolescent pregnancy and fertility are reduced, but not eliminated, when statistical controls for family income and parental education are introduced (Miller & Moore, 1990; Moore et al., 1986). Taken together, then, all of this evidence implies that the normative and attitudinal context of the black community is more conducive to conditions favoring adolescent pregnancy risk than is the case among other racial or ethnic groups.

Socioeconomic Status
and Adolescent Pregnancy

Adolescent pregnancy and fertility also vary according to socioeconomic status (SES). Lower-income adolescents, particularly those who live in poverty, and those with less educated parents initiate sexual activity earlier and have higher pregnancy rates and birthrates than do higher-status teens (Furstenberg, 1991; Hogan & Kitagawa, 1985; Moore et al., 1986; Voydanoff & Donnelly, 1990). As Miller and Moore (1990) point out, this effect may be due to a "perceived lack of options and desirable alternatives for the future," and to differential "community norms and supervision practices" (p. 1030) of families in different socioeconomic strata. According to Voydanoff and Donnelly (1990):

> Because a whole series of conditions correlated with poverty are tied to sexual activity among young people, this relationship is not surprising. Poor families, for instance, are more likely to be headed by a female and to be large. Both of these conditions contribute to the likelihood that parental supervision of dating activities will be reduced. This autonomy provides more opportunities for sexual initiation and activity. (p. 28)

Also involved is the fact that adolescents from lower socioeconomic backgrounds tend to have lower educational and occupational aspirations, and to experience more problems in school, than do others. This leads to a relatively limited range of perceived life opportunities and to a greater propensity to engage in sexual activity, to employ contraception less often and less effectively, and to experience a greater probability of becoming pregnant (Furstenberg, 1991; Hayes, 1987; Moore et al., 1986). Adolescents in the High School and Beyond study who reported lower educational aspirations, more problem behavior in school, and more episodes of depression in the previous month were more willing than others to consider having a child outside of marriage (Abrahamse et al., 1988). As Furstenberg (1991) notes, disadvantaged youths lack the motivation for actively seeking ways to prevent pregnancy.

> Early childbearing owes its persistence to the fact that many women —not just disadvantaged black youth—have relatively little to lose by having a first birth in their teens or early 20s. . . . Without a strong belief that means of mobility are available, teens in disadvantaged communities are likely to display indifferent efforts to prevent pregnancy from occurring. . . . Without providing teenagers, females and males alike, a stronger reason to postpone parenthood, many will fail to use birth control even if it is freely available. (p. 136)

Socioeconomic status, aspirations, and expectations are just some of the variables associated with the risk of pregnancy in adolescence. Adolescent pregnancy risk is a complex issue that has been the subject of considerable empirical study over the past 15 years.

ADOLESCENT PREGNANCY RISK

Given the statistics and trends reviewed in the previous section, research attention continues to be directed at the fundamental question of why some adolescent females and males assume the risk of experiencing a pregnancy while others do not. Adolescent pregnancy risk is determined by two clusters of behavior: *sexual activity*, which includes the timing of first intercourse, the frequency of subsequent sexual encounters, and the number of sexual partners; and *contraceptive behavior*, which includes contraceptive decision making at first intercourse, the frequency of contraceptive efforts during subsequent sexual encounters, and the effectiveness of any contraceptive measures that are employed. Pregnancy risk varies as a function of these two behavioral domains; the greater the level of sexual activity and the lower the frequency of effective contraceptive use, the greater the pregnancy risk.

Knowledge about the determinants of adolescent sexual activity has been reviewed elsewhere in this volume (see Chapter 3) and will not be repeated here. In this section, I will review the trends in sexually active adolescents' use of contraception in terms of frequency and effectiveness. Variables identified as determinants of contraceptive use in the research literature will also be discussed. The reader should note, however, that the research literature on adolescent contraceptive behavior is vast and cannot be reviewed comprehensively here. A number of recent reviews provide excellent summaries of the studies conducted to date (see Hayes, 1987; Miller & Jorgensen, 1988; Miller & Moore, 1990; Voydanoff & Donnelly, 1990). Additionally, with a few notable exceptions (e.g., Blum & Resnick, 1982; Finkel & Finkel, 1975; Robinson, 1988; Sonenstein, Pleck, & Ku, 1989), most of what we know about adolescent contraception is based on large surveys of sexually active adolescent females.

Trends in Adolescent Contraceptive Use

It is generally recognized that the high rate of adolescent pregnancy in American society relative to other developed nations is attributable to the relatively infrequent and ineffective use of contraception among sexually active adolescents. As Jones et al. (1986) point out, the rate of sexual activity in the United States is comparable to other nations examined in their study (France, Canada, Sweden, England and Wales, and the Netherlands). Clearly, then, higher pregnancy rates in the United States are a reflection of the higher pregnancy risk assumed by sexually active American adolescents who do not employ contraception consistently or effectively.

In reviewing a number of national surveys of sexually active adolescent females, conducted in 1976, 1979 (Zelnik & Kantner, 1980), and 1982 (National Survey of Family Growth [NSFG]; Pratt, Mosher, Bachrach, & Horn, 1984), Trussell (1988) made a number of revealing observations about adolescent contraceptive use. Only 48% of sexually active adolescent females surveyed in the 1982 NSFG used any method of contraception at first intercourse, and many used nonmedical methods that have relatively low rates of user effectiveness (47% used a condom, 27% employed withdrawal, and another 9% relied on other methods, whereas only 17% used the pill). In the 1979 national survey conducted by Zelnik and Kantner (1980), 66% of the sexually active 15- to 19-year-olds reported never or only sometimes employing a contraceptive method.

Adolescents also tend to delay the acquisition of a family planning method until well after the initiation of sexual activity. In a later analysis of the 1982 NSFG data, Mosher and Horn (1988) reported that only 17% of the sexually active women aged 15-24 made their first family planning visit before they began having intercourse, and only another 10% made their first family planning visit during the same month as first intercourse. The remaining 73% waited an average (median) of 23 months after first intercourse to seek family planning services.

The result of this ineffective use or nonuse of contraception at first and subsequent episodes of sexual intercourse among adolescents is a high probability of unintended pregnancy. Zabin, Kantner, and Zelnik (1979) reported that 20% of all first adolescent pregnancies in their 1976 survey occurred within 1 month after first intercourse, and about 50% occurred within 6 months after sexual activity began. Among adolescent females who reported always using a contraceptive method, the likelihood of experiencing a pregnancy was reduced drastically relative to those who reported never using contraception. Only 11% of the contraceptors had experienced pregnancy after 2 years following first intercourse, compared to 66% of the noncontraceptors.

More recent data provides evidence that the effective use of contraception in the sexually active adolescent population is increasing to some degree. Miller and Moore (1990), for example, report estimates that only 10% to 20% of sexually active adolescents today use no contraceptive method of any kind. Sonenstein et al. (1989) compared 17- to 19-year-old males interviewed in 1979 with another sample interviewed in 1988 and found that condom use increased from 20% to 54% at first intercourse and from 21% to nearly 58% for the most recent intercourse. The percentages using no method or an ineffective method of contraception at last intercourse also declined substantially, from 51% in 1979 to 21% in 1988; this was also the case for first intercourse (from 71% in 1979 to 39% in 1988). The researchers attributed these trends in accelerating condom use to increased awareness of and concern about acquired immune deficiency syndrome (AIDS) in the adolescent population, in conjunction with the increased accessibility of condoms and media attention to their use. Nonetheless, although these trends are promising, the percentages reporting no use or ineffective use of contraception remain sufficiently high to warrant continuing concern about teen contraceptive behavior and the resulting risk of unintended adolescent pregnancy in American society.

Determinants of Adolescent Contraceptive Use

Relatively few adolescents, male or female, consciously plan to experience a pregnancy when they do (Furstenberg, 1991), and few report a desire to become pregnant when they begin to have sex (Miller & Moore, 1990). Why, then, do so many sexually active teens risk pregnancy by delaying the acquisition of an effective family planning method, by using ineffective methods, or by using no method at all? An extensive body of research literature provides much needed insight in addressing this question. The variables associated with contraceptive use and nonuse are found at many levels of analysis.

Psychological and Individual Variables

The decision to use contraception requires a number of qualities that are often lacking in the adolescent: knowledge, information, motivation, personal and interpersonal skills, and a positive self-concept. Miller and Moore (1990) provide a clear picture of the complexity of the contraceptive decision and actual contraceptive behavior that face adolescents, many of whom still have "one foot in childhood" and who lack the psychological, emotional, and social maturity of adulthood.

At the most basic level, the adolescent has to recognize that he or she is or will be sexually active. The young person also has to understand that sexual intercourse leads to pregnancy and that methods of birth control can prevent pregnancy. The possibility that pregnancy could happen has to be personalized, and the adolescent has to feel that pregnancy would be a negative occurrence. In addition, the social, economic, and psychic costs of obtaining and using a method of birth control must be weighed against the perceived risks and costs of pregnancy. The use of contraception may need to be negotiated with the partner. Moreover, this calculation must be repeated regularly, since most birth control methods require action on a daily basis or with every act of sex. (p. 1031)

Given the complex nature of the decision, empirical evidence suggests that effective contraception among adolescents is *less* likely to occur when:

1. the individual desires a pregnancy, or has no reason to care one way or the other because she or he sees little to lose if a pregnancy should occur (Furstenberg, 1991; Jorgensen, 1981; Shah, Zelnik, & Kantner, 1975);

2. the individual fails to accept her or his own sexuality and views the sexual self with guilt or feelings of discomfort (i.e., a negative sexual self-concept) (Lindemann, 1974; Winter, 1988);

3. the individual lacks the level of cognitive development required in making complex decisions of the type required by contraceptive use (i.e., ability to conceptualize and weigh costs and benefits, to engage in effective problem solving, to internalize and integrate information, and to overcome the egocentric thought patterns of childhood) (Cvetkovich & Grote, 1981; Cvetkovich, Grote, Bjorseth, & Sarkissian, 1975; Jorgensen, 1981);

4. the individual has low educational and occupational aspirations and expectations and lacks the incentive to move up the socioeconomic ladder (Furstenberg, 1991; Hayes, 1987; Moore et al., 1986);

5. the individual lacks accurate knowledge about human sexuality and the facts relating to reproduction, effective contraceptive methods, health risks and benefits of various family planning methods, the ways they work, and their accessibility in the community (Kantner & Zelnik, 1973; Moore & Burt, 1982; Robinson, 1988; Shah, Zelnik, & Kantner, 1975);

6. the individual holds unfavorable attitudes toward birth control (either specific effective methods or in general) or believes that birth

control use will interfere with the pleasurable, "spontaneous" nature of sexual intercourse (Jorgensen, 1980; Moore et al., 1986; Shah, Zelnik, & Kantner, 1975; Sonenstein, 1986);

7. the individual is unable or unwilling to plan for sexual encounters that might be sporadic or unexpected, as is often the case in sexually active adolescent relationships (Sonenstein, 1986; Zelnik, Kantner, & Ford, 1981); or

8. the adolescent male believes that contraceptive use is the female's responsibility, and the adolescent female believes that it is the male's responsibility (Finkel & Finkel, 1975; Robinson, 1988).

It is also well-known that older sexually active adolescents use contraception more effectively and more consistently (Hayes, 1987; Voydanoff & Donnelly, 1990). In other words, age is correlated highly with most of the variables identified above: The older the adolescent, the greater the level of cognitive development, knowledge about sexuality and family planning methods, development of educational and occupational aspirations, acceptance of one's sexuality, and so on.

Social Networks:
Peers, Parents, and Partners

Adolescent contraceptive use also is shaped by the teenager's involvement with friends, family, and sexual partners. Parents and friends, for example, appear to be the most important influence in encouraging sexually active adolescents and young women to seek professional family planning services. Based on the 1982 NSFG data, Mosher and Horn (1988) reported that 51% of adolescents and young women making first family planning visits to private doctors were referred by parents or other relatives, who were also the referral source for 24% whose first visit was to a family planning clinic. Friends were the referral source for 44% of those attending family planning clinics and 22% of those making first family planning visits to private doctors. School counselors, teachers, and sex partners (boyfriends) were the least likely referral sources.

In a large study of adolescent females attending family planning clinics in Maryland, Nathanson and Becker (1986) found that both peers and parents were involved in supporting the girls' attendance. Peers became more influential in the contraceptive acquisition process, however, when the adolescent desired to avoid parental detection or if parents otherwise were perceived to be nonsupportive. The researchers referred to this as a type of "fallback strategy" (Nathanson & Becker, 1986, p. 520); friends were not called upon for support if parents were already involved in the process. Parental involvement and support for seeking contraceptive services was greater for black adolescents and was the least likely for whites with well-educated mothers.

When parents and adolescents are able to communicate about sexuality and the need for responsible family planning behavior, more effective and consistent use of contraception is likely to follow. Research reviewed by Hayes (1987) and Miller and Jorgensen (1988) shows that such discussions can provide the adolescent with information about reproduction and contraception and can convey positive and supportive attitudes from the parent. Research reported by Jorgensen and Sonstegaard (1984) also found that when sexually active adolescents perceived their parents to support their use of contraceptives, they were more likely to be effective contraceptive users, particularly if they were motivated to comply with their parents' wishes.

The nature of the sexually active couple's relationship can also influence the effectiveness of contraceptive behavior in adolescence. For example, Jorgensen, King, and Torrey (1980) found that adolescent females who reported that they had more power and influence in their relationships with their boyfriends, and who were more satisfied with the quality of those relationships, were more likely than others to report consistent and effective contraceptive use. This finding replicated an earlier study of college-age men and women (Thompson & Spanier, 1978), which found that partners had more influence over whether or not effective contraception was employed than did either parents or peers. Communication within the relationship and the degree of involvement were both correlated with partner influence on contraceptive behavior.

Social Structural and Demographic Variables

In summarizing the research on racial differences in adolescent contraceptive behavior, Moore et al. (1986) and Voydanoff and Donnelly (1990) concluded that white adolescents are somewhat more likely than blacks to employ a contraceptive method at first intercourse.

Blacks, however, have been found to be more likely to use an *effective* medical method at first intercourse. In their 1988 national survey of 15- to 19-year-old males, Sonenstein et al. (1989) found similar results: Blacks were more likely to have used ineffective or no contraceptive method at first intercourse than were nonblacks (49% vs. 36%) but were more slightly more likely (9% vs. 6%) to have used an effective female method (e.g., the pill, IUD). The picture changed considerably, however, when examining contraception at *last* (i.e., most recent) intercourse. Sonenstein et al. (1989) found that blacks were more likely than either whites or Hispanics to report using a condom at last intercourse, whereas whites were more likely than either blacks or Hispanics to have used an effective female method without a condom at last intercourse. Hispanics were the most likely to report using no method, whereas blacks were least likely to report use of an ineffective or no method (31% for Hispanics versus 23% for whites and 20% for blacks). Thus it appears that blacks are more likely to report having improved in their overall contraceptive behavior from first to most recent intercourse relative to other groups. For all groups, however, the rate of inconsistent and ineffective contraceptive use in the sexually active adolescent population is substantially greater than in the general adult population.

Black-white differences in contraceptive use are reduced substantially when statistical controls for social class, family stability, and religion are invoked. Among both blacks and whites, the higher the social status, the greater the probability of contraception at first and subsequent episodes of sexual intercourse. This finding is consistent with the positive correlation between adolescent educational and occupational aspirations and contraceptive use that was reported above.

There is some evidence to suggest that although more religious adolescents delay sexual activity relative to others, those who do become sexually active are less likely to use contraception or to do so in a less consistent fashion (Studer & Thornton, 1987). This suggests that religious youths who become sexually active are struggling with the morality of their sexual decision making. To employ contraception in a premeditated manner would be admitting to themselves and to their partners that they are actually planning or intending to do something that is "wrong" within the context of their religious value system. Thus it may be that religious adolescents are more likely than others to report that they did not employ contraception to prevent pregnancy because sexual intercourse was unplanned or "just happened."

Also to be considered is the availability of affordable, convenient, and confidential family planning services in the community. According to Hayes (1987), teenagers are less likely to seek contraceptive services if the latter are perceived to be too expensive, if they require parental notification or approval, or if they are inconvenient in terms of travel time or appointment schedules. Research has shown that greater clinic attendance by sexually active teens is associated with family planning programs that provide (a) special outreach and follow-up activities geared for adolescents; (b) free services to teens; (c) visits without having to schedule an appointment; (d) understanding of cultural beliefs and practices of patients; (e) clinic hours that are convenient for students; (f) a diversity of locations and provider types; (g) understanding of teens' concern that parents will be told of their visits; (h) easier and less embarrassing access to male methods among potential adolescent male clients; and (i) a staff that expresses warmth, caring, and rapport with teen clients (Moore et al., 1986). As Furstenberg (1991) noted, however, the provision of convenient and affordable family planning services is no guarantee that sexually active teens will take advantage of them. The genuine motivation to prevent an unwanted pregnancy is a necessary condition, and it is often lacking in today's population of sexually active adolescents who, despite the easy access to affordable and confidential family planning services, do not avail themselves of them in a timely or consistent manner.

THE RESOLUTION
OF ADOLESCENT PREGNANCIES

When faced with a pregnancy, adolescent females and males are confronted with decisions that have important implications for their present and future lives. Also affected are the lives of their family members and, of course, of the offspring that is conceived. Decisions must be made in regard to abortion versus bringing the pregnancy to term; marriage versus single parenthood; adoption versus keeping the child; and raising the child oneself versus having the child raised by other family members (e.g., parents or grandparents). These decisions are influenced, to varying degrees, by male partners, friends, parents, and other significant others (e.g., schoolteachers or counselors, clergy); they may be carefully thought through, or they may be "spur of the moment" and haphazard (Voydanoff & Donnelly, 1990).

Trends in Adolescent Pregnancy Resolution

As noted earlier in this chapter, less than one half of all adolescent pregnancies result in live births, and slightly more than 40% are terminated by induced abortion; the remainder are stillborn or miscarried. Among those mothers who carry their babies to term, only a small percentage (around 5%) relinquish their babies for adoption, whereas the balance keep their babies to be raised by themselves and/or other family members.

A declining number of adolescent mothers are choosing to marry prior to delivering the child. According to analyses conducted by Furstenberg (1991), 85% of all births to teens in 1960 were to mothers who were married at the time. This proportion decreased to 34%, or just one in three, by 1988. The trends in racial differences are also noteworthy. For example, black adolescent mothers are much less likely than whites to marry the child's father in order to "legitimate" the birth. In 1988, 92% of all births to black teens were to those who were unmarried at the time, compared to only 54% among white adolescent childbearers (Furstenberg, 1991). The black-white gap in the proportion of teen births that are out of wedlock, however, has narrowed considerably over the past 30 years. A declining proportion of white adolescent mothers today are choosing to marry the child's father. In 1988, for example, white adolescents produced 53% of all unmarried births to teenagers, compared to 42% in 1975 and only 37% in 1960 (Furstenberg, 1991).

The Abortion Decision

Perhaps the first decision many pregnant teens face is whether or not to seek an abortion. Following the landmark U.S. Supreme Court decision in 1973 legalizing abortion in the United States, this option became much more viable for those experiencing an unintended or unwanted pregnancy. For some, the decision is clear-cut and easy: Either abortion is out of the question, for one reason or another, or it is the only answer to the problem created by the unwanted pregnancy.

Complicating the decision for many other pregnant adolescents, however, have been the quite serious moral, political, and religious controversies that surround the abortion issue, many of which have led to court cases and lawsuits challenging one or more aspects of the 1973 Supreme Court decision. Some of these are particularly relevant to adolescents: Is parental notification and/or approval required for pregnant adolescents seeking abortion? What if the teen's parents are separated or divorced? If notification or approval is required, is it needed from both parents? Under what circumstances can a parental notification or approval requirement be waived? Can federal funds be used to subsidize the abortions of low-income adolescents? The abortion debate rages on with no clear view of when, if ever, these thorny issues will be resolved satisfactorily. In the meantime, the abortion decision is made even more trying for many pregnant teens who must struggle under this cloud of ambivalence relating to abortion in our society.

A substantial body of research literature bearing on the variables associated with the decision to obtain an abortion has been recently reviewed by Hayes (1987), Miller and Moore (1990), and Voydanoff and Donnelly (1990). The decision to seek and to obtain an abortion among pregnant adolescents is more likely among:

1. those who are not highly religious or a member of a fundamentalist religious organization;
2. those with higher educational and occupational aspirations, and those whose parents are of higher SES and who have higher levels of education;
3. those who are in school, performing well in school, and who have never dropped out of school;
4. those who remain unmarried during their pregnancies and whose family members (especially mothers), friends, or male partners support or encourage the abortion decision;
5. those who have convenient access to medically safe, legal abortion facilities in their communities;
6. younger adolescents (under age 15) and older adolescents (age 18 or 19);
7. those who are financially self-supporting;
8. those who have not disclosed or discussed their pregnancies with their mothers;

9. those who are able to project themselves realistically into the future by envisioning what their lives would be with or without experiencing adolescent parenthood;

10. those who do not desire to have a child, whose pregnancy was unintended, and who believe that to have a child as a teenager is extremely poor timing;

11. those who have a relatively favorable attitude toward abortion as a legitimate choice for terminating an unwanted pregnancy and who are not flatly opposed to abortion on moral or religious grounds; and

12. those who have been previously pregnant.

What are the consequences of the abortion decision? What impact does the abortion decision have on adolescents who choose it to resolve a pregnancy? Recent evidence reported by Zabin, Hirsch, and Emerson (1989), based on a sample of 360 black teenage women in Baltimore, sheds some light on this question. It was found that those who chose abortion were no more likely than those in two comparison groups (a group of adolescent childbearers and a nonparent group) to report psychological problems 2 years later. Those who chose abortion were far more likely to be in school or to have completed high school, however, and they were better off financially. They also were less likely to have experienced a repeat pregnancy and were more likely to be practicing contraception in the 2 years after their abortions.

The Marriage Decision

Adolescent pregnancy does not necessarily involve two adolescents. In many cases, the male partner is older than the female, often 2 to 3 years older, and is himself not an adolescent. In any event, marriage to legitimate an adolescent pregnancy has profound implications for the life course of both the teenage girl and her male partner (to be discussed more fully later in this chapter), whatever age he might be.

As noted previously, the proportion of black teenage mothers marrying is less than 10%, whereas the proportion of white teen mothers marrying had declined to 46% by 1988. Clearly, marriage and parenthood are not linked as closely as they once were in the adolescent population (as is the case in the adult population as well) (Furstenberg, 1991). For blacks, marriage is less likely because fewer black males of marriageable age are either advancing in school or employed at a level that can sustain a growing family. In commenting on the relatively disadvantaged social and economic context in which the black American family resides, Moore et al. (1986) noted that

> high unemployment rates in the black community pose a barrier to establishing an economically viable marriage. Whether it is a young couple faced with a premarital pregnancy but lacking job prospects or a married couple faced with repeated spells of unemployment, not having earnings to rely on undercuts the ability of blacks to form and maintain marriages. . . . Setting up a married household may also be more difficult for blacks because access to housing that is suitable or acceptable is more limited. (p. 109)

The economic constraints in the black community appear to be accompanied by normative support for early childbearing. Black adolescents hold more tolerant attitudes toward out-of-wedlock childbearing and expect more favorable reactions toward their pregnancies from parents and partners. Survey evidence also has found that black adolescents, more often than whites, express a preference for having children *before* they are married (Abrahamse et al., 1988; Clark, Zabin, & Hardy, 1984).

In addition to racial differences in the propensity to marry, research recently reviewed by Hayes (1987), Miller and Moore (1990), and Voydanoff and Donnelly (1990) shows that the decision to marry the male partner is *less* likely among pregnant adolescents who:

1. have a general willingness to become a single parent, particularly if it is accompanied by the prospect of financial assistance from the family of origin or from the government;
2. are younger, with the highest probability of marriage occurring among older white adolescents;
3. are from lower SES families; or
4. are enrolled full-time in a post-high school educational program.

The Adoption Decision

Among those pregnant adolescents who carry their babies to term, only a small minority (about 5%) will relinquish them for adoption.

As noted earlier, this percentage was substantially higher prior to 1973, when abortion was legalized in the United States.

Again, the recent literature reviews of Hayes (1987), Miller and Moore (1990), and Voydanoff and Donnelly (1990) provide information to identify the variables associated with the adoption decision. According to Hayes (1987), adolescents who choose adoption are more similar in some ways to those who choose abortion than they are to pregnant teens who choose single parenthood. Teenage mothers are more likely to relinquish the child for adoption if they:

1. are younger, white, and come from families of higher SES;
2. have higher educational and occupational aspirations and are performing satisfactorily in school;
3. live in families who have adopted a child, or know others who have had positive adoption experiences;
4. live in two-parent family structures, have parents who have more influence on their decision making, and have partners whom they have known for less time and who have less influence;
5. have higher levels of religiosity;
6. have friends who support the adoption decision;
7. have a realistic future time perspective that does not glamorize parenthood and that allows them to envision what their lives would be like if they kept a child versus relinquishing it for adoption.

What is the impact of the adoption decision on the adolescent childbearer? Are they any better or worse off than those who keep their babies? Data provided by McLaughlin, Manninen, and Winges (1988) in a study of 123 child rearers and 146 relinquishers found that those who relinquished their infants for adoption were more likely than the teen mothers to have completed vocational training, to have higher educational aspirations, to delay marriage, to be employed 6 months after the birth, and to live in higher-income households. The child rearers, on the other hand, were more likely to experience a repeat pregnancy and to resolve those pregnancies by abortion. These differences remained even when controlling potentially important background variables that might have explained the outcome advantages for the relinquishing group (higher SES, parents' education, etc.). Both groups were satisfied with their decisions, although the relinquishers were slightly less satisfied.

CONSEQUENCES OF ADOLESCENT PREGNANCY
AND PARENTHOOD

A number of authors (see, e.g., Hayes, 1987; Jorgensen, 1986; Makinson, 1985; Moore & Burt, 1982; Trussell, 1988; Voydanoff & Donnelly, 1990) have reviewed the physical and health, psychological, social, and economic consequences of adolescent pregnancy and childbearing. Although the literature is far too vast to review comprehensively here, it is clear that overwhelming evidence exists to show that adolescent parenthood is associated with adverse consequences at all levels of analysis.

It is also clear , however, that responses to teen pregnancy and early childbearing vary widely from one adolescent mother and her family to the next, and that any consequences associated with this situation also vary accordingly (Furstenberg, 1991). Some adapt and succeed in parenthood and in achieving a satisfactory quality of life, whereas others do not. As Furstenberg (1991) points out, adolescents vary in the availability of resources and in their ability to employ them when confronted with unintended pregnancy and parenthood:

> That many teenage mothers and their families respond resourcefully to the challenge of managing motherhood is undeniable. . . . It is likely that the timing of the first birth has minimal effects on the segment of teen parents who are extremely poor before the birth of their first child (though it may well have adverse effects on their offspring). Also, early parenthood may have only modest effects on the most capable women, who possess the resources to respond to the added demands of child care. The burden of early parenthood might well be greatest for those capable of attaining economic self-sufficiency but lacking the resiliency to respond effectively to additional stresses. (pp. 135, 137)

The Question of Causality

Evidence is mounting to show that a number of identified "consequences" are not as directly a result of adolescent pregnancy and parenting per se as once was thought, and that methodological problems in earlier studies limit their generalizability. In commenting on the literature relating to the medical and health consequences of adolescent pregnancy, Trussell (1988) noted that many studies suffer from such methodological limitations as flawed experimental designs, inappropriate analytical techniques, and small and unrepresentative samples. It is also methodologically difficult to separate the effects of early childbearing from other variables that are associated with it. For example, Makinson (1985) reviewed medical evidence from several developed countries and concluded that many of the adverse health consequences for adolescent mothers and their children, such as maternal complications from pregnancy and delivery, are more a result of the poor prenatal care and low social class that tend to characterize pregnant teens than of the biological age of the mother. Many adolescents delay the seeking of prenatal care, not thinking or wanting to acknowledge that they might be pregnant until it is too late to prevent complications. Adolescent nutrition habits also tend to be poor relative to older women, which is part of an overall tendency to neglect their physical health. This problem is exacerbated in lower socioeconomic strata, where the probability of adolescent pregnancy is higher.

There is evidence, however, to suggest that biological age of the mother per se may indeed lead to adverse health consequences among the youngest adolescent mothers—those below the age of 15 (Hayes, 1987; Makinson, 1985). For these young mothers, biological immaturity has been linked to such pregnancy complications as toxemia, anemia, prolonged labor, and premature labor, as well as relatively high rates of maternal death. Their infants are significantly more likely than those of adult women to be premature and of low birth weight.

Furstenberg (1991) discussed the "selective recruitment" hypothesis of adolescent pregnancy and parenthood in relation to the longer-term social and economic consequences that typically are attributed to early childbearing. According to this view, those who become teenage parents are systematically different prior to their pregnancies than those who do not become pregnant, and these preexisting differences explain variance in the long-term consequences of adolescent pregnancy that is not explained by the pregnancy and childbearing per se. The poverty status, school-related problems, lower educational and occupational aspirations, and family instability more characteristic of teen parents than of later childbearers all are associated independently with truncated educational careers, reduced occupational achievement, and future family instability. Many teens who grow up in such circumstances will encounter bleak educational and occupational futures regardless of whether or not they experience an adolescent pregnancy. As noted by Furstenberg (1991), however, research has yet to determine the relative impact of preexisting socioeconomic background variables versus adolescent pregnancy and childbearing on the educational and economic futures of these early childbearers.

The putative consequences of adolescent pregnancy and parenting reported in the research literature therefore must be viewed in the context of the considerations discussed above. Teenage pregnancy per se may not be the primary causal variable in some instances. The most we can say at this time is that the following outcomes at least are associated with adolescent pregnancy and parenting, either causally or in conjunction with other variables that co-vary with early childbearing. In all likelihood, adolescent pregnancy and childbearing place additional limitations and burdens upon the current well-being and future life chances of adolescent parents and their offspring beyond what they might otherwise have faced.

Medical and Health-Related Outcomes

A number of outcomes have been linked to adolescent pregnancy and, as noted above, are more likely to occur among the youngest pregnant adolescents. These include anemia, hypertension, abnormal deliveries, uterine dysfunctions, pregnancy-related infections, postpartum hemorrhaging and abnormal bleeding, premature rupture of the uterine membrane, and maternal mortality. Infants born to teenagers are more likely than others to be premature and of low birth weight; to have physiological abnormalities, including epilepsy, spinal and head injuries, low IQ and mental retardation, blindness, deafness, and nervous disorders; to be stillborn; to be miscarried; to be aborted voluntarily; and to die during infancy.

Psychological Outcomes

Relative to women whose first childbearing occurs after 20 years of age, teen mothers are more likely to experience stress, feelings of helplessness, despair, and depression; suicide and suicide attempts; and a sense of personal failure and low self-esteem. Although research on teenage fathers is sparse, there is some evidence to suggest that they, too, experience heightened psychological stress and anxiety relative to their older adult counterparts (Elster & Hendricks, 1986; Robinson, 1988).

Social and Economic Outcomes
for Adolescent Parents

Early childbearing has also been linked to numerous longer-term outcomes for the mother, the father, their families of origin, and the child that is born. In contrast to those who begin childbearing as adults, teenage mothers and fathers are less likely to complete high school or to earn a college degree. They are more likely to experience unemployment and poverty as adults, to be dependent upon government welfare programs (particularly unmarried adolescent mothers), and to work in lower-paying and less skilled occupations that yield lower lifetime earnings. These income differences relative to older mothers are not as severe as once was thought, however, and they tend to decline over time (as teenage mothers enter their late 20s and early 30s) (Hayes, 1987). The fertility histories of teenage childbearers are marked by more than the desired number of children (i.e., family planning continues to be problematic for them), larger family sizes, and higher levels of marital discord and divorce should they decide to marry (Trussell & Menken, 1978).

The relatively low educational attainment of teen parents explains much of their limited occupational futures. It is therefore important to understand differences within the adolescent parent population in regard to who is more or less likely to continue in school following the transition to early parenthood. Adolescent parents are more likely to return to school and to complete high school or college degree objectives if they are black, if they remain unmarried, if they are able to prevent a repeat pregnancy within 5 years, and if they live with their parents (Hayes, 1987; Voydanoff & Donnelly, 1990). There is conflicting evidence, however, relating to the age of the adolescent when she becomes a parent. Hayes (1987) concluded that the younger the adolescent mother, the more likely she is to complete high school. This is attributed to the fact that younger adolescents are more likely to reside in the parental home, to stay unmarried, and to receive encouragement and support that will promote the completion of education. Older adolescent mothers undergo other transitions, such as marrying or seeking employment to support oneself and one's child, that force school dropout.

Evidence provided by Upchurch and McCarthy (1989) from a national longitudinal study, however, shows that the younger the adolescents when their first child was born, the less likely they were to be high school graduates. More research is needed to confirm what effect, if any, age of the adolescent has on the chances of completing high school.

Social and Economic Outcomes of the Children of Adolescents

The children of adolescent parents also experience, on the average, more problems and developmental difficulties than do children born to older parents. Beyond the medical and health-related problems identified above, the children of teen parents experience lower levels of academic achievement and more problems in school. Scores on intelligence and other cognitive tests are lower, and measures of socioemotional development show that they are more likely to have problems in dealing with emotions and in controlling their behavior in socially appropriate ways. They are significantly more likely than children born to older parents to become pregnant and parenting adolescents themselves, but this trend is more common among whites than among blacks. In addition, when such "second generation" teen parenting does occur, these children of adolescent parents find themselves in more dire socioeconomic straits than their mothers were when they were teen parents (Furstenberg, Levine, & Brooks-Gunn, 1990). Their educational and economic outlooks are bleaker, and they appear to be more vulnerable to long-term welfare dependence and impoverishment.

The relatively poor educational histories of many children born to adolescent parents generally are attributed to the conditions that seem to foster teen pregnancy in the first place. These children have mothers whose own educational attainment is limited, who have lived a life of resource deficits, and who may lack the ability, motivation, discipline, encouragement, and support necessary to promote their children's school performance (Hayes, 1987). Their mothers are more likely to be poor and to have grown up in disadvantaged neighborhoods, attended lower-quality schools, and experienced relatively high rates of family instability (Hayes, 1987).

Despite these barriers, however, Furstenberg et al.'s (1990) 20-year follow-up study of children born to adolescent mothers in the late 1960s found that the majority had graduated from high school and currently were either in school or employed. Only a small number were on public assistance, and two thirds had avoided experiencing an adolescent pregnancy. This led to the conclusion that

> early childbearing is neither inevitable—nor even the modal pattern —among the offspring of urban, black teenage mothers. . . . The great majority of offspring of teenage mothers are not repeating the pattern of their parents. . . . Of those teenagers without children, most had completed high school, and many went on to college. (Furstenberg, 1990, pp. 60-61)

These findings are consistent with those of Horowitz, Klerman, Kuo, and Jeckel (1991), who followed up on 180 unmarried pregnant black 13- to 18-year-olds first studied in 1967-1969. Eighty-one percent of their female children, and 89 percent of their male children, had not experienced parenthood by age 19. Those who did become teenage parents were more likely to have mothers who had experienced lifelong depression and were more likely to have been removed from a nurturing, stable environment at an early age.

In sum, the research evidence suggests that multiple life trajectories are possible among adolescent parents and their children as they grow up (Miller & Moore, 1990). Although teenage pregnancy and the conditions associated with it create barriers to individual development of the children born to adolescent parents, they are not as severe and as insurmountable as was once believed.

Social and Economic
Outcomes for Families

The families of adolescent parents also are affected by the early childbearing of their children. Miller and Moore (1990) and Voydanoff and Donnelly (1990) have reviewed research that shows a wide diversity of living arrangements following the birth of a child to an adolescent mother, and these arrangements vary by race. The large majority of adolescent mothers (about 75% in 1984) reside in the household of a parent or other relative, at least for a short time following the child's birth, whereas the remainder establish their own households. The unmarried adolescent mother is the most likely to reside in a parent or other relative's household.

Children born to black adolescents are about twice as likely as those born to whites to live with the teen mother and her relatives, most often in her mother's household (Hogan, Hao, & Parish, 1990). Though a significant number of lower-income white (58%) and Hispanic (48%) adolescent mothers and their babies in a 1984 study resided with the mother's male partner in the time period shortly after the birth, either in their own separate household or in a relative's, black fathers were present in only 15% of the cases (Marsiglio, 1987). Catholic males, and those who fathered a child at age 17 or older, were more likely than others to be living with the adolescent mother and their child. Higher-income whites are the most likely group to form a family unit comprising the teen mother, father, and child (77%), and most of these families form separate households. Living in the parental home is only a transitory stage for most adolescent parents, however, as the percentage residing with relatives declines sharply over time in all racial groups.

Adolescent childbearing often places demands on the physical and social resources of many teen parents' families. Assistance and support are most likely to be given if the teen mother and the child reside in the parental home, and least likely if she resides with the partner in a separate household (Voydanoff & Donnelly, 1990). Although many teen parents do receive significant amounts of help from their families, nearly one third of black adolescent mothers and one half of whites reported little or no support in Hogan et al.'s (1990) 1984 national study.

When support is provided, it comes in the form of financial assistance, child care, and transportation, as well as psychological and emotional support for the young mother. White adolescent mothers are more likely to receive support in the form of financial assistance, whereas support for black mothers is more likely to be housing and child care. The level of support provided varies according to the resource availability of the family, but those who do receive assistance in the parental household are somewhat more likely to complete high school, to be free of welfare dependency, and to be employed (Furstenberg & Crawford, 1978).

Furstenberg (1991), however, warns that we should not be overly optimistic about the potential benefits of adolescent mothers and their offspring residing with their extended kin, particularly in terms of the quality of care and socialization the child receives. Their presence in the parental home creates potentially "complex child care systems that are unwieldy, conflict-ridden, and unstable" (p. 132). Problems can arise in forging a satisfactory division of labor, being able to afford the additional expenses involved with the childbearing, and undergoing the heightened levels of emotional stress introduced into the family system by the new arrangement. We lack the research evidence necessary to draw any firm conclusions about the impact that coresidence of adolescent parents and their offspring has on the extended family system.

Economic Costs to Society

Citing estimates provided by the Center for Population Options in 1986, Voydanoff and Donnelly (1990) concluded that adolescent childbearing in the United States costs billions of dollars annually. Public welfare benefits provided to adolescent parents come in the form of Medicaid, Aid to Families with Dependent Children (AFDC), food stamps, and other health-related economic support programs. It is estimated that the federal government spent $16.65 billion on all adolescents and their children who were receiving benefits in 1985. It also is estimated that the entire cohort of children born to adolescent mothers in 1985 will eventually cost the government $6.04 billion in welfare support over the next 20 years. This is $2.42 billion more than would have been spent if these children been born to adult women. For a child born to an adolescent mother in 1985, it was estimated that the government would provide $15,620 to support that child until age 20. This is $6,248 more than the average welfare costs would have been had these children been born when their mothers were adults. The cost is greater for children born to younger mothers ($18,089 for those under age 14) than to older mothers ($14,481 for those over age 18). In sum, the economic costs of adolescent childbearing are substantial.

Outcomes of Adolescent Parenting

A number of studies have suggested that adolescent parents are more prone to abuse and maltreat their children (Bolton, Laner, & Kane, 1980; de Lissovoy, 1973; Gelles, 1986). This problem has been attributed to a number of factors, including the unrealistic expectations that teen parents are more likely to hold for the child's development and behavior; stressful ties to relatives, spouses, and the job market; frustration caused by having to compromise educational and occupational goals; economic insecurity and low income; and isolation from meaningful peer relationships as a result of pregnancy and parenthood.

More careful analysis of this situation, however, shows that the conditions associated with adolescent pregnancy risk (e.g., low socioeconomic background, poor educational and occupational prospects, and family instability) account for much of the variance in abusive or neglectful behavior of adolescent parents (Hayes et al., 1987; Voydanoff & Donnelly, 1990). Additionally, studies have reported that a nontrivial proportion of teenagers are effective parents who display few differences relative to older mothers (Bolton & Belsky, 1986; Furstenberg, Brooks-Gunn, & Morgan, 1987; Roosa & Vaughn, 1984). Clearly, there is substantial variation within the adolescent parent population in regard to success in overcoming the hurdles imposed by premature parenthood, including the quality of parenting behavior. Some are able to recover socially and economically and are on track with their children toward productive adult lives (Hayes, 1987). Many others, however, struggle with their circumstances and experience significant problems in competently playing parental roles.

Regardless of whether age or other variables associated with teen pregnancy risk are responsible, adolescent parents are more likely than others to demonstrate ineffective parenting styles. They vocalize to their infants less, experience more anxiety and frustration in parenting, have fewer positive exchanges with their children, and hold more negative attitudes toward the parenting role. They also are more likely to perceive their infants as being difficult to deal with. All of these differences contribute to the socioemotional and cognitive problems and delays that children of adolescent parents experience (discussed above), and possibly to a "delayed" propensity to engage in abusive behavior with their children (Miller & Moore, 1990).

PROSPECTS FOR THE FUTURE

Adolescent pregnancy and parenthood will continue to remain part of the American social fabric for years to come, barring some unforeseen shift in social policy or adolescent behavior. For those who wish to see a substantial reduction in the rate of adolescent pregnancy, the current outlook is not favorable.

Social Policy and Adolescent Pregnancy

In regard to policy, serious initiatives have been undertaken at both the federal and state levels to support research on the antecedents and outcomes of pregnancy risk in the adolescent population. Owing directly to this support, our understanding of this phenomenon has grown substantially over the past two decades. This knowledge, however, has yet to be translated into a consistent line of prevention programs that could potentially have the effect of reducing the level of adolescent pregnancy risk experienced in our society year after year. Until this happens, our adolescent pregnancy rate will remain among the highest in the developed world.

Our preventive efforts are scattered, hit-and-miss programs that are applied unevenly across states and communities. As noted at the outset of this chapter, this situation is a result of competing moral, political, and religious agendas that literally have stalled our efforts to develop effective solutions to the adolescent pregnancy problem. Some interventions focus on promoting sexual abstinence among teens, attempting to help them internalize the ability to say no to sexual activity, while forbidding the teaching of family planning methods as a means of reducing pregnancy risk. Evaluation studies of abstinence-based programs are few, but those that have published data are not finding the hoped-for changes in attitudes and behaviors that would augur a significant reduction in pregnancy risk in high-risk communities (Christopher & Roosa, 1990; Jorgensen, 1991; Roosa & Christopher, 1990). Other programs incorporate contraceptive information, whereas still others actually provide family planning services and contraceptive prescriptions. Even these school-based health clinics have failed to yield consistent effects in reducing pregnancy risk-related attitudes and behaviors in the target populations (Kirby, Waszak, & Ziegler, 1991).

Although some programs are offered through community and religious organizations, a wider net is cast by those offered through public and private schools. In either type of setting, however, their application is inconsistent. Though a few school programs might recognize that effective sex education begins with the young elementary school child, most others wait until secondary grades to begin discouraging sexual behavior that, for many, has already begun and has become a regular feature of adolescent relationships. Although the dynamics of adolescent pregnancy risk are often found within the dyadic relationship of the teen female and male partner, prevention programs often isolate females into one group and males into another. There is considerable variance in the degree to which sex education interventions are geared to the level of cognitive development of the target group. Some involve parents and have the strong support and involvement of the local schools and community groups, but most do not. Many are abbreviated in duration and content; address issues of sexuality and teen pregnancy in isolation from critical and related life-planning issues (e.g., educational and occupational goal setting); ineffectively address the strong influences that peers, partners, and the media have on the sexual values, attitudes, and behavior of contemporary teens; and simply lack the necessary "punch" to effect genuine behavior change in this age group. In sum, in view of our haphazard and confused social policies bearing on pregnancy prevention programs, it is little wonder that the problem of adolescent pregnancy risk in American society has yet to be solved.

Adolescent Pregnancy Risk Behavior

Adolescent pregnancy is most directly a result of sexual intercourse that is unaccompanied by consistent use of an effective contraceptive method. What are the prospects for a significant change in either of these behavioral dimensions of pregnancy risk? At this point, the prospects do not look good.

In regard to sexual activity, no serious scholar involved in the adolescent pregnancy research domain forecasts a change in adolescent sexual behavior. The vast majority of adolescents are sexually active, the proportion who become so has increased over the years (albeit more slowly in the 1980s than the 1970s), and there is no sign to indicate that the trend will reverse. Sexual activity is being initiated at younger ages and with a greater average number of partners during the adolescent years.

What are the reasons for this consistently upward trend in adolescent sexual activity in American society? It is agreed generally that the trend is associated with the increasingly tolerant attitudes toward human sexuality, either within or outside of marriage, that characterize contemporary society in general. These attitudes of adult society are reflected in potent mass media influences (e.g., television, radio, movies, and advertising of all types).

Regardless of how one might evaluate the desirability or undesirability of this trend toward sexual openness, images of the "fun" and "feel good" aspects of sex are prolific, yet they are unaccompanied by messages of the interpersonal responsibilities and potentially adverse developmental sequelae of precocious sexual activity for teenagers. How confusing it must be for adolescents to be encouraged on the one hand via cultural messages to experience the joys of sex, and then to be told on the other that sexual abstinence and saying no is the only acceptable course. It obviously will take more than superficial attempts at sex education, encouragement to "just say no," and even an epidemic of a highly fatal sexually transmitted disease (AIDS) to effect a meaningful change in the sexual behavior of American adolescents. Without a significant shift in the sociocultural context of human sexuality in contemporary society, we cannot expect to see a change in adolescent participation in sexually active behavior.

In regard to contraception and responsible family planning behavior, the prognosis for adolescents is equally bleak. Because a good amount of adolescent sexual activity, particularly the first episode of sexual intercourse, is reported to be unplanned, we cannot expect teenagers to bring to this experience a rational plan for pregnancy prevention. To employ contraception is an act of recognizing that sexual intercourse is going to take place, which is incompatible with the excuse that it is unplanned or "just happens." Also, as long as educators, policymakers, policy enforcers, and the general public believe that to teach adolescents about responsible birth control endorses adolescent sexual activity and grants it legitimacy, we are unlikely to see a notable improvement in the contraceptive behavior of American adolescents. Ironically, many who oppose abortion also oppose the most effective means of abortion prevention for adolescents—responsible contraceptive behavior.

In significant ways, therefore, we in the "adult society" of America are doing a disservice to our adolescent youth. We espouse inconsistent and confusing messages about sex and sexuality, and we hold ambivalent attitudes toward contraception for the sexually active teenager that seem to shift continuously with the political winds. Neither do we give many adolescents, those who must face grim socioeconomic futures with a feeling of hopelessness, adequate reason to do all that they can to prevent a teen pregnancy. Such a situation keeps pregnancy risk, in the societal aggregate, at a high level. In all likelihood, when we next take stock of where we stand relative to other developed nations in regard to our adolescent pregnancy rate, we will again be at or near the top of the list.

This prognosis begs for a wholesale change in our approach to the adolescent pregnancy problem. As the cartoon character Pogo said, "We have met the enemy, and it is us." Adolescents are a reflection of our collective adult selves, and their pregnancy-risking behaviors are understandable in the context of our own permissive behavior and conflicting value systems relating to acceptable means of pregnancy prevention. Unless we in adult society reframe the two indicators of pregnancy risk, sexual activity and contraceptive use, in a more socially responsible manner, we can expect to see little improvement in the socially and sexually responsible behavior of our adolescent population.

REFERENCES

Abrahamse, A. F., Morrison, P. A., & Waite, L. J. (1988). Teenagers willing to consider single parenthood: Who is at greatest risk? *Family Planning Perspectives, 20,* 13-18.

Alan Guttmacher Institute. (1976). *Eleven million teenagers.* New York: Author.

Alan Guttmacher Institute. (1981). *Teenage pregnancy: The problem that hasn't gone away.* New York: Author.

Bachrach, C. A. (1986). Adoption plans, adopted children, and adoptive mothers. *Journal of Marriage and the Family, 48,* 243-253.

Blum, R. W., & Resnick, M. D. (1982). Adolescent decision-making: Contraception, abortion, motherhood. *Pediatric Annals, 11,* 797-805.

Bolton, F. G., Jr., & Belsky, J. (1986). The adolescent father and child maltreatment. In A. B. Elster & M. E. Lamb (Eds.), *Adolescent fatherhood* (pp. 123-140). Hillsdale, NJ: Lawrence Erlbaum.

Bolton, F. G., Jr., Laner, R. H., & Kane, S. P. (1980). Child maltreatment risk among adolescent mothers: A study of reported cases. *American Journal of Orthopsychiatry, 50,* 489-504.

Christopher, F. S., & Roosa, M. W. (1990). An evaluation of an adolescent pregnancy prevention program: Is "just say no" enough? *Family Relations, 39,* 68-72.

Clark, S. D., Jr., Zabin, L. S., & Hardy, J. B. (1984). Sex, contraception, and parenthood: Experience and attitudes among urban black young men. *Family Planning Perspectives, 16,* 77-82.

Cvetkovich, G., & Grote, B. (1981). Psychosocial maturity and teenage contraceptive use: An investigation of decision making and communication skills. *Population and Environment, 4,* 211-225.

Cvetkovich, G., Grote, B., Bjorseth, A., & Sarkissian, J. (1975). On the psychology of adolescents' use of contraception. *Journal of Sex Research, 11,* 256-270.

de Lissovoy, V. (1973). Child care by adolescent parents. *Children Today, 2,* 22-25.

Elster, A. B., & Hendricks, L. (1986). Stress and coping strategies of adolescent fathers. In A. B. Elster & M. E. Lamb (Eds.), *Adolescent fatherhood* (pp. 55-65). Hillsdale, NJ: Lawrence Erlbaum.

Finkel, M. L., & Finkel, D. J. (1975). Sexual and contraceptive knowledge, attitudes and behavior of male adolescents. *Family Planning Perspectives, 7,* 256-260.

Furstenberg, F. F., Jr. (1991). As the pendulum swings: Teenage childbearing and social concern. *Family Relations, 40,* 127-138.

Furstenberg, F. F., Jr., Brooks-Gunn, J., & Morgan, S. P. (1987). Adolescent mothers in later life. New York: Cambridge University Press.

Furstenberg, F. F., Jr., & Crawford, A. G. (1978). Family support: Helping teenage mothers to cope. *Family Planning Perspectives, 10,* 322-333.

Furstenberg, F. F., Jr., Levine, J. A., & Brooks-Gunn, J. (1990). The children of teenage mothers: Patterns of early childbearing in two generations. *Family Planning Perspectives, 22,* 54-61.

Furstenberg, F. F., Jr., Morgan, S. P., Moore, K. A., & Peterson, J. L. (1987). Race differences in the timing of first intercourse. *American Sociological Review, 52,* 511-518.

Gelles, R. J. (1986). School-age parents and child abuse. In J. B. Lancaster & B. A. Hamburg (Eds.), *School-age pregnancy and parenthood* (pp. 347-360). New York: Aldine DeGruyter.

Hayes, C. D. (Ed.). (1987). *Risking the future: Adolescent sexuality, pregnancy, and childbearing* (Vol. 1). Washington, DC: National Academy Press.

Henshaw, S. K., & Van Vort, J. (1989). Teenage abortion, birth and pregnancy statistics: An update. *Family Planning Perspectives, 21,* 85-88.

Hofferth, S. L., & Hayes, C. D. (Eds.). (1987). *Risking the future: Adolescent sexuality, pregnancy, and childbearing* (Vol. 2). Washington, DC: National Academy Press.

Hogan, D. P., Hao, L., & Parish, W. L. (1990). Race, kin networks, and assistance to mother-headed families. *Social Forces, 68,* 797-812.

Hogan, D. P., & Kitagawa, E. M. (1985). The impact of social status, family structure, and neighborhood on the fertility of black adolescents. *American Journal of Sociology, 90,* 825-855.

Horowitz, S. M., Klerman, L. V., Kuo, H. S., & Jeckel, J. F. (1991). Intergenerational transmission of school-age parenthood. *Family Planning Perspectives, 23,* 168-172, 177.

Jones, E. F., Forrest, J. D., Goldman, N., Henshaw, S. K., Lincoln, R., Rosoff, J. I., Westoff, C. F., & Wulf, D. (1986). *Teenage pregnancy in industrialized countries.* New Haven, CT: Yale University Press.

Jorgensen, S. R. (1980). Contraceptive attitude-behavior consistency in adolescence. *Journal of Population, 3,* 174-194.

Jorgensen, S. R. (1981). Sex education and the reduction of adolescent pregnancies: Prospects for the 1980s. *Journal of Early Adolescence, 1,* 38-52.

Jorgensen, S. R. (1986). *Marriage and the family: Development and change.* New York: Macmillan.

Jorgensen, S. R. (1991). Project Taking Charge: An evaluation of an adolescent pregnancy prevention program. *Family Relations, 40,* 373-380.

Jorgensen, S. R., & Sonstegaard, J. S. (1984). Predicting adolescent sexual and contraceptive behavior: An application and test of the Fishbein model. *Journal of Marriage and the Family, 46,* 43-55.

Jorgensen, S. R., King, S. L., & Torrey, B. A. (1980). Dyadic and social network influences on adolescent exposure to pregnancy risk. *Journal of Marriage and the Family, 42,* 141-155.

Kantner, J. F., & Zelnik, M. (1973) Contraception and pregnancy: Experience of young unmarried women in the United States. *Family Planning Perspectives, 5,* 21-35.

Kirby, D., Waszak, C., & Ziegler, J. (1991). Six school-based clinics: Their reproductive health services and impact on sexual behavior. *Family Planning Perspectives, 23,* 6-16.

Lindemann, C. (1974). *Birth control and unmarried young women.* New York: Springer.

Makinson, C. (1985). The health consequences of teenage fertility. *Family Planning Perspectives, 17,* 132-139.

Marsiglio, W. (1987). Adolescent fathers in the United States: Their initial living arrangements, marital experience and educational outcomes. *Family Planning Perspectives, 19,* 240-251.

McLaughlin, S. D., Manninen, D. L., & Winges, L. D. (1988). Do adolescents who relinquish their children fare better or worse than those who raise them? *Family Planning Perspectives, 20,* 25-32.

Miller, B. C., & Jorgensen, S. R. (1988). Adolescent fertility-related behavior and its family linkages. In D. M. Klein & J. Aldous (Eds.), *Social stress and family development* (pp. 210-233). New York: Guilford.

Miller, B. C., & Moore, K. A. (1990). Adolescent sexual behavior, pregnancy, and parenting: Research through the 1980s. *Journal of Marriage and the Family, 52,* 1025-1044.

Moore, K. A., & Burt, M. R. (1982). *Private crisis, public cost: Policy perspectives on teenage childbearing.* Washington, DC: Urban Institute.

Moore, K. A., Simms, M. C., & Betsey, C. L. (1986). *Choice and circumstance: Racial differences in adolescent sexuality and fertility.* New Brunswick, NJ: Transaction Books.

Mosher, W. D., & Horn, M. C. (1988). First family planning visits by young women. *Family Planning Perspectives, 20,* 33-40.

Nathanson, C. A., & Becker, M. H. (1986). Family and peer influence on obtaining a method of contraception. *Journal of Marriage and the Family, 48,* 513-525.

Pratt, W. F., Mosher, W. D., Bachrach, C. A., & Horn, M. C. (1984). Understanding U. S. fertility: Findings from the National Survey of Family Growth Cycle III. *Population Bulletin, 39,* 1-42.

Robinson, B. E. (1988). *Teenage fathers.* Lexington, MA: D. C. Heath.

Roosa, M. W., & Christopher, F. S. (1990). Evaluation of an abstinence-only adolescent pregnancy prevention program: A replication. *Family Relations, 39,* 363-367.

Roosa, M. W., & Vaughn, L. (1984). A comparison of teenage and older mothers with preschool age children. *Family Relations, 33,* 259-265.

Shah, F., Zelnik, M., & Kantner, J. F. (1975). Unprotected intercourse among unwed teenagers. *Family Planning Perspectives, 7*, 29-44.

Sonenstein, F. L. (1986). Risking paternity: Sex and contraception among adolescent males. In A. B. Elster & M. E. Lamb (Eds.), *Adolescent fatherhood* (pp. 31-54). Hillsdale, NJ: Lawrence Erlbaum.

Sonenstein, F. L., Pleck, J. H., & Ku, L. C. (1989). Sexual activity, condom use and AIDS awareness among adolescent males. *Family Planning Perspectives, 21*, 152-158.

Studer, M., & Thornton, A. (1987). Adolescent religiosity and contraceptive usage. *Journal of Marriage and the Family, 49*, 117-128.

Thompson, L., & Spanier, G. B. (1978). Influence of parents, peers, and partners on the contraceptive use of college men and women. *Journal of Marriage and the Family, 40*, 481-492.

Trussell, J. (1988). Teenage pregnancy in the United States. *Family Planning Perspectives, 20*, 262-272.

Trussell, J., & Menken, J. (1978). Early childbearing and subsequent fertility. *Family Planning Perspectives, 10*, 209-218.

Upchurch, D. M., & McCarthy, J. (1989). Adolescent childbearing and high school completion in the 1980s: Have things changed? *Family Planning Perspectives, 21*, 199-202.

Vinovskis, M. A. (1988). *An "epidemic" of adolescent pregnancy? Some historical and policy considerations.* New York: Oxford University Press.

Voydanoff, P., & Donnelly, B. W. (1990). *Adolescent sexuality and pregnancy.* Newbury Park, CA: Sage.

Winter, L. (1988). The role of sexual self-concept in the use of contraceptives. *Family Planning Perspectives, 20*, 123-127.

Zabin, L. S., Hirsch, M. B., & Emerson, M. R. (1989). When urban adolescents choose abortion: Effects on education, psychological status and subsequent pregnancy. *Family Planning Perspectives, 21*, 248-255.

Zabin, L. S., Kantner, J. F., & Zelnik, M. (1979). The risk of adolescent pregnancy in the first months of intercourse. *Family Planning Perspectives, 11*, 215-222.

Zelnik, M., & Kantner, J. F. (1980). Sexual activity, contraceptive use and pregnancy among metropolitan-area teenagers: 1971-1979. *Family Planning Perspectives, 12*, 230-237.

Zelnik, M., Kantner, J. F., & Ford, K. (1981). *Sex and pregnancy in adolescence.* Beverly Hills, CA: Sage.

6. Aberrant Sexual Experiences in Adolescence

Annette U. Rickel
Marie C. Hendren
Wayne State University

INTRODUCTION

The experience of adolescence is perhaps one of the most complex periods of physical and psychological growth and development. The maturation of sex organs, hormonal changes, and acquisition of sex-role identity can be a challenging and difficult period for the adolescent and her or his parents. Although the opportunity and desire on the part of adolescents to explore their developing sexuality is not a unique experience of modern society, the evolving roles of men and women since the early 1900s suggest a heightened expectation for early sexual experiences (Rickel & Allen, 1987). The mixed pressures for both abstinence and participation in sexual activity are a normal experience for adolescents, and one in which each cohort of teens successfully survive relative to their peer experiences (Rickel, 1989). When the sexual experiences of adolescence include those that are forced upon the individual or perpetrated by family members, these aberrant experiences can result in a variety of emotional and psychological problems.

The categories of aberrant sexual experiences to be discussed in this chapter include intrafamilial sexual abuse/incest, stranger and date rape, and prostitution. The prevalence of these experiences is widely accepted as being conservative as a result of underreporting by the victims and caretakers. Additionally, procedures and criteria for reporting can lead to ambiguity and underreporting. One example is the Uniform Crime Report (UCR) published by the Federal Bureau of Investigation. Compliance in submitting incidence reports with the UCR is not mandatory, and thus not all law enforcement agencies submit data. Furthermore, those agencies that do comply with the UCR reflect only those incidents bound over for trial; reports of more serious crimes that are bargained down to lesser offenses are not identified. Ambiguity in the language used to define sexual abuse/incest is also a factor contributing to the varied statistics on incidence.

A review of the literature shows that the prevalence of sexual abuse for both sexes before the age of 18 years is between 19% and 31% (Coons, Bowman, Pellow, & Schneider, 1989). The incidence of father-daughter incest is reported between 1% and 4.5% for this same population. Unless specifically stated otherwise, reports of sexual abuse may include family members, neighbors, teachers, and family friends. Although early childhood sexual abuse is suspected to be equally prevalent among both sexes, the incidence for adolescent boys is less common than for girls. This difference may be attributed to reporting discrepancies between boys and girls, as well as the perception that adolescent boys are not as vulnerable as their female counterparts. With the enactment of the Child Abuse and Neglect Prevention Treatment Act in 1974, there has been an increase in the reports of sexual abuse.

The societal stigma of incest is believed to inhibit the reporting of such cases by both the victim and the caretaker. Fear of the nonabusing parent's disbelief, feelings of guilt, and fear of retaliation by the perpetrator are often cited as reasons for the victim not to report abuse. Concern about legal repercussions, loss of economic support, and dissolution of family bonds are reported as strong inhibitors for parental reporting (Farrell, 1988).

Research on father-daughter incest often combines biological, step-, foster, and adoptive fathers into a single category, because they all typically occupy the same role of parental authority. The definition of incestuous acts varies within studies from fondling to intercourse; the latter usually does not occur until puberty. The fear of pregnancy and the seriousness of the act often serve as catalysts for the victim to report the incident (Farrell, 1988). Perhaps in keeping with the fear of the incest taboo, Farrell found that less serious abuse is more likely to be reported than very serious abuse. Although a majority of reported cases are long-term incestuous relations between the victim and perpetrator, singular occurrences and short-term relations in adolescence also occur. Long-term abuse is often disclosed at puberty, when the victim becomes more confident of her or his ability to cease the abuse.

Research in the area of sibling incest is scant, with a conservative prevalence estimate of 13% for the general population (Daie, Witztum, & Eleff, 1989). Controversy exists in the literature concerning the importance placed on the effects of sibling incest. Findings from research on adult victims suggest such lasting effects as emotional scarring that can impair adult relationships, similar to the long-term effects of father-daughter sexual abuse.

As with intrafamilial sexual abuse/incest, the reporting of rape (both stranger and date) is believed to be conservative. The Victimization Crime Report (VCR) cited 121,380 rape victims (including all ages) in 1988. Of this number, 58.5% were committed by a person known to the victim. These data were obtained by a survey conducted from a random sampling of the population; by interviewing victims, the VCR can identify incidents not reported to law enforcement agencies. The same inhibitors that keep victims from reporting these crimes to the authorities, however, also influence admission to the VCR.

Research by Hall and Gloyer (1985) suggests that the incidence of rape for adolescents is higher than in any other age group. In a review of a longitudinal study of adolescent girls, 5% to 11% per year reported sexual assaults by peers (Gidycz & Koss, 1989). A random telephone survey of 508 adolescents revealed 12% of the females as citing rape or sexual assault. Adolescent victims report that fears of their parents' reactions to the rape and of peers learning of the incident are strong deterrents for reporting.

When the assault is perpetrated by an acquaintance, additional factors can confound the willingness to report. Adolescents are often unclear as to what constitutes a rape when it is committed by a date or "friend." Victims of date rape may feel guilt and responsibility concerning their decision to be in the company of their attacker. These feelings may induce the victim to perceive the occurrence as normal or deserved.

The prevalence of prostitution among the adolescent population is possibly the most complex to ascertain. The revolving door of the legal system in prosecuting minors, lack of parental presence in the environment, and the secluded underground environment in which these youths typically live combine to keep this activity nearly invisible from our society. The UCR reported 2,116 arrests of females between the ages of 10 to 18 for prostitution in 1989. There were 996 arrests of males between the ages of 10 to 18 for prostitution in the same year. That adolescent prostitutes are often runaways should underscore the concern for the 72,385 female runaways reported in the UCR in 1989.

A review of the literature on male and female prostitutes reveals early childhood sexual abuse and incest as a recurring characteristic in this population. Prevalence of this characteristic varies within the literature between 28.5% and 65% for female prostitutes and between 10% and 85.5% for male prostitutes (Seng, 1989). This early experience is thought to condition these children to view sex as a means of communication with adults while retaining a level of control as prostitutes that was lacking in their earlier victim-abuser relationships. Additionally, the low self-esteem characteristic of sexually abused children aids the pimp and the prostitute in keeping the latter in this self-abusing profession.

There are psychological and environmental differences between male and female prostitution. Female prostitutes most often are managed by a pimp and service a male clientele. Male prostitutes typically operate independent of a pimp and service other males, and thus their activity is homosexual in orientation. Although homosexual activity is the dominant experience of male prostitutes, these adolescents are as likely to define themselves as being heterosexual as well as homosexual in their personal orientation.

INTRAFAMILIAL SEXUAL ABUSE AND INCEST

As noted in the introduction, a comprehensive understanding of the prevalence of intrafamilial sexual abuse is difficult to ascertain. The terms *sexual abuse* and *incest* suggest on the surface two isolated typologies of abuse, yet incest certainly may be defined as sexual abuse and vice versa. In fact, much of the literature uses the terms interchangeably. This often occurs because of ambiguity in the language and a lack of uniform consensus on the specific acts that would differentiate between the two. For example, the term *incest* may be used when a singular occurrence of fondling is at issue or in defining a long-term sexual victimization of a child in which intercourse took place.

The discussion that follows will often use the terms *sexual abuse* and *incest* interchangeably except when describing findings of individual studies. The terms used by these researchers will be used solely in discussing their findings so as not to stray from the intent of the authors. Caution should be used in interpreting the conclusions and findings reviewed in the literature. The risk of blaming the victim and placing the responsibility for the abuse on others rather than the perpetrator is a real issue that is present both in the family and in agencies charged with treatment and intervention.

Father-Daughter Incest/Sexual Abuse

Reports of father-daughter sexual abuse have crossed all racial, ethnic, and economic barriers. Findings by Paveza (1988) on risk factors in father-daughter sexual abuse revealed a higher frequency of abuse in blue-collar families. This discrepancy from much of the literature may be attributable in part to the increased opportunities afforded white-collar families for private intervention versus public intervention. Another common finding in the literature is that significantly more families were involved in second marriages.

Five prevalent characteristics were isolated as risk factors associated with father-daughter sexual abuse (Paveza, 1988). These factors, listed in descending order of their risk ratio, are lack of mother-daughter closeness, marital dissatisfaction, spousal violence, and low income. Paveza (1988) argues for support of the controversial findings of income as a risk factor stating that a negative correlation exists between income and physical abuse in families. He further hypothesizes that the internal inhibitors that are diminished allow physical abuse in economically strained families and may also allow potential for sexual abuse. This argument is also supported by the finding of spousal violence as a risk factor in families of father-daughter sexual abuse.

A review of the literature supports findings of marital satisfaction and mother-daughter closeness as risk factors. Typologies of incest compiled by Gupta and Cox (1988) cite case studies that illustrate poor spousal relationships and emotionally distant relations between mother and daughter. Research by Levang (1989) investigating theories of father-daughter incest found additional support for these characteristics. Levang's study included three groups of families: those with daughters who were incest victims, those with daughters having an oppositional disorder, and control families. Spouses of incest victims were the least likely among the three groups to demonstrate warm and genial communication. The mother-daughter dyads in the incest group displayed very little intercommunication, appearing distant and isolated from each other.

A common scenario illustrating the familial environment where incest has happened allows a better understanding of this occurrence. Internal and external stressors placed on spouses who are unable or unwilling to attend effectively to the needs of the spousal relationship turn the spouses' attention to other means for their individual needs to be met. Children often attempt to compensate for marital discourse by a multitude of avenues. Older children may be compelled to assume a role of mediator or attempt to side with one parent. The insecurity of the family bond and the resulting dysfunctional roles adopted result in a shift of the appropriate closeness between father and daughter.

Intensive research by Meiselman (1990) and Blume (1990) has revealed the physical environment often associated with father-daughter incest. The sexual assault typically takes place at night, with the perpetrator approaching the child while she is asleep. Many victims report feigning sleep in an attempt to avoid dealing with the occurrence and in hopes that the perpetrator will lose interest. When the abuse occurs during waking hours, the abuse is still more likely to happen in the home. The child is often isolated in her bedroom or living room while other family members are still at home. This scenario is conducive to portraying normal family activities to other family members because the child is not removed from the home or family unit.

The use and abuse of alcohol was also found as a prevalent characteristic of the abusing parent. When the victim has other female siblings, there is often a characteristic present in the victim that is seen as vulnerable to the perpetrator. The victim may be of lower intelligence or have a physical handicap. When the victim finds a means of ceasing the abuse (often by running away), the abuser will often turn to the next daughter.

Father-Son Incest

Although the incidence and reported cases of father-son incest are low, a review of the literature and examinations of case histories by Williams (1988) and Pierce (1987) have identified common characteristics among this population. Physical abuse toward other family members, as well as violence concurrent with the sexual abuse, are common characteristics of the families studied. The use of sexual abuse and violence is often utilized by the father to symbolize his authority and power in the family unit (Horton, Johnson, Roundy, & Williams, 1990).

The homosexual nature of father-son incest suggests a homosexual orientation of the perpetrator. A review of case histories (Halpern, 1987; Pierce, 1987; Williams, 1988) has identified cases of homosexual experiences of the perpetrator prior to the incest, admitted homosexual orientation, and denial of homosexual orientation. Excerpts of statements by perpetrators denying homosexual ideation state that the incestuous act was one of love and affection for the son rather than a homosexual expression (Williams, 1988). Analysis of the psychosocial histories of abusers have revealed early childhood sexual and physical abuse in their families of origin. Adolescent boys sexually abused by their fathers often are inhibited by the dual taboo of incest and homosexuality and thus are not likely to report an incident.

Alcoholism is often a central issue in incestuous families. In many of the reported incidences, the father was intoxicated during the abuse, and some perpetrators may report not recalling the abuse (Pierce, 1987; Williams, 1988). Although quality of the spousal relationship has been identified as a risk factor in father-daughter incest, this characteristic is not identified as strongly in father-son incest; however, the barriers defining healthy parental and child roles and functions obviously are blurred and dysfunctional. Additionally, although mothers often initially deny having prior knowledge of the incestuous abuse, further investigations reveal that they were aware and chose not to intervene—often because of the violent nature of their spouse and the feared physical retaliation (Pierce, 1987).

Maternal Incest

Incest between a mother and son or daughter is the rarest form of incest reported. Such incidents between mother and child usually occur under the guise of natural maternal caretaking during early childhood. The sexual abuse usually involves genital stimulation while giving the child a bath or applying skin lotion.

Research by Horton et al. (1990) suggests that the lack of information on female offenders is attributable to the dominant theoretical perspectives of child sexual victimization containing inherent biases viewing women as sexually passive and men as sexually aggressive. These historically accepted theories depict such abuse as male power and superiority versus female passive victimization, thus relegating the less frequent reports of female offenders to the status of a "freak" occurrence and not incorporating these incidents into theories to explain their existence.

Alcoholism and drug abuse are a common characteristic of female offenders. A review of the findings from case studies by Chasnoff, Burns, Schnoll, Burns, Chisum, & Kyle-Spore (1986) revealed isolation of the mothers, loneliness, and no current sexual relations as common variables in female offenders. Participation of both parental figures may also occur with female offenders, as well as the involvement of more than one child in incestuous victimization. Early childhood sexual abuse and rape are frequent experiences of the female offender.

When more blatant incestuous acts occur between a mother and son, the son can have greater problematic reactions compared to victims of more common forms of incest (Meiselman, 1990). The incestuous mother-son dyad typically is one of inappropriate emotional enmeshment, where the child is dependent on the mother and one or both parties suffer severe psychological disturbance. The mother has used the son as her primary source of intimacy since early childhood and does not initiate intercourse until puberty. Whereas threats and force are used by the perpetrator in father-daughter incest, emotional manipulation is utilized in mother-son incest.

Sibling Incest

A review of the literature by Wiehe (1990) suggests that one third of sibling incest occurs during adolescence. Most often the abuse is heterosexual, and the perpetrator is an older male sibling. Many incestuous acts are initiated prior to the victim being old enough to realize that the act is sexual abuse. None of the subjects in Wiehe's study reported fighting back when abused; sibling abuse in adolescence often is accompanied by physical violence and threats that keep the victim from reporting the incident.

Wiehe (1990) and Meiselman (1990) found that sibling abuse typically occurs while an older sibling is "in charge" of the younger sibling(s). Similar to father-daughter incest, most often the abuse occurs at night, with the sibling approaching the victim while he or she is asleep. Again, the victim often feigns sleep in an attempt to avoid dealing with the abuse.

Meiselman (1990) found that sibling incest occurs more often in large families. The familial environment frequently is one in which the parents are emotionally and/or physically absent. The sibling perpetrator often is acting out family problems and learned incestuous behavior through her or his own victimization (Horton et al., 1991). Wiehe (1990) found that when the mother is aware that her daughter has become sexually active, she is less likely to believe the daughter's reports of sibling sexual abuse.

Effects on Victims and Considerations for Intervention

A myriad of problematic emotional and behavioral disorders arise from the experience of intrafamilial sexual abuse/incest. Most studies on effects are done on adult or mixed populations; their findings have illuminated both the immediate and long-lasting effects on incest victims. Poor self-esteem, depression, difficulty in interpersonal relationships, and continued self-blame are common emotional characteristics that can last into adulthood (Blume, 1990; Meiselman, 1990; Wiehe, 1990). Problematic behavioral characteristics reported by researchers are sexual dysfunction, eating disorders, and alcohol and drug addiction.

The manner in which an incest victim acts out her or his victimization in adolescence was researched by Meiselman (1990) and Seng (1989). Running away, chemical dependency, and prostitution are common outcomes that often may be interrelated. An incest victim may view leaving home as the only means to stop the abuse. The lack of options available to minors without parental sheltering can be conducive to procurement into prostitution. Alcohol and drugs often are employed as a means of escaping from a poor self-image and the reality of a dysfunctional family unit. Seng (1989) found that early chemical abuse is a common characteristic of incest victims who enter into prostitution.

The feelings of shame and self-blame apparent in incest victims induce them to feel "ruined" and in need of punishment. The sexual acting out of promiscuity reflects the child's confusion of sexuality with affection and a desire to regain a sense of control over her or his sexuality that was denied in the experience of coerced sex.

Suicidal ideation and self-mutilation are common characteristics present in adolescent victims. These characteristics both serve as an escape from the trauma of incest and confirm the victim's strongly held contention that she or he is a bad person deserving of punishment. Somatic complaints and hysterical symptoms may also be present in adolescent victims. Seizure disorders with no physical basis can be symbols of the traumatic experience. The resulting attention paid to the adolescent's illness offers a secondary gain by allowing an avenue of escape from further victimization.

Many victims may lack apparent affect in response to the abuse. The need to suppress and deny the feelings and memories allows the adolescent to engage more fully in the natural business of adolescence. A review of the literature suggests, however, that the apparent escape from symptomology is temporary. Post-traumatic stress disorder can be a common experience of adult victims of intrafamilial sexual abuse and incest.

PROSTITUTION

Intensive research by Campagna and Poffenberger (1988) and Cates (1989) offers an intimate insight into the environment and experience of adolescent prostitution. The illicit activity of prostitution too often is accompanied by high-risk activities that further aid in the delinquency and endangerment of these children. The following descriptions of the female and male experiences highlight the lifestyles and inherent hazards associated with adolescent prostitution.

The Female Experience

The most lucrative population of prostitutes is adolescent girls, with the youngest females typically commanding the highest price. This fact alone ensures that there will always be a market for the exploitation of young girls. The financial gain made in the prostitution of adolescents, however, will not be found in the pocketbooks of the girls. Rather, the pimps, madams, and marketers who control the life-styles of these girls retain the profits.

Adolescent female hustlers can be found working in the streets, brothels, truck stops, and sundry locales. A majority of these girls (especially the youngest) are most likely to be working in sheltered work sites, such as a brothel. The sheltering of young girls allows more privacy from public scrutiny, thus diminishing chances for detection and arrest. Because most underage prostitutes are runaways, they often are sold or traded by their pimps along a circuit of sheltered domiciles and sex rings across state lines. Keeping these girls mobile and working outside their home states ensures that the girls will not be recognized by clients or others who may come in contact with them. This constant mobility also serves to break any ties the adolescent might have to her community and makes the development of new bonds difficult and temporary.

Once the procurement of a child into prostitution has succeeded, other types of exploitation may be experienced. The use of child prostitutes in pornographic film and photography, and in the blackmailing of clients, is not uncommon. The environment of hustling, by virtue of its illicit nature, is conducive to adapting to other illegal activities. The use of illegal drugs and alcohol, theft, and violence are common characteristics of adolescent prostitution.

The young girl often is introduced to the use of drugs and alcohol by her procurer. This action minimizes her resistance during the apprenticeship phase of indoctrination into this new life-style. The psychological and physiological dependence thus enhances the procurer's control over the girl. The pimp's use of violence (actual or threatened) further aids in undermining the victim's self-esteem and potential empowerment.

The Male Experience

Male adolescent prostitutes typically do not earn as much as their female counterparts. The reasons for this are twofold: First, the average "trick" costs less, and secondly, male prostitutes typically service fewer clients per workday. The latter reason is related to the nature of the sexual activity that typically is requested; male prostitution is characterized by homosexual activity whereby the hustler is asked to engage in passive sex and to achieve an orgasm, thus limiting the number of clients that can be serviced. When the male hustler is managed by a pimp, the financial profits are awarded to the pimp, who leaves a small percentage to the adolescent. Most male prostitutes, however, enjoy a free-lance status not afforded their female counterparts.

Whereas sheltered domiciles are common sites for female prostitution, male prostitution most often occurs on the streets and in transportation terminals, adult bookstores, bath houses, and truck stops. A boundary usually separates the street territory designated to either male or female prostitution. This segregation ensures less competition between the genders and decreases confusion among potential clients.

The environment encompassing male prostitution invites exploitative and illicit activities similar to those in female prostitution. Substance abuse and the use of boys in pornography and blackmail are common experiences. The potential for violence is particularly epidemic for this population; a mutual distrust commonly is reported by both hustler and client. Young boys may be taken to secluded areas where they are bound, beaten, and left without their promised fees. Likewise, male prostitutes may set up their clients to be ambushed and robbed. These frequent experiences leave both parties wary of each other and prepared to respond violently by carrying weapons.

The indoctrination of boys into prostitution is typically different from that of girls (Campagna & Poffenberger, 1988). As with females, most male prostitutes are runaways. A youth finding himself on the streets without a means of support may learn quickly of the demand for male prostitutes. Befriending a peer on the street, the adolescent may be told that prostitution is an easy way to earn a few dollars. The perceived peer support makes the transition easier for the adolescent (Cates, 1989; Schaffer & DeBlassie, 1984). Alternatively, the boy may be approached by a potential client offering him money or temporary lodging for sex. The adolescent thus may happen upon this life-style without prior intention of selling himself for sex. Within the population of male prostitutes, there exist both homosexually and heterosexually oriented youths. Youths identifying themselves as homosexually oriented may use prostitution as a means of combining business with pleasure.

The Etiology of Prostitution and
Issues for Preventive Intervention

There is no easy or definitive explanation as to what elements build a foundation that may lead to prostitution for adolescents. The examination of studies done to identify common life experiences among this population, however, does illuminate possible at-risk characteristics.

The common experience of intrafamilial sexual abuse and/or incest can foster characteristics that leave the victim vulnerable to procurement into prostitution. The poor self-esteem correlated with a history of abuse may support the transition to prostitution: The demoralizing experience of prostitution confirms the child's poor self-image while serving as a tool for the manipulation of the child by a pimp.

The lack of control a child has over the experience of sexual victimization may be seen as regained in the prostitute-client relationship. Interviews with sexually abused prostitutes indicate that such adolescents mistakenly perceive a role reversal wherein they are in control of their sexual experiences and decision making with the client. Token gifts given to an abused child by the perpetrator mimic the transaction of sex for profit. This latter experience may indirectly undermine the child's innocence concerning the experience and instill a sense of cooperation or implicit consent to the act.

The dynamics in which many adolescent prostitutes were reared are typically dysfunctional and unstable. Broken homes, foster homes, and absent parents coupled with inconsistent economic and emotional parental support are the typical family history. Parents and guardians often are so handicapped emotionally by their own personal problems that they are inept in their role as caretakers for their children.

Children reared in dysfunctional families often develop problematic behavioral and emotional characteristics (Thomas, Rickel, Butler, & Montgomery, 1990). Research on prostitution with children from dysfunctional families reveals that truancy, poor academic performance, quitting school, running away, and drug abuse are all commonly shared behavioral characteristics. Problematic emotional characteristics such as depression, poor self-image and suicidal tendencies are highly representative of the prostitution-involved children researched.

The child victim of intrafamilial sexual abuse certainly may be said to be a product of a dysfunctional family. And though the literature reveals intrafamilial sexual victimization as a frequent experience of underage prostitutes, many underage prostitutes do *not* share this early childhood experience. Rigorous examination of behavioral and emotional characteristics of sexually abused adolescents involved in prostitution and of sexually abused adolescents not involved in prostitution was conducted by Seng (1989). Important differences between the two suggest that the behavioral characteristics of quitting school, running away, and drug and alcohol abuse are significantly more frequent characteristics for the prostitution-involved adolescent. A further difference in the variable of running away lies in the frequency of running away: Whereas many sexually abused children reported running away at least once, significantly more prostitution-involved children reported running away 11 or more times.

The use of drugs and alcohol by adolescent prostitutes is almost a natural extension of the life-style. As noted earlier, addiction often is encouraged by pimps as a means of control. Additionally, the use of drugs may appear as an attractive escape to a child trapped in the unpleasant world of prostitution. Drug use prior to procurement into prostitution also may enable such a transition; the means of obtaining illegal substances, by virtue of its illicit nature, puts the child in contact with unscrupulous individuals. Subsequent addiction and its economic needs may foster favorable conditions for entry into prostitution.

The conservative attitude prevalent in our society toward sex education and the expression of homosexuality also may indirectly enable conditions favorable for leading to prostitution. As noted earlier, many male prostitution-involved adolescents chose prostitution in order to express their sexual desires as well as to earn money. A homosexually oriented adolescent has very little, if any, socially accepted means of discussing her or his sexuality and related concerns. The film industry's attempts to portray the coming out of gay men sympathetically reflect society's ambivalence. Parental rejection, being ostracized by peers, and dissolution of family bonds are representative of the events portrayed in these films.

The realization of the adolescent that she or he is attracted to the same sex must certainly make her or him feel alone and separate from family and friends. Any sexual exploration desired by the adolescent thus is conducted, by necessity, in a shroud of secrecy and fear. Strangers and casual acquaintances may appear to be the only safe persons with whom to experiment with one's sexuality. For an individual who has inadequate support in her or his life, such a life-style may eventually decrease inhibitions concerning other activities that also lack public approval and acceptance.

RAPE: STRANGER AND ACQUAINTANCE/DATE

As noted in the introduction, the violent assault of rape is increasing. Although there are cases of male rape victims, they are far less common, and the perpetrators are most likely to be male. It has been postulated that 15% to 25% of women will experience completed rape in their lifetime (Calhoun & Atkeson, 1991). That this crime typically is perpetrated by men against women has enabled a general consensus in the literature that the psychology of our society may foster the prevalence of this crime.

Rape myths and societal responses to reports of rape often support the underlying belief that the victim is responsible for her victimization and that the offender is ruled by biological impulses or was seduced (Freeman, 1989). The issues involved in date rape exemplify the power of rape myths in serving as an effective barrier to the conviction of a reported offender (Holmes, 1991; Holmstrom & Burgess, 1988). Additionally, that 58.5% of rapes reported in the 1988 VCR were committed by persons known to the victim underscores the inherent danger in the acceptance of these myths.

Despite the advances toward more egalitarian roles for men and women in recent history, women still are perceived as vulnerable, weak, helpless, and dependent on men. Simultaneously, men are viewed as superior, aggressive, and self-reliant. These themes can be seen depicted in literature and film, both mirroring society's perceptions and fostering their validity. Rape myths are perpetuated in film and romance novels in which the woman comes to love her attacker or, after crying "no" to advances, responds passionately to subsequent force. The common rape myths of "she really wants it," "she was looking for it," and "she enjoyed it" are commonly reported beliefs of men and women alike (Holmes, 1991).

Rape is assumed to occur more often among strangers; however, most rapes actually are perpetrated by someone known to the victim. The term *acquaintance rape* was coined to include all forms of prior familiarity between the victim and attacker, from casual acquaintances at the workplace to a close friend or date. As a result of the increasing awareness of rapes committed between "friends," the term *date rape* has come into popular usage. The incidence of date rape is suspected of being grossly underreported (Calhoun & Atkeson, 1991; Holmes,1991; Quina & Carlson, 1989).

Research was conducted by Muehlenhard (1988) on young adults' attitudes toward date rape and how it relates to their own dating habits. Muehlenhard found that rape justifiability ratings and sex willingness were highest in dating scenarios where the woman initiated the date, where she went to the male's apartment, and/or when the male paid for the dating expenses. Additionally, Muehlenhard found that rape justifiability ratings were higher for men than for women and higher for persons who held traditional attitudes about male and female roles.

A study by Jenkins and Dambrot (1987) looked more directly at young peoples' belief in rape myths and their reactions toward scenarios depicting legally defined acts of rape. Jenkins and Dambrot found that sexually aggressive males who believed in the rape myths were less likely to view the scenarios as rape, blamed the victim more often, and saw the victim as "deserving" forced intercourse. Females who agreed with the rape myths also tended to blame the victim and to see the victim as "deserving" intercourse.

Results from the aforementioned studies, coupled with the publicized scenario awaiting victims who pursue prosecution of their assailants, aid in the underreporting of date rape incidents. Uncertainty over whether a crime was committed, doubts about their own guilt, and fear of not being believed can inhibit many victims. Even when rape is reported, chances for successful conviction are least likely when the perpetrator was known to the victim (Holmstrom & Burgess, 1988). Research conducted by Holmstrom and Burgess (1988) found that the "ideal" rape victim is one who did not know her or his attacker, was a virgin or had only one partner at the time, sustained physical damage, had an eyewitness, and was a different race than the perpetrator.

Victims of date rape can never satisfy these ideal criteria for obtaining a conviction. Victims should, however, be armed with as much knowledge about the legal system and possible outcomes so as to make informed decisions concerning their role in the legal process. The trauma of a trial and losing a conviction can exacerbate the trauma of the rape (Holmstrom & Burgess, 1988). Successful resolution of the problematic reactions to a rape is affected by such mitigating variables as social support, restoration of the victim's sense of self-control/mastery, and the meaning ascribed to the rape by others as well as the victim (Koss & Harvey, 1991). The legal process places the victim in a position to prove her victimization publicly, especially in cases of acquaintance rape. The legal process and negative results can exacerbate the victim's sense of guilt, depression, and isolation. Research by Koss and Harvey (1991) underscores the effect of rape myths on jury outcomes, citing among reasons given for acquittals the victim telling her rapist to "fuck off," which was interpreted by the jury as sexually exciting.

Effects on Victims
and Crisis Intervention

Victims of rape perpetrated by either strangers or acquaintances experience a disruption of their normal physical and psychological state. The mental health advocate should take care to be sensitive to the impact of the legal, medical, and familial roles upon the victim. Although there are many individual differences among rape victims and among their experiences, there are many common behavioral and emotional reactions shared in the aftermath of rape.

The most common effects of rape on victims include a disruption of behavior and thoughts, reliving the incident in nightmares and waking thoughts, humiliation and shame, guilt, anger, and low self-esteem (Calhoun & Atkeson, 1991; Quina & Carlson, 1989). Fear and anxiety are possibly the most pervasive problems endured by rape victims (Calhoun & Atkeson, 1991).

The acute crisis phase for the intervention of rape trauma is generally the first 6 weeks following the assault (Quina & Carlson, 1989); however, individual factors regarding both the experience of the attack and the victim's psychological history affect the outcome. Victims having a history of poor mental health and adjustment prior to the rape are at greater risk for long-term problems with depression. Also at greater risk are victims whose rape experience was very violent and/or prolonged (Calhoun & Atkeson, 1991; Holmstrom & Burgess, 1988).

Research by Calhoun and Atkeson (1991) suggests that 37% of rape victims are between 11 and 17 years of age. As noted earlier, most rapes are committed by persons known to the victims, with many of these attacks occurring during the course of a date. These two facts support the importance of implementing educational methods of rape prevention in the schools. Abolishing the rape myths and promoting more egalitarian relationships as a social ideal for our adolescents are commonly advised criteria for diminishing the rate of date rape (Calhoun & Atkeson, 1991; Holmes, 1991; Quina & Carlson, 1989).

CONCLUSION

The complex and pervasive issues surrounding the sexual victimization of children, which likewise inhibit reporting, make intervention a challenging task. When intervention is possible, it is necessary for the mental health professional to address the dynamics of all family relationships for treatment to be most effective. Psychotherapeutic intervention for the victim as well as other family members may be advised.

Group therapy with adolescents who have endured similar traumas in their families can offer additional support toward improved mental health. This intervention technique allows members of the group who are further along in their treatment to serve as role models to newer members. Additionally, feelings of isolation and loneliness can be addressed as the group members share their common histories and goals.

Successful intervention with adolescents involved in prostitution may be the most difficult to achieve because of the inherent barriers in reaching them, including the fact that they are frequently runaways. Knowledge garnered from studies on the behavioral and emotional characteristics prevalent in adolescents prior to procurement into prostitution, however, may provide insight into effective preventive interventions. Because these children often come from families where the parental guardians are physically and/or emotionally absent, community- and school-based prevention/intervention programs may be the most effective in identifying individuals at risk.

REFERENCES

Blume, E. S. (1990). *Secret survivors*. New York: John Wiley.

Calhoun, K. S., & Atkeson, B. M. (1991). *Treatment of rape victims: Facilitating psychological adjustment*. New York: Pergamon.

Campagna, D. S., & Poffenberger, D. L. (1988). *The sexual trafficking in children*. Medfield, MA: Auburn House.

Cates, J. A. (1989). Adolescent male prostitution by choice. *Child and Adolescent Social Work, 6*(2), 151-156.

Chasnoff, I. J., Burns, W. J., Schnoll, S. H., Burns, K., Chisum, G., & Kyle-Spore, L. (1986). Maternal-neonatal incest. *American Journal of Orthopsychiatry, 56*, 4, 577-580.

Coons, P. M., Bowman, E. F., Pellow, T. A., & Schneider, P. (1989). Post-traumatic aspects of the treatment of victims of sexual abuse and incest. *Psychiatric Clinics of North America, 12*(2), 325-335.

Daie, N., Witztum, E., & Eleff, M. (1989). Long-term effects of sibling incest. *Journal of Clinical Psychiatry, 50*(11), 428-431.

Farrell, L. T. (1988). Factors that affect a victim's self-disclosure in father-daughter incest. *Child Welfare, 67*(5), 463-468.

Freeman, J. (Ed.). (1989). *Women: A feminist perspective.* Palo Alto, CA: Mayfield.

Gidycz, G. A., & Koss, M. P. (1989). The impact of adolescent sexual victimization: Standardized measures of anxiety, depression, and behavioral deviancy. *Violence and Victims, 4*(2), 139-149.

Gupta, G. R., & Cox, M. (1988). A typology of incest and possible intervention strategies. *Journal of Family Violence, 3*(4), 299-312.

Hall, E. R., & Gloyer, G. (1985). How adolescents perceive sexual assault services. *National Association of Social Workers, 10*(2), 120-128.

Halpern, J. (1987). Family therapy in father-son incest: A case study. *Social Casework, 68*(2), 88-93.

Holmes, R. A. (1991). *Sex crimes.* Newbury Park, CA: Sage.

Holmstrom, L. L., & Burgess, A. W. (1988). *The victim of rape: Institutions' reactions.* New York: John Wiley.

Horton, A. L., Johnson, B. L., Roundy, L. M., & Williams, D. W. (Eds.). (1990). *The incest perpetrator.* Newbury Park, CA: Sage.

Jenkins, M. J., & Dambrot, F. H. (1987). The attribution of date rape: Observer's attitudes and sexual experiences and the dating situation. *Journal of Applied Social Psychology, 1*(10), 875-895.

Koss, M. P., & Harvey, M. R. (1991). *The rape victim.* Newbury Park, CA: Sage.

Levang, C. A. (1989). Father-daughter incest families: A theoretical perspective from balance theory and GST. *Contemporary Family Therapy, 11*(1), 28-43.

Meiselman, K. C. (1990). *Resolving the trauma of incest.* San Francisco: Jossey-Bass.

Muehlenhard, C. L. (1988). Misinterpreting dating behaviors and the risk of date rape. *Journal of Social and Clinical Psychology, 6*(1), 20-37.

Paveza, G. J. (1988). Risk factors in father-daughter child sexual abuse. *Journal of Interpersonal Violence, 3*(3), 290-306.

Pierce, L. H. (1987). Father-son incest: Using the literature to guide practice. *Social Casework, 68*(2), 67-74.

Quina, K., & Carlson, N. L. (1989). *Rape, incest, and sexual harassment: A guide for helping others.* New York: Praeger.

Rickel, A. U. (1989). *Teen pregnancy and parenting.* New York: Taylor & Francis.

Rickel, A. U., & Allen, L. (1987). *Preventing maladjustment from infancy through adolescence.* Newbury Park, CA: Sage.

Schaffer, R., & DeBlassie, R. R. (1984). Adolescent prostitution. *Adolescence, 19*(75), 689-696.

Seng, M. J. (1989). Child sexual abuse and adolescent prostitution: A comparative analysis. *Adolescence, 24*(95), 665-675.

Thomas, E., Rickel, A. U., Butler, C., & Montgomery, E. (1990). Adolescent pregnancy and parenting. *Journal of Primary Prevention, 10*(3), 195-206.

Wiehe, V. R. (1990). *Sibling abuse: The hidden physical, emotional, and sexual trauma.* Lexington, MA: Lexington Books.

Williams, M. (1988). Father-son incest: A review and analysis of reported incidents. *Clinical Social Work Journal, 16*(2), 165-179.

7. Sexually Transmitted Diseases

Carl G. Leukefeld
University of Kentucky

Harry W. Haverkos
National Institute on Drug Abuse

Sexually transmitted diseases, commonly referred to as STDs in the United States by public health practitioners and health care professionals, present a formidable challenge for the United States and other countries as we move into the coming decades. This challenge is particularly difficult for adolescents and for practitioners who provide services to adolescents and their families. Although current data are limited, the existing data indicate that both the incidence (i.e., the number of new cases) and the prevalence (i.e., the number of actual cases) of STDs are increasing for the United States and, more specifically, for its adolescents. Yet it seems that members of the general public, as well as many professionals who come into contact with adolescents and their health needs, are turning their heads away from what are becoming major issues.

Although adolescents are healthy, as many as one in five of the 31 million U.S. adolescents could have at least one serious health problem (Office of Technology Assessment, 1991). An important associated factor is the limited health care that is currently available to the U.S. general population, including adolescents. Like adults, adolescents at greatest risk for health problems are overrepresented in poor and minority racial and ethnic groups. The Office of Technology Assessment (OTA, 1991) reports that contemporary data indicate that adolescents have a number of documented health problems in a variety of areas: family problems, social problems, lack of recreational opportunities, chronic physical illnesses, nutrition and

AUTHORS' NOTE: This article was prepared in part by an employee of the United States federal government as part of official duties; therefore, the material is in the public domain and may be reproduced or copied without permission.

161

fitness problems, dental and oral health problems, AIDS and other sexually transmitted diseases, pregnancy and parenting, mental health problems, alcohol and tobacco use, illicit drug abuse, delinquency, and homelessness.

The interrelatedness of adolescent problems is important to recognize, as is the clustering of these behaviors in what have been labeled "high-risk adolescents" by both practitioners and researchers. These high-risk adolescents have been studied and, among other things, have been described as exhibiting problem behaviors (Jessor & Jessor, 1977). Thus, for both clinical and research purposes, adolescent behaviors should not be examined in isolation. In addition to general health data, there are a number of specific studies in the alcohol, drug, and juvenile justice areas that have focused on high-risk adolescent behaviors (see, e.g, Hawkins, Lishner, Jenson, & Catalano, 1987; Jessor & Jessor, 1977). These data point not only to the risky situations in which some adolescents seem to find themselves constantly but also to the apparent invulnerability with which adolescents face life in day-to-day situations.

With this background, the purpose of this chapter is to focus on sexually transmitted diseases that can affect adolescents. We will discuss the incidence and prevalence of selected STDs among adolescents, examine trends, and provide rudimentary aspects of clinical management. We then will review general behavioral approaches to alter sexual behavior, provide a personal letter from one of the authors to his children as an example of parent-child communication on this issue, and review the Centers for Disease Control (CDC) guidelines regarding the use of condoms. Additional medical information regarding the diversity of STDs is provided by Benenson (1985) and Holmes et al. (1990).

RATES OF ADOLESCENT STDs

Before discussing specific adolescent STD trends and rates, it is important to note that gathering information on teenage sex habits, rates of pregnancy, AIDS prevalence, and STD rates, as well as data regarding other risky adolescent behaviors, has not been without controversy. In fact, a recent decision by Health and Human Services Secretary Louis Sullivan reaffirmed this fact when he canceled federal support for a 5-year survey of the sexual behaviors of 24,000 teenagers that included questions related to these areas of adolescent behaviors, including STDs (American Public Health Association, 1991).

Although there are inconsistencies in reporting STDs, including varied definitions used by the 50 states, there are available data that underscore the fact that STDs are a problem for adolescents (Miller, Turner, & Moses, 1990). There are also estimates of STD rates among adolescents. Figure 7.1 presents an overview of selected estimates (using available data) for national and local areas of U.S. adolescents infected with HIV or other sexually transmitted diseases. These data were developed by the Office of Technology Assessment and are based on the multiple data sources listed below the figure. The highest rates estimated in this figure are for chlamydia and candidiasis at 37% and 38%, respectively, with gonorrhea estimated at 18.5%. Clearly, these estimates provide a sense of the severity and high rates of STDs in the U.S. adolescent population.

SEXUALLY TRANSMITTED DISEASES

STDs comprise a variety of diseases transmitted by sexual activity through the exchange of bodily fluids such as semen, vaginal fluids, and blood; an individual can get a sexually transmitted disease by having sex with an infected person. As many as 20 different sicknesses can be labeled as STDs. Among the more common STDs are chlamydia, herpes, gonorrhea, genital warts, syphilis, hepatitis B, HIV infection (i.e., AIDS), crabs, and trichomoniasis.

Table 7.1 (Burroughs Wellcome, 1990) presents an overview of symptoms, diagnosis, and therapy for 10 common STDs. The viral STDs (genital herpes, genital warts, hepatitis B, cytomegalovirus, and HIV) can be treated but usually are not cured. For bacterial STDs (e.g., syphilis, gonorrhea, and the parasitic infections), curative therapies are available.

The control of STDs is based on four concepts (CDC, 1989): (a) education of persons at risk on the modes of disease transmission and the means of reducing the risk of transmission; (b) detection of infection in asymptomatic persons and in those who are symptomatic but unlikely to seek diagnostic and treatment services; (c) effective diagnosis and treatment or persons who are infected; and (d) evaluation, treatment, and counseling of sex partners of persons

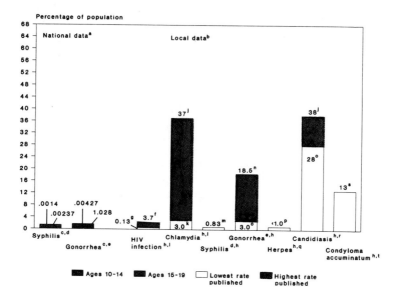

Figure 7.1. U.S. Adolescents With HIV Infection or Sexually Transmitted Diseases: National and Local Estimates
(notes for figure on facing page)

with an STD. Both the medical aspects and interventions attempting to change sexual behaviors that put patients at risk are important for effective STD control. Much is known about the medical aspects of STD control; less is known about effective behavioral change strategies.

Four of the most common STDs (gonorrhea, syphilis, chlamydia, and AIDS) are reviewed here to present details about the epidemiology and rudimentary clinical aspects of medical management of these diseases. The CDC in Atlanta, Georgia, collects reports of gonorrhea, syphilis, and AIDS. Chlamydial infections are not reportable nationwide. Although the CDC national reporting systems are the best available, most experts agree that significant underreporting is the rule rather than the exception, and that publicly funded clinics and hospitals have more complete reporting than those in the private sector.

Figure 7.1. Continued

SOURCE: Office of Technology Assessment, 1991, based on the sources noted below.

NOTE: National data are not drawn to same scale as local data.

a. The Centers for Disease Control (CDC) in the U.S. Department of Health and Human Services collects national data on syphilis and gonorrhea, but national data on other STDs are not available. CDC recommends that states report particular STDs, but has no authority to require such reporting (48.274). Thus there is no uniformity in state reporting requirements for STDs. Even in the states that do report STDs, there are incomplete reporting requirements for STDs, differences in reporting by public and private health sources, and limitations in the specificity of diagnostic tests (17.123).

b. Local data are obtained from different studies using varying sample sizes. The studies and selected pertinent details of each study are list in footnotes below.

c. This is a population incidence rate, which is the measure of the number of new cases of a particular disease or condition occurring in a population during a given period of time.

d. Syphilis is caused by the bacterium *Treponema palladium*.

e. Gonorrhea is caused by the bacterium *Neisseria gonorrhoeae*.

f. This figure is from a study conducted on 510 runaway and homeless youth, age 18 or under, who were residing in Covenant House in New York City in 1987-1988 (200).

g. This figure is from a study conducted on 12,344 adolescent mothers (age 18 or under) of newborns, who were age 20 months or less, in upstate New York in 1987-1988 (162). The same study tested 12,871 adolescent mothers (age 18 or under) of newborns in New York City and found a clinical prevalence percentage of 0.72.

h. This is a clinical prevalence rate, which is a measure of the number of individuals in a given clinical population who have a specific disease or other condition at a designated time (or during a particular period).

i. HIV is the virus associated with AIDS.

j. This figure is from a study conducted on 115 low-income, pregnant, predominantly black females, ages 13 to 19, who were receiving prenatal care in the Johns Hopkins Adolescent Pregnancy Program (69).

k. These data are from a study conducted on 948 sexually active asymptomatic adolescent males, ages 13 to 19, who were attending teen or detention clinics in San Francisco, CA (188).

l. Chlamydia infection (formal name, "nongonoccal urethritis") is caused by the bacterium *Chlamydia trachomatis*.

m. This figure is from a study conducted on 2,521 adolescent males and females, ages 9 to 18, who were in the New York City Juvenile Detention Center (4).

n. This figure is from a study conducted on 567 adolescent males and females who were visiting the Adolescent and Young Adult Clinic of the Children's National Medical Center in Washington, DC (45).

o. This figure is from a study conducted on 100 low- and middle-income, sexually active, adolescent females from urban areas, who were attending the Adolescent Clinic of the Children's Hospital Medical Center in Cincinnati, OH (185).

p. This figure is from a study conducted on 376 inner-city, low-income females, ages 12 to 18, who were seeking contraceptive counseling at the Teen Accent Clinic in Birmingham, AL (163).

q. Herpes in caused by the herpes simplex virus (HSV).

r. Candidiasis is caused by the bacterium *Candidiasis albicans*.

s. This figure is from a study conducted on 89 low-income, sexually active, primarily black females, ages 13 to 19, who were attending an adolescent clinic of the University of Maryland Hospital in Baltimore, MD (128).

t. Condyloma acuminatum is caused by human papillomavirus.

Gonorrhea

Gonorrhea is the most commonly reported STD in the United States. The U.S. incidence of gonorrhea increased beginning in the 1960s, declined in the mid-1970s, and declined further in every year during

Table 7.1 Overview of Common Sexually Transmitted Diseases

STD	Symptoms	Diagnosis	Therapy	Result if Left Untreated
Chlamydia	Pain and burning when urinating, discharge	Lab exam of fluid from the infected area	Antibiotic pills that kill bacteria	Pelvic infections (PID); sterility (can't have children)
Crabs	Severe itching	Visual	Over-the-counter or prescription lotion	Continuing symptoms
Cytomegalovirus (CMV)	No symptoms; fever or fatigue; severe illness in people with damaged immune systems	Lab exam of fluids or skin; blood test	Shots to slow progress of serious eye infection in people with immune damage	Healthy people—symptoms go away but may come back; people with immune damage—severe mononucleosis, blindness, dangerous blood disorders, lung damage
Genital herpes	Pain and burning when urinating, red bumps/blisters in genital area	Lab exam of fluid from the sore	Pills and ointment	Prolonged and more severe symptoms
Genital warts	Bumpy warts on/near genitals	Visual	Burning or liquid removal of warts	May lead to some cancers
Gonorrhea	Pain or burning when urinating, yellow discharge	Lab exam of fluid from infected area	Antibiotic pills that kill bacteria	PID; sterility
Hepatitis B	Nausea, vomiting, stomach pain, yellow skin	Blood tests	Pills, shots to treat symptoms/complications, not disease	Liver damage

HIV/AIDS	Swollen glands, weight loss, open sores, permanent diarrhea	Blood tests	Drugs (pills) that slow progress of virus, drugs that fight infections	Dangerous infections; disease progresses faster
Syphilis	Chancre sore, rash, genital ulcers	Lab exam of tissue, fluids/blood test	Penicillin shots to kill bacteria	Blindness, heart disease, brain damage
Trichomoniasis	Itching in/around vagina, strawberry-colored rash	Lab exam of fluids, urine test	Pills	Men—prostate damage; women—continuing symptoms

SOURCE: Adapted from Burroughs Wellcome Company (1990).

the 1980s except for one (Barnes & Holmes, 1984; Hook & Holmes, 1985). In 1990, 689,854 cases of gonorrhea were reported to the CDC. Among 10- to 14-year-olds, 11,737 cases were reported (2,854 boys and 8,882 girls); among 15- to 19-year-olds, 197,062 cases (29% of all cases) were reported (117,846 boys and 96,324 girls) (Joe Blount, CDC, personal communication).

The increased incidence in the 1960s and early 1970s was seen primarily among white females (presumably resulting from the increased availability of oral contraceptives and intrauterine devices) and homosexual men. The decreases observed between the mid-1970s and the mid-1980s were attributed to the awareness of adverse effects and concomitant decreased usage of oral contraceptives and intrauterine devices among women and to decreased promiscuity among homosexual men in the 1980s caused by fear of AIDS. Recently, several STDs have increased including gonorrhea (partially as a result of penicillinase-producing strains of *Neisseria gonorrhoeae*, or PPNG), syphilis, and chancroid (CDC, 1987, 1988a, 1988c). These increases have been attributed to sexual promiscuity associated with drug abuse and to reallocation of STD resources into the field of AIDS. The abuse of cocaine, especially "crack" usage, has been associated recently with several outbreaks of gonorrhea.

Gonorrhea is caused by a bacterium (*Neisseria gonorrhoeae*) and predominantly affects the mucous membranes of the lower genito-urinary tract and, less frequently, the rectum, oropharynx, and conjunctivae. Gonorrhea usually presents as purulent penile discharge in men and as urethritis or cervicitis in women. The incubation period is 2 to 8 days. Asymptomatic carriers occur in both sexes but are more common in females.

The most rapid diagnostic test for men is Gram's stain of urethral discharge, which shows intracellular gram-negative diplococci (Gram's stain of urethral or cervical discharge in women is unreliable because of the presence of nonpathogenic *Neisseria* species). For both sexes, cultures for *N. gonorrhoeae* should be plated immediately on warm chocolate agar or Thayer-Martin medium and incubated in a carbon dioxide incubator.

The currently recommended regimen to treat uncomplicated urethral, endocervical, and rectal gonorrhea is ceftriaxone 250 milligrams intramuscularly (one dose only) and doxycycline 100 milligrams orally twice a day for 7 days. Doxycycline is used to treat co-existing chlamydial infection, which is documented in up to 45% of gonorrhea cases in some populations (CDC, 1989). The cost to a pharmacy of the ceftriaxone-doxycycline regimen is approximately $10.

Chlamydial Infections

Although gonorrhea is the most commonly reported STD among adolescents, there are several STD experts who believe that chlamydial infections are more common among teenagers and cause more lower genital tract infections than gonorrhea. Chlamydial infections, however, are not reportable in all 50 states. Inferences about the extent of chlamydial infections are based on pilot studies. Several investigations of adolescent populations have found cervical chlamydial infection rates in females and urethral infections in males to be about twice as common as gonorrhea. In virtually all studies, teenage women have a higher risk for chlamydial infection than older women. The reason for the higher rates of chlamydial infection among teenagers is unknown (Cates, 1990). Some investigators estimate that 3 to 4 million cases of chlamydial infection occur each year in the United States.

Chlamydia trachomatis is a obligate, intracellular organism that contains both DNA and RNA, has a cell wall and ribosomes, and can be inhibited by antibiotics. At one time, chlamydiae were considered to be large viruses, but they are now classified as bacteria. The clinical spectrum of *C. trachomatis* infection closely resembles that of gonorrhea. Both agents cause urethritis in both sexes and can cause other problems, such as epididymitis, cervicitis, salpingitis, proctitis, and arthritis. About 40% of women with documented gonorrhea will have a coexisting chlamydial infection. About one fourth of men with gonorrhea will also have a chlamydial infection.

Pelvic inflammatory disease (PID) results from untreated gonorrhea and/or chlamydial infection in women and can have serious health impacts in future years. Acute PID increases one's risk for recurrent PID, chronic pelvic pain, infertility, and ectopic pregnancy. "Silent" or subclinical PID also increases one's risk for these complications (Cates, 1990).

In the last decade, several new, less costly methods of testing cervical swabs and penile discharge for chlamydial infections have been developed. Antigen detection methods are used by several hospitals and clinics. A gene probe methodology for chlamydial RNA and DNA costs about $6 per test. Enzyme-linked immunosorbent assay

(ELISA) techniques of antigen detection cost about $3 per test but are not as sensitive or specific as the gene probe methodolgy. Direct examination of cell scrapings, isolation in cell culture, and serologic testing for antibodies to chlamydia are also available.

The CDC recommends that all asymptomatic high-risk women be screened for chlamydial infection and treated if positive. Priority groups for chlamydia testing are high-risk pregnant women, adolescents, and women with multiple sex partners. Periodic surveys for chlamydia should be performed in clinical settings to determine the local chlamydial prevalence in patients with gonorrhea. Doxycycline 100 milligrams orally twice per day for 7 days or tetracycline 500 milligrams four times per day for 7 days is the recommended regimen. Pregnant women should be *not* be treated with doxycycline or tetracycline; erythromycin base 500 milligrams orally four times per day for 7 days is the recommended regimen for pregnant women. Sex partners of patients with chlamydia infection should be treated if contact was within 30 days of the onset of symptoms. Chlamydial reinfection from untreated sexual partners to the index case is common (CDC, 1989).

Syphilis

The incidence of syphilis in the United States decreased shortly after World War II following the introduction of penicillin, but the incidence has increased recently (Fichtner et al., 1983). Syphilis declined from 1982 to 1985, largely as a result of decreases among gay men; however, this trend reversed in the last half of the 1980s, when the incidence of primary and secondary syphilis increased 85% (from 27,131 cases in 1985 to 50,224 reported cases in 1990) (Joe Blount, CDC, personal communication). For 1990, 307 cases of primary and secondary syphilis were reported among 10- to 14-year-olds (43 boys and 264 girls). Among 15- to 19-year-olds, 5,200 cases (10% of all cases) were reported in 1990 (1,872 boys and 3,328 girls) (Joe Blount, CDC, personal communication). Overall, the greatest increases occurred in New York, California, and Florida, which together reported more than half of all U.S. cases. The increases in syphilis were reported predominantly among black and Hispanic heterosexual men and women (CDC, 1988b; Pepin et al., 1989).

Syphilis is a chronic systemic infection caused by a bacterium (*Treponema pallidum*). The disease may present in a variety of ways.

The most common presentations are as a chancre at the inoculation site (primary syphilis), a disseminated form that commonly includes a maculopapular rash and nontender lymphadenopathy (secondary syphilis), and aortitis and/or inflammation of the central nervous system (tertiary syphilis). The incubation period for the primary lesion is usually 2 to 6 weeks; secondary syphilis usually occurs 2 to 12 weeks later. Tertiary syphilis may appear within a few years of infection or remain latent and then appear between 20 and 40 years later.

Blood or serologic testing is the most common method of syphilis diagnosis. Two types of serologic tests are employed. Nontreponemal tests, such as the Venereal Disease Research Laboratory (VDRL) test and rapid plasma reagin (RPR), are used for initial screening and during follow-up. Treponemal tests, such as fluorescent treponemal antibody-absorption (FTA-ABS) and *T. pallidum* hemagglutination assay (MHA-TP or TPHA), are specific and distinguish false-positive from true positive nontreponemal tests. Once positive, the treponemal tests remain positive for life. Diagnosis of primary and secondary lesions can also be made by dark-field microscopy; however, this is difficult in outpatient settings unless an experienced microscopist is available (CDC, 1989).

Therapy for syphilis varies by stage of illness. Benzathine penicillin G 2.4 million units intramuscularly (1.2 million units in each hip) in one dose is recommended for primary and secondary syphilis and early latent syphilis of less than 1 year in duration. For latent syphilis of more than 1 year in duration and for cardiovascular syphilis (with normal lumbar puncture exam), benzathine penicillin G 2.4 million units intramuscularly weekly for 3 successive weeks is recommended. The treatment of neurosyphilis has not been studied adequately. Present treatments include either aqueous penicillin G 2.4 million units intravenously every 4 hours for 10 days or procaine penicillin G 2.4 million units intramuscularly daily plus probenecid 500 milligrams orally daily for 10 days, each followed by benzathine penicillin G 2.4 million units intramuscularly for 3 weeks. Concomitant HIV disease with syphilis is common (CDC, 1989), and some investigators recommend that all patients with HIV infection and syphilis receive treatment adequate for neurosyphilis. More research is needed to determine the optimal therapies.

HIV Infection (AIDS)

The acquired immunodeficiency syndrome (AIDS) is the fastest-growing and most lethal of the STDs. Unknown before 1980, AIDS has been reported and is increasing in frequency on all inhabited continents. Approximately 60% of all persons with AIDS have died. In 1990, 43,339 AIDS cases of Kaposi's sarcoma and/or life-threatening opportunistic infections in the United States were reported to the CDC. About 120 new cases are reported to the CDC each day. Among 13- to 19-year-olds, 168 cases (boy:girl ratio about 3:1) were reported in 1990. The most common exposure categories for adolescents with AIDS are hemophilia/coagulation disorder (32%), heterosexual contact (21%), and male homosexual/bisexual contact (16%) (CDC, 1991).

The number of AIDS cases, however, does not describe adequately the extent of the problem among adolescents. AIDS is caused by human immunodeficiency virus (HIV), an RNA virus that is transmitted from person to person through sexual contact; exposure to infected blood, blood products, and possibly other bodily fluids; and from mother to child during pregnancy and nursing. Because of the long latency period from infection to diagnosis of AIDS (estimated to average 10 to 12 years), many adult AIDS cases probably were infected as adolescents. Among 20- to 24-year-olds, 1,637 new AIDS patients were reported in 1990. The most common exposure categories for 20- to 24-year-olds with AIDS are male homosexual/bisexual contact (50%), use of injected drugs (18%), and heterosexual contact (12%). The HIV seroprevalence rate among adolescents in the United States is difficult to estimate because of the paucity of studies; however, HIV seroprevalence rates as high as 5.3% of runaway youths in New York City and 8.2% of runaways in San Francisco suggest that HIV infection has gained a significant foothold in the adolescent population (Rotheram-Borus, Koopman, Haignere, & Davies, 1991; St. Louis et al., 1990).

HIV counseling and testing are recommended for all persons with an STD (CDC, 1989). Antibody testing for HIV begins with a screening test (usually an ELISA test) and, if positive, is followed by a more specific confirmatory test (generally a Western blot assay). Systems for additional follow-up, counseling, support systems, and partner notification should be made available to all HIV-positive individuals.

Although a cure for AIDS has not yet been discovered, zidovudine (formerly referred to as azidothymidine, or AZT) has been documented to prolong survival among AIDS patients who have recovered from at least one episode of *Pneumocystis carinii* pneumonia and to delay the onset of AIDS of HIV-infected individuals with less than 500 CD4 T-lymphocytes (Fischl et al., 1987; Volberding, Lagakos, Koch, et al., 1990). Nausea, myalgias, insomnia, and severe headaches commonly are reported by recipients as zidovudine side effects, and severe anemia and leukopenia frequently result in discontinuation of therapy (Richman et al., 1987). One hundred milligrams by mouth five times daily is the currently recommended dosage; the drug costs about $1.50 per capsule. A second drug, dideoxyinosine, has been approved recently by the Food and Drug Administration (FDA) for treatment of HIV infection.

Management of the complications of HIV infection and AIDS will require more expert care. Hospitalizations of AIDS patients becomes more common as the disease progresses. Prophylactic therapy for *Pneumocystis carinii* pneumonia is indicated for patients who recover from *Pneumocystis pneumonia* and for HIV-infected individuals who have CD4 T-lymphocyte counts less than 200 per cubic millimeter. Trimethoprim/sulfamethoxazole 160/800 milligrams orally per day or pentamidine 300 milligrams by aerosol monthly are the recommended regimens.

PREVENTION APPROACHES

Prevention has been conceptualized in different ways (Leukefeld & Bukoski, 1991). Sensitivity to prevention approaches can afford a better understanding of the importance of applying tailor-made and specifically designed prevention approaches for adolescents. The current AIDS campaign developed by the CDC and the cocaine campaign from the National Institute on Drug Abuse serve as examples of such targeted media efforts to change behaviors, especially for adolescents.

Even with targeted messages, it is important to have credible messages for the target audience, especially for adolescents. In the case of STDs (including AIDS), however, there is disagreement about the content of the message. On the one hand, there are those who advocate that prevention messages should be nonspecific; on the other hand, there are those who emphatically state that messages should move away from what Shilts (1987) has called "AIDS talk" and focus on specific behaviors. In this situation (where the rubber meets the road, so to speak), there is debate and disagreement.

It is clear, however, that abstinence from sexual activity is the most effective method for preventing the spread of sexually transmitted diseases. Education is also an important part of preventing STDs. Like that for other behaviorally driven disorders, prevention of STDs among adolescents should focus on specific behaviors within an educational context. Risk assessment may be a beginning step toward systematically examining adolescent sexual behaviors. This examination may be difficult, given the highly charged sensitivities that surround sexual issues in our culture.

There seems to be almost universal agreement among public health officials that discussing abstinence from sexual activity is a start but is not the only approach for preventing the spread of STDs. Indeed, condoms must be discussed explicitly; although they do not provide total protection from STDs, they can reduce risk if used properly. There is some evidence that spermicides, particularly nonoxynol-9, may provide some additional protection for HIV infection. A possible approach for parents is to combine their own values with feelings in discussions of HIV/STD prevention. It must be stressed that this is not the only way to present this kind of information, but it can be useful for encouraging discussion and for framing thinking about AIDS and STDs. An example is the following letter, which was developed by one of the authors of this chapter for his children (Leukefeld, 1987). The letter subsequently was published by the National Association of Social Workers in the following form:

> There are lots of things your mother and I have tried to give you. Most of the time we explain that our "gifts of wisdom" are for your own good. We say we will pray for you. We badger you, hoping you'll change your behavior. And we speak about life and death, about religion, values and ethics. And just occasionally we all get confused.
>
> In all of our discussions, however, survival skills always seem to come to the fore. Many of these skills are the customs, traditions, and beliefs passed from generation to generation. But there seems to be a constant supply of new survival skills and customs that we must learn. Sometimes we learn the hard way. Sometimes the easy. Sometimes there is no easy way.

And so now I want to tell you about AIDS and the HIV virus that causes AIDS. Talking about AIDS means talking about sex. As your parent I am still scared to talk with you about sex. I don't know why. I guess most parents would rather let schools teach about sex as I was taught in the sixth grade. I learned then that a man's sperm fertilizes a woman's egg through sexual intercourse—an experience called by so many names and also by a four letter word polite people don't use. From the biological perspective, sex relates to an erection, insertion, climax, and ejaculation. And as you read this you're probably thinking that you already know this anyway, which is just what I thought. I will only remind you that just because you know something can be done, doesn't mean it should be.

You know that your mother and I are religious people. Now, with the risk of AIDS, not committing adultery is taking on new importance. Other adults have similar considerations to make.

But for you, I think it's simple—don't have sex. No negotiation. Just no sex. Period. You have probably heard some say that sexual experimentation and taking risks are part of adolescence, part of growing up. What I am saying is that experimentation is dangerous. It has got to stop for you and everyone else. Maybe even television and movies will change as more people realize that sexual experimentation can kill.

In addition to being your father, however, I am also a public health social worker. Wearing that hat, I see the importance of spreading information to control the AIDS virus. Here are some of the facts public health professionals cite when we talk about AIDS.

We get AIDS from having sexual relations with other people—both heterosexual and homosexual. You can get AIDS from just one other person, if that person is infected—even if that person looks perfectly healthy. You can also get it by using intravenous drugs from contaminated needles and syringes. Mothers with AIDS can pass the virus to their children. There is no cure for AIDS, and there is no vaccine to prevent its spread. We only have one drug now which may prolong the lives of those with AIDS.

You should also know that once someone gets the AIDS virus he or she will always have it. And when one is a virus carrier, there is about a 30 percent chance (one in three) of getting AIDS and dying. Carriers will always run the risk of spreading it to others. I am compelled to tell you once again—no sex and no drugs.

That aside, listen carefully. This part is hard for your dad—but easier for me as a public health professional. What if you are going to have sexual intercourse? (Don't do it, says your dad again. But, what if?) Just remember, even if people say they have received the

AIDS test and don't have AIDS because the test was negative, it doesn't mean much. It only provides information to the point in time the test is taken. That means that anything happening after that time is not taken into account. Anyway, I'd really caution you about a relationship with the kind of person who brags about having been tested for AIDS.

There is one potential form of protection, but it is not without risks. The protection is a condom. There are two kinds of condoms, those made of animal intestines, which are not effective, and those made of latex. They have been used for years in efforts to prevent pregnancy and to control sexually transmitted diseases like syphilis, gonorrhea, and herpes. Latex condoms are about 90 percent effective in preventing other sexually transmitted diseases, and it appears that they are similarly effective in preventing AIDS transmission. But condoms are not foolproof.

Here we come to the delicate part. I need to tell you how to use a condom, much as I don't want to. First a word of caution—don't use petroleum products or jellies (like Vaseline) with condoms. The latex breaks down with petroleum jellies and the virus is able to pass through the condom. A condom comes packed in a sealed pouch. and it's rolled up like the base of a balloon. Make sure the package is sealed and new because condoms deteriorate when they get old. When they are, they can break apart. That's a disaster because sperm and the HIV virus will move through the latex.

When the condom is put on, it gets rolled over the male's erect penis. Space must be left at the end—a reservoir at the tip of the condom to catch the sperm. The end is pinched and pulled before rolling it on. After sex, the condom must be held at the base of the penis when it is removed so the sperm remains in the condom. You got it?

Whew! That's enough for now. I'm glad I told you. I'm a little scared in the back of my mind that you'll use this information to have sexual experiences. It's probably a baseless fear. I think I know better than that and really do feel better that you have this information. If you have any questions, your mom and dad are here for you. Never forget that we love you and wish only that you live well and wisely as you can.

Love, Dad

Unfortunately, science has not advanced enough to provide fool-proof methods to prevent the spread of sexually transmitted diseases, and we will rely on behavioral interventions for the near (and possibly distant) future. The following information was developed by the Centers for Disease Control (CDC, 1989, p. ix) with the goal of understanding the *limitations* of using condoms; clearly, they are not foolproof.

1. Latex condoms should be used, because they may offer greater protection against HIV and other viral STDs than natural membrane condoms.
2. Condoms should be stored in a cool, dry place, out of direct sunlight.
3. Condoms in damaged packages or those that show obvious signs of age (e.g., those that are brittle, sticky, or discolored) should not be used. They cannot be relied upon to prevent infection or pregnancy.
4. Condoms should be handled with care to prevent puncture.
5. The condom should be put on before any genital contact to prevent exposure to fluids that may contain infectious agents. Hold the tip of the condom and unroll it onto the erect penis, leaving space at the tip to collect semen, yet ensuring that no air is trapped in the tip of the condom.
6. Only water-based lubricants should be used. Petroleum- or oil-based lubricants (e.g., petroleum jelly, cooking oils, shortenings, and lotions) should not be used, because they weaken the latex and may cause breakage.
7. Use of condoms containing spermicide may provide additional protection against STD. Vaginal use of spermicide along with condoms, however, is likely to provide still greater protection.
8. If a condom breaks, it should be replaced immediately. If ejaculation occurs after condom breakage, the immediate use of spermicide has been suggested; however, the protective value of postejaculation application of spermicide in reducing the risk of STD transmission is unknown.
9. After ejaculation, care should be taken so that the condom does not slip off the penis before withdrawal; the base of the condom should be held throughout the withdrawal. The penis should be withdrawn while still erect.
10. Condoms should never be reused.

DISCUSSION

So what does this mean for those who work with adolescents? In addition to the need for awareness about STDs, we all need to know about their implications for adolescents, and we need to be unencumbered enough to plan prevention activities. We know there are specific things we can do to educate adolescents, and in particular those adolescents at high risk for STDs, if these actions are initiated. Understandably, there are those who might argue, given the nature of adolescence and the increase of STDs and HIV among adolescents, that all adolescents are at high risk and that prevention approaches thus should be initiated for all adolescents. Clearly, many teens believe that they are not at risk because of their infrequent and sporadic sexual behavior (Grieco, 1987), but this seems far from what is seen happening in both data and clinical accounts.

Two traditional settings are used for prevention interventions. The first and the most traditional setting is the school. Health education and other science courses have been used to provide information about STDs and their transmission. These prevention activities are dependent, by and large, upon the school district, which has control over all curricula (including health information and information related to prevention). Preventive educational activities are varied and frequently are uneven from district to district. Videos and films have been used, as well as skills training interventions, especially in the area of drug abuse (Botvin, Baker, Resnick, Filazzola, & Botvin, 1984), and these present possible approaches and models for application in the area of STDs. Other methods that can be used to channel prevention interventions and to target mass media are community interventions focused on high-risk neighborhoods and targeted groups within those neighborhoods (Leukefeld, Battjes, & Amsel, 1991). Finally, and most important, planned and targeted preventive interventions for adolescents are needed that are related to their high-risk behaviors, including those that involve STDs. We need to move beyond the stage of providing information alone and toward recognition by parents and others of the seriousness of these diseases.

REFERENCES

American Public Health Association. (1991, September). *The nation's health*. Washington, DC: Author.

Barnes, R. C., & Holmes, K. K. (1984). Epidemiology of gonorrhea: Current perspectives. *Epidemiologic Reviews, 6*, 1-30.

Benenson, A. S. (Ed.). (1985). *Control of communicable diseases in man*. Washington, DC: American Public Health Association.

Botvin, G. J., Baker, E., Resnick, N. L., Filazzola, A. D., & Botvin, E. M. (1984). A cognitive-behavioral approach to substance abuse prevention. *Addictive Behaviors, 9,* 137-147.

Burroughs Wellcome Company. (1990). *STD.* Research Triangle Park, NC: Author.

Cates, W. C. (1990). The epidemiology and control of STDs in adolescents. In M. Schydlower & M. S. Shafer (Eds.), *AIDS and other sexually transmitted diseases* (pp. 409-427). Hanley & Belfus.

Centers for Disease Control. (1987). Penicillinase-producing *Neisseria gonorrhea*— United States, 1986. *Morbidity and Mortality Weekly Report, 36,* 107-108.

Centers for Disease Control. (1988a). Continuing increase in infectious syphilis— United States. *Morbidity and Mortality Weekly Report, 37,* 35-38.

Centers for Disease Control. (1988b). Relationship of syphilis to drug use and prostitution—Connecticut and Philadelphia, Pennsylvania. *Morbidity and Mortality Weekly Report, 37,* 755-758.

Centers for Disease Control. (1988c). *Sexually transmitted disease statistics: 1987.* Atlanta, GA: Author.

Centers for Disease Control. (1989). 1989 sexually transmitted diseases treatment guidelines. *Morbidity and Mortality Weekly Report, 38*(Suppl. 8),1-43.

Centers for Disease Control. (1991). *HIV/AIDS surveillance report, January.* Atlanta, GA: Author.

Fichtner, R. R., Aral, S. O., Blount, J. H., Zaidi, A. A., Reynolds, G. H., & Darrow, W. W. (1983). Syphilis in the United States: 1967-1979. *Sexually Transmitted Diseases, 10,* 77-80.

Fischl, M. A., Richman, D. D., Grieco, M. H., Gottlieb, M. S., Volberding, P. A., Laskin, O. L., Leedom, J. M., Groopman, J. E., Mildvan, D., Schooley, R. T., Jackson, G. G., Durack, D. T., King, D., & AZT Collaborative Working Group. (1987). The efficacy of azidothymidine (AZT) in the treatment of patients with AIDS and AIDS-related complex: A double-blind, placebo-controlled trial. *New England Journal of Medicine, 317,* 185-191.

Grieco, A. (1987, March). Cutting the risks for STDs. *Medical Aspects of Human Sexuality,* 70-77.

Hawkins, J. D., Lishner, D. M., Jenson, J. M., & Catalano, R. (1987). Delinquents and drugs: What the evidence suggests about prevention and treatment programming. In B. Brown & A. Mills (Eds.), *Youth at risk for substance abuse* (pp. 81-131). Rockville, MD: Alcohol, Drug Abuse and Mental Health Administration.

Holmes, K. K., Mardh, P., Sparling, P. F., Wiesner, P. J., Cates, W. C., Lemon, S. M., & Stamm, W. E. (1990). *Sexually transmitted diseases* (2nd ed.). Hightstown, NJ: McGraw-Hill.

Hook, E. W., III, & Holmes, K. K. (1985). Gonococcal infections. *Annals of Internal Medicine, 102,* 229-243.

Jessor, R., & Jessor, S. L. (1977). *Problem behavior and psychological development: A longtudinal study.* New York: Academic Press.

Leukefeld, C. G. (1987). A government official talks to to his children about AIDS. In National Association of Social Workers, *AIDS: We need to know, we need to care* (pp. 7-13). Silver Spring, MD: National Association of Social Workers.

Leukefeld, C. G., Battjes, R. J., & Amsel, Z. (1990). Community prevention efforts to reduce the spread of AIDS associated with intravenous drug abuse. *AIDS Education and Prevention, 2*(3), 235-243.

Leukefeld, C. G., & Bukoski, W. J. (Eds.). (1991). *Prevention research: Methodological issues*. Washington, DC: Government Printing Office.

Miller, H. G., Turner, C. F., & Moses, L. E. (1990). *AIDS: The second decade*. Washington, DC: National Academy Press.

Office of Technology Assessment. (1991). *Adolescent health, Vol. 1: Summary and policy options*. Washington, DC: Government Printing Office.

Pepin, J., Plummer, F. A., Brunham, R. C., Piot, P., Cameron, W., & Ronald, A. R. (1989). The interaction of HIV infection and other sexually transmitted diseases: An opportunity for intervention. *AIDS, 3*, 3-9.

Richman, D. D., Fischl, M. A., Grieco, M. H., Gottlieb, M. S., Volberding, P. A., Laskin, O. L., Leedom, J. M., Groopman, J. E., Mildvan, D., Hirsch, M. S., Jackson, G. G., Durack, D. T., Nusinoff-Lehrman, S,. & AZT Collaborative Working Group. (1987). The toxicity of azidothymidine (AZT) in the treatment of patients with AIDS and AIDS-related complex: A double-blind, placebo-controlled trial. *New England Journal of Medicine, 317*, 192-197.

Rotheram-Borus, E., Koopman, C., Haignere, C., & Davies, M. (1991). Reducing HIV sexual risk behaviors among runaway adolescents. *Journal of the American Medical Association, 266*, 1237-1241.

Shilts, R. (1987). *And the band played on*. New York: St. Martin's.

St. Louis, M. E., Rauch, K. J., Petersen, L. R., Anderson, J. E., Schable, C. A., Dondero, T. J., & Sentinel Hospital Surveillance Group. (1990). Seroprevalence rates of human immunodeficiency virus infection at sentinel hospitals in the United States. *New England Journal of Medicine, 323*, 213-218.

Volberding, P. A., Lagakos, S. W., Koch, M. A., et al. (1990). Zidovudine in asymptomatic human immunodeficiency virus infection: A controlled trial in persons with fewer than 500 CD4-positive cells per cubic millimeter. *New England Journal of Medicine, 322*, 941-949.

8. Promoting Sexual Responsibility in Adolescence

Gary M. Blau
Thomas P. Gullotta
Child and Family Agency of Southeastern Connecticut

Ellen, an articulate and popular 14-year-old, arrived at the junior high school-based health clinic complaining of stomach cramps and nausea. She told the nurse practitioner that she "hadn't been herself" for several months, and that she constantly was tired and irritable. Ellen also noticed that she had gained almost 10 pounds in the past 3 months, but she figured this was because of "overeating." When asked about her menstrual cycle, Ellen could not respond. She couldn't remember the approximate date of her last period, and she didn't understand what that had "to do with anything anyway." Ellen also denied any sexual activity and stated that her family "doesn't believe in premarital sex." Not surprisingly, the urine test showed that Ellen was indeed pregnant. In fact, according to the ultrasound, Ellen was entering her last trimester, and her lack of knowledge and emotional denial had delayed necessary prenatal care. Ellen was devastated by the discovery and required intense crisis intervention services. Her family had to be told, obstetrical appointments had to be scheduled, and plans had to be made.

Contrast Ellen's case with Sarah's. Sarah is 15 years old and speaks easily of the many sexual partners she has had. Sarah states that she "knows how to use sex," and that she learned about sex from her stepfather when she was 7. He died when Sarah turned 11, and it was at that time when Sarah began "going to bed" with many people. Although Sarah did not want to become pregnant, she rarely if ever used birth control. Shortly after her 15th birthday, she was told that she was going to have a baby. Sarah was not surprised, but she became increasingly frightened when the doctor suggested she be tested for AIDS.

Unfortunately, these stories are not uncommon. Neither is the story of Willie, a 15-year-old who boasted that he had slept with dozens of girls. One morning, Willie woke up with painful sores covering his genital area. At first he figured it was "just a rash," so he ignored the condition. After about a week, the sores dried up and began to go away. Willie decided that it "must have been nothing." Two months later his "rash" came back. This time Willie went to his school clinic, and they informed him that he had herpes. Willie asked for some medication to "get rid of this" and was surprised when he was told that the herpes virus would be with him for the rest of his life.

The one thing all of these youngsters share is that they now are faced with an unwanted pregnancy or a sexually transmitted disease. How can this be prevented? How do teenagers learn to make responsible decisions about sex? How can parents, teachers, mental health professionals, and prevention experts help teenagers understand and accept the physical, emotional, and social dimensions of sexual behavior?

Teenagers engage in sex. This simple truth has been well documented in several national samples (Alan Guttmacher Institute, 1981; Burt, 1986; Fielding, 1978; Westoff, Calot, & Foster, 1983). Current estimates indicate that teenage pregnancy accounts for almost 13% of all births in the United States (Kean, 1989). In fact, the United States has rates of teenage pregnancy and abortion that are among the highest of any developed country (Jones et al., 1985). For this reason, many authors have referred to teenage pregnancy as an "epidemic" (Beck & Davies, 1987). As Jorgensen (see Chapter 5) points out, however, there continues to be controversy as to whether teen pregnancy should be considered an epidemic. Vinovskis (1988), for example, states that the term *epidemic* has been used as an alarmist tactic to propel teenage pregnancy into the political arena. Furstenberg (1991), in response to this allegation, agreed that the term was misleading (especially in light of the slight decline in teenage fertility rates in the past two decades) but stated that the use of an emotionally charged word such as *epidemic* served to draw attention to a significant national problem. Unfortunately, despite more than two decades of public concern about adolescent sexual behavior, the overall rates of adolescent sexual activity either have increased or have remained constant (Furstenberg, Brooks-Gunn, & Chase-Lansdale, 1989; Morrison, 1985), and more than 1.3 million adolescents will become pregnant this year alone (S. Gordon, 1983; Jorgensen, Chapter 5).

Although many Americans espouse the virtue of abstinence and saying no to sexual intercourse, it is clearly evident that this country's youths continue to be sexually active. The risks and costs associated with adolescent sexuality are many. Because the use of contraceptive material occurs, on average, 6 to 12 months after the onset of sexual activity, adolescent pregnancy is a primary concern. In a large national sample, Zabin, Kantner, and Zelnik (1979) found that the risk of pregnancy is 20% in the first month of unprotected intercourse and 50% if unprotected intercourse continues for 6 months. Pregnant teenagers and their babies are at greater risk for obstetrical complications, including premature birth and low birth weight, prenatal mortality, anemia, toxemia, congenital abnormalities, and mental and physical handicaps (Reppucci, Mulvey, & Kastner, 1983).

In addition, as Campbell (1968) articulately stated, a parenting teenager has "90 percent of her life's script written for her" (p. 238). Convincing evidence indicates that most adolescent mothers will not complete high school, will require some form of government assistance, will be abandoned by the child's father, and most likely will need peripheral services such as mental health involvement and financial aid (Gordon, 1983; Hayes, 1987). Hardy (1987) writes that although the long-term consequences of teenage childbearing are more severe for the mother and child, adolescent fathers may also suffer educational and economic disadvantages, increased levels of personal stress, and higher levels of pathology compared to adolescents who were not fathers.

Recent evidence also indicates that society incurs staggering financial costs as a result of adolescent pregnancy. In 1979, the Stanford Research Institute estimated that $8.3 billion of taxpayer money was spent on adolescent pregnancy. More recently, given increased health care costs, government expenditures have been estimated at $16 billion annually (Burt, 1986). Although both of these estimates include federal, state, and local funding for financial assistance, health care, nutritional supplements, and special services for the teenage mother and her child, many professionals believe that these are gross underestimates and fail to account for such other factors as the loss of job productivity. In addition, the most affected persons are teenagers who already are poor and lack resources. That is, although adolescent pregnancy occurs in all levels of society, the more affluent families tend to terminate the pregnancies (Hardy, 1987).

Thus childbirth most often occurs among those who have the fewest resources to prevent its occurrence or to cope with its consequences.

Although the negative consequences of adolescent pregnancy can be evidenced by the emotional, social, medical, and financial outcomes, another serious concern is the high risk for sexually transmitted diseases (STDs). Hardy (1987) states that sexually active adolescents are more likely to have multiple partners and less likely to use adequate protection. A teenager may not become pregnant, but she or he may acquire a sexually transmitted disease. Teenage females have the third highest rate of STDs (behind homosexual men and prostitutes). Cates and Rauh (1985) report that female teenagers have the highest rates of gonorrhea, cytomegalovirus, chlamydia, cervicitis, and pelvic inflammatory disease compared to any age group. S. Gordon (1983) estimates that more than 1 million cases of STDs occur each year in the adolescent population. A specific example was reported by Leukefeld and Haverkos in Chapter 7: These authors, citing a personal communication with Joe Blount of the Centers for Disease Control (CDC), indicate that more than 200,000 cases of gonorrhea were reported to the CDC in 1990 for youngsters below the age of 19, and almost 12,000 of these cases were from children aged 10 to 14.

Of additional concern is that the risks of acquired immune deficiency syndrome (AIDS) are increasing (Flora & Thoresen, 1988). Furstenberg et al. (1989) report that although few adolescents have been diagnosed with AIDS, the numbers have doubled in recent years, and the incidence appears to be increasing. Curran et al. (1988) indicate that one fifth of all AIDS cases occur in 20- to 29-year-olds. Because the incubation period for the AIDS virus can easily be 7 years or more, this suggests that these cases may have originated in adolescence. These costs are not included in the previous cost estimates, and the outcomes obviously can be tragic.

The significant impact of adolescent sexual behavior provides the clear justification for preventive efforts. Preventive efforts, however, have been plagued with controversy and debate. In fact, many individuals believe that adolescent sexuality is nothing more than a moral dilemma and refuse to acknowledge that adolescents are sexual beings (Reppucci et al., 1983). Therefore, their logic is simple: Because adolescents should not be sexual, promoting sexual responsibility is unnecessary and may even encourage sexual experimentation. It is for this reason that some school systems do not have sex education programs. The documented evidence, however, refutes this logic. In fact, we believe that denying the reality of adolescent sexuality, demanding abstinence, or blaming teenagers for having sexual desires not only is antiquated but, from a public health perspective, clearly is ill-advised.

It is our intention in the remainder of this chapter to review several adolescent pregnancy prevention efforts. For clarity, the prevention efforts will be divided into four distinct categories: education, promotion of social competency, community organization/ systems intervention, and natural caregiving (Gullotta, 1987; Gullotta & Adams, 1982).

EDUCATION

Of all the proposed preventive strategies, education is the most widespread (Zelnik & Kim, 1982). In general, the primary purpose of these programs is to teach teenagers about the human reproductive system. Education programs have also targeted increasing adolescents' knowledge about contraceptive use (Brooks-Gunn & Furstenberg, 1989). Most sex education courses take place in the schools, and the typical program is 8 to 10 hours in length. Topic areas often include adolescent body changes (e.g., development of primary and secondary sexual characteristics), anatomy and physiology of the reproductive system, the consequences of pregnancy and childbearing, and information about common venereal diseases. Other possible topics include the nature of sexual activity, relationships and intimacy, and the use of contraceptive materials.

The majority of sex education programs take place in junior and senior high schools; elementary school programs are rare. In fact, Brooks-Gunn and Furstenberg (1989) report that there is currently no systematic review of sex education programs in elementary schools. For junior high students, sex education typically focuses on puberty, reproductive anatomy, and dating, but it is not until senior high that sex education includes such topics as family planning, contraceptive methods, and abortion. Emotionally charged topics such as masturbation and homosexuality often are omitted, even in the high schools (Orr, 1982).

The use of education to promote sexual responsibility stems from survey evidence indicating that adolescents' knowledge about sex and sexuality is highly inadequate (Onyehalu, 1983), and that teenagers thus become pregnant because they lack knowledge about effective birth control and sexuality. Onyehalu (1983) states that most information about sex comes from the peer group and is fraught with misconceptions and misinformation. One would assume that teenagers have a basic understanding of the relation between intercourse and pregnancy and of the mechanisms of fertility, but this is simply not true. In fact, a variety of survey studies have found that adolescents have extremely faulty information regarding sexuality (Cvetkovich & Grote, 1983; DeAmicus, Klorman, Hess, & McAnarney, 1981; Evans, Selstad, & Welcher, 1976; Miller, 1976; Zelnik & Kantner, 1977). Adolescents in these studies did not know that fertility begins at menarche, that they could become pregnant the first time they had intercourse, or that the timing of intercourse during the fertility cycle was important in conception.

Teenagers' knowledge about contraceptive behavior also has been investigated (Morrison, 1985). Although teenagers can name at least one birth control method or identify several, they have considerable difficulty understanding the proper procedures for use (Freeman, Rickels, Mudd, & Huggins, 1980; Lieberman, 1981; Nadeson, Notman, & Gillon, 1980; Oskamp & Mindick, 1983). Of interest is that adolescents' attitudes toward the use of contraceptives have been correlated with knowledge and use. Furstenberg, Shea, Allison, Herceg-Bacon, and Webb (1983) found that such negative attitudes toward sexuality as the anticipation of guilt and fears about what others might think, as well as concerns about the effects of contraception on pleasure and intimacy and ambivalence regarding contraceptive effectiveness, lead adolescents away from learning about or using contraceptives. Other studies have corroborated these findings (DePietro & Allen, 1984; Gilchrist & Schinke, 1983; Schinke, Blythe, Gilchrist, & Burt, 1981).

As a result, many professionals have promoted the importance of educating adolescents and reducing their negative attitudes. Conceptually, the idea is that if accurate information about sex and sexuality is provided, there will be a concomitant change in attitudes and behavior. Therefore, increasing knowledge will reduce the negative consequences of adolescent sexuality, including pregnancy and sexually transmitted diseases. Not surprisingly, however, research on the impact of sex education programs has been equivocal. Although it is easy to document an increase in knowledge, it is more difficult to document behavioral change. It is important to note that, contrary to initial concerns, sex education does not seem to promote or increase sexual behavior (Furstenberg, Moore, & Peterson, 1986). There are mixed results, though, regarding the impact of these programs on such factors as delaying onset of intercourse or contraceptive use.

Although sex education programs can occur virtually anywhere (e.g., home, church), the majority of programs are implemented in schools (Brooks-Gunn & Furstenberg, 1989). Schools offer the unique opportunity to reach all youngsters in a particular vicinity. The advent of school-based health clinics has served further to intensify educational efforts in the schools (Dryfoos, 1985). Medical and mental health staff are readily available to develop and implement pregnancy prevention programs. Perhaps the best-known educationally based school program has been documented by Edwards, Steinman, Arnold, and Hakanson (1980). Fertility rates in their St. Paul, Minnesota, sample dropped from 79 to 26 per 1,000 between 1973 and 1984. In addition, the proportion of dropouts for teenage girls with babies decreased from 45% to 10%, and more than 80% of the participants reported continued use of contraceptives after a 2-year interval between pre- and posttest.

Another innovative program has been evaluated recently by Zabin, Hirsch, Smith, Streett, and Hardy (1986). This educationally based program was implemented outside of Baltimore, Maryland, with a predominantly black inner-city population. Although similar in scope to the St. Paul, Minnesota, project, several important distinctions have been noted. First, the populations were quite disparate. The Baltimore sample included junior and senior high students, whereas the St. Paul sample contained only senior high students. In addition, the Baltimore project included more students from low SES families and reportedly had a greater proportion of sexually active students as compared to the St. Paul sample (Zabin et al., 1986). Second, contraceptives were supplied by the same staff and at the same location as other clinical services because the Baltimore clinic was located off school grounds. School-based clinics, such as the one developed in St. Paul, are often unable to dispense contraceptives because of legal restraints. For example, in the two school-based health clinics that we administrate, political and social pressures necessitated a specific disclaimer about services involving sexual behavior: The clinics cannot prescribe or dispense birth control products, nor make referrals for abortions. If this statement were not included, we suspect that the city and the board of education may have rejected the clinics. This constraint, however, was not required of the Baltimore project.

A third program distinction was that the Baltimore project was not designed to be a comprehensive health service facility. Rather, the clinic was only open after school hours and offered limited medical interventions. The primary project goal was to open an educational and counseling service with an adjunct medical component. A social worker and a nurse practitioner (or nurse midwife) were available to assist in classroom presentations, to counsel individuals or small groups, and to provide limited health care. Finally, this project differed substantially from other pregnancy prevention efforts because of the research component. As a condition of service, all students must complete a comprehensive questionnaire, and these data serve as a baseline from which to evaluate program effectiveness. Thus far, results from this project are extremely encouraging. Clinic utilization rates have increased dramatically, and contraceptive use also has increased. Longitudinal data (i.e., pregnancy rates, fertility, abortion) have not been evaluated systematically as yet; however, initial results indicate increased knowledge about sexuality and reproduction and more conservative attitudes toward sexual behavior (Zabin et al., 1986).

Another school-based pregnancy prevention program was conducted by Herz, Reis, and Barbera-Stein (1986). These researchers compared the impact of three variations of family life education programs for 172 junior high students. The study was conducted in an economically disadvantaged inner-city neighborhood in Chicago, and all three programs were implemented in one of three participating schools. The three education programs were varied by their intensity, instructional methods, and teacher quality, and program effectiveness was compared along the dimensions of knowledge and attitude change. Male and female social workers and nurses from a neighborhood health agency co-taught the curriculum, and a standardized instructional package provided the foundation for the programs (Herz et al., 1986; Wilson & Kirby, 1984). In program I, didactic instruction was augmented by role playing, values clarification, and discussions of personal responsibility and decision making. In programs II and III, the majority of time was spent in didactic instruction. Programs II and III differed in that program II was held during the school day, and program III was held after school. Not surprisingly, attendance in the after-school program became problematic. Although the attendance rate averaged 95% for program II, attendance for program III averaged only 46%.

The conclusions drawn from this project clearly indicated that the more intensive the program, the better the results. Participants in program I made greater gains in knowledge about contraception, reproductive physiology, and the consequences of teen pregnancy and parenthood when compared to the other groups. In addition, students in program I learned more birth control methods than those in the other two groups. Further, participants in program I tended to take more responsibility for contraceptive behavior and were less willing to engage in sexual intercourse. These findings have led some to suggest that education alone does not reduce the rates of teen pregnancy. In fact, although education may be a necessary component in pregnancy prevention programs, it may not be sufficient to bring the changes needed to prevent unwanted teen pregnancies. Rather, as Herz et al. (1986) found, pregnancy prevention efforts must be more comprehensive in their approach and take a broader perspective if they are to be successful.

Another more recent development in educationally based programs has been the inclusion of teenage males. Most investigations and programs have preferred to focus on young women, and less attention has been given to young men (Furstenberg et al., 1989). Despite this, Brooks-Gunn and Furstenberg (1989) indicate that 40% of girls rely on "male methods" of contraceptive behavior (i.e., condoms, coitus interruptus). Very little descriptive research has been done, however, regarding boys' knowledge or attitudes about contraceptive use. Boys traditionally know very little about reproduction, menstrual cycles and contraceptive methods, and by ignoring the needs of the teenage male, preventionists neglect a key component in pregnancy prevention efforts (Watson & Kelly, 1989).

Watson and Kelly (1989) state that this is irresponsible: "When one realizes that a male teenager can impregnate a different female every few hours, seven days a week, it is not wise to leave him unattended any longer" (p. 454). These researchers have called for an increase in preventive services for adolescent males and have developed the Young Men's Sexuality Awareness Program in Norfolk, Virginia. This program was set up originally as a teenage fathers' support group, but the scope has been expanded to male adolescents who are at risk of becoming fathers. The group meets biweekly for ten 90-minute sessions; topics covered include reproduction, values clarification, dating and communication, sexually transmitted diseases and AIDS, and contraception. To hold the attention of the participants, audiovisual presentations are used, and specific instruction is given on the proper use and care of condoms. The authors also provide several suggestions for program developers interested in reaching the male adolescent. First, topics must be timely and eye-catching, such as "getting the most out of relationships" or "the ABCs of dating." In addition, incentives such as refreshments and field trips are important to enhance participation. Finally, choosing locations that normally are frequented by male adolescents (e.g., recreational centers, boys' clubs and the YMCA) is recommended. According to Watson and Kelly (1989), these facilities are geared to reach out to youth and act as a natural location compared to a classroom setting. Of course, as found in the Herz et al. (1986) study, after-school or outreach programs may be confounded by attendance difficulties. Watson and Kelly (1989), however, prefer this mode of intervention over classroom activities.

The unfortunate reality is that sex education programs for adolescents have not met with consistent results. In their review of teen contraceptive compliance, Beck and Davies (1987) report that most programs increase sexual knowledge, but few are notable in their effects on other outcome variables (e.g., increased use of contraception, reduced rates of pregnancy). In addition, programs designed to promote sexual abstinence (i.e., saying no to sexual activity) have not demonstrated success in reducing high-risk behaviors in teenagers (Christopher & Roosa, 1990; Jorgensen, 1991). As a result of the equivocal evidence, some researchers have argued for the need to augment educationally based programs. Specifically, programs that include skill enhancement and competency promotion have been suggested.

COMPETENCY PROMOTION

Competency enhancement and skill training have received increasing interest and support in the field of mental health and are cited frequently as an approach to primary prevention (Durlak,

1983; Felner, Jason, Moritsugu, & Farber, 1983; Gullotta, 1987). Teaching problem-solving skills (e.g., consequential thinking, goal-directed behaviors, and effective interpersonal functioning) is thought to enable an individual to cope with stress and to adapt successfully to different environmental circumstances (Spivack & Shure, 1979; Weissberg & Elias, 1991). Using this conceptual framework, the idea is that teenagers can do nothing with the information they acquire if they do not possess adequate skills and behavioral repertoires (Schinke et al., 1981). Similarly, adolescents must also be prepared developmentally to assimilate the knowledge (D. E. Gordon, 1990; Proctor, 1986; Romig & Bakken, 1990). Teenagers must be capable of comprehending and evaluating the consequences of their actions, be assertive in communicating their needs and beliefs, and feel competent regarding their feelings and themselves. Thus, even if a teenager has knowledge, she or he may still cause an unwanted pregnancy because she or he failed to think through a behavioral decision, or because she or he could not emit the behavioral responses necessary for avoidance.

Conceptualizing adolescent pregnancy in this manner has given rise to cognitive-behavioral skills training programs. Gilchrist and Schinke (1983) and Schinke (1984) report on several competency-based pregnancy prevention efforts. These programs do present information on birth control, but the main focus is on decision making, interpersonal communication, and assertiveness training. A specific example of this type of preventive intervention can be found in Schinke et al. (1981). These researchers provided pregnancy prevention programs to 83 urban vocational school students. An experimental, posttest-only control group design was used to evaluate effectiveness. Small groups were assigned ($N < 8$), and a curriculum was developed that included sessions for sex education lectures and problem solving. Longitudinal data (6-, 9-, and 12-month follow-up) revealed that the treatment groups had higher self-reported contraceptive compliance than control groups. Significant effects also were found regarding improved communication and more favorable attitudes toward sexuality. Interestingly, although Schinke et al. (1981) believed this last finding to be important in developing responsible sexual behaviors, others have not felt the same way. In fact, many believe that more favorable attitudes about sexuality lead to increased sexual behavior (Reppucci, 1987). As will be discussed in a subsequent section, however, acceptance of one's sexuality may be an important precursor to effective contraceptive use.

The empirically based support for competency enhancement programs has led to a variety of program refinements and improvements (Beck & Davies, 1987). One such modification was developed and studied by Jay, DuRant, Shoffitt, Linder, and Litt (1984). These researchers were interested in the effects when peer counselors are used as part of a competency-based intervention procedure. It was believed that competency would be enhanced by incorporating peer role models, because the intervention would become more meaningful. Participants were females aged 14 to 19 and came from a low SES minority background. Random assignment to experimental groups was performed, and sessions were held at a hospital clinic. Of particular interest was the use of urine testing to determine oral contraceptive compliance; this objective measure served to eliminate previous methodological criticisms levied against self-report data. Results of this study indicated that adolescents counseled by peers had significantly higher contraceptive compliance rates at 1- and 2-month follow-ups. These same adolescents also demonstrated a lower attrition rate compared to nurse-led groups. The inclusion of positive peer role models thus may hold promise for future pregnancy prevention efforts.

A more recent advance for competency-based preventive interventions has been offered by Danish (1991). In response to the positive findings associated with the use of peer role models, Danish and his associates have developed a primary prevention curriculum for the Richmond, Virginia, public school system that is based on peer mentoring and is designed to increase positive goal-directed behaviors. Specifically set up for seventh-grade students, participants are taught the steps toward reaching goals and the importance of avoiding obstacles that may interfere with goal attainment (e.g., drug use, unsafe sexual behavior). The focus is on helping the adolescent learn what to say yes to rather than simply teaching them to say no. Several programs have been developed and implemented during the past 4 years, and all are covered under the rubric of "Going for the Goal." In essence, the "Going for the Goal" projects are a collection of activities designed to promote healthy behaviors and functioning and to reduce the potential for negative outcomes, such as an unwanted pregnancy.

One such activity that is particularly germane to this chapter is the ACT program. ACT (for Athletes Coaching Teens) is a peer mentoring program in which athletes act as group leaders and facilitators (Danish, Howard, & Farrell, 1991). Peer mentors are chosen by their schools based on demonstrated accomplishment and leadership ability. Although originally intended to target athletes as mentors, the program has been expanded to allow any student the opportunity to become a peer leader.

Once selected, peer leaders receive intensive training in communication, teaching performance, and leadership. They also learn the "Going for the Goal" curriculum that was developed to increase social competency and goal-directed behavior. The curriculum is broken into seven 45-minute workshops; role playing, discussion, and activities provide the learning environment. In the first session, entitled "Dare to Dream," participants discuss the importance of dreams and the need to dream about the future. Session two, "Setting Goals," teaches the characteristics of a reachable goal and emphasizes the need to set goals that are important and salient. Sessions three, four, and five ("Making a Goal Ladder," "Roadblocks to Reaching Goals," and "Overcoming Roadblocks") deal specifically with procedures toward goal attainment. Teen pregnancy is brought up in session four as a significant roadblock toward reaching a goal, and a problem-solving strategy called STAR is taught in session five. STAR is an acronym that reminds participants to "Stop and chill out," "Think of choices," "Anticipate the consequences of choices," and "Respond with the best choice." Session six, "Rebounds and Rewards," teaches participants how to rebound from temporary setbacks and how to develop rewards when they experience accomplishment. The final session, "Putting Your ACT Together," integrates and applies the information to issues brought up in previous sessions. Danish (1991) indicated that more than 680 students from five different schools have participated in the ACT program, and more than 110 peer leaders have been selected and trained. Initial results indicate that the students who participated in the project showed significantly more positive expectations for their futures, higher self-esteem, more knowledge of problem solving, greater use of restraint and control in their behavior, and less personal distress compared to control groups. Danish, Howard, and Farrell (1991), however, are skeptical of short-term impact data. Though the initial results are promising, evaluation involving a longitudinal component will be necessary prior to any definitive conclusions. The researchers conclude, however, that the inclusion of competency enhancement activities may be an important element in pregnancy prevention efforts.

COMMUNITY ORGANIZATION
AND SYSTEMS INTERVENTION

Although the preponderance of pregnancy prevention efforts have been sex education programs and, to a lesser extent, competency-based programs, some professionals have considered these techniques restrictive and myopic (Allen, Philliber, & Hoggson, 1990; Reppucci, 1987; Reppucci, Mulvey, & Kastner, 1983). Reppucci (1987), for example, writes that an individually based approach neglects the environmental and social ecological factors that influence adolescent decision making about sexual behavior. In other words, the broader community and systems organization must be examined to address the issue of unwanted adolescent pregnancy.

Many authors have speculated that society has offered mixed messages to today's teenager (Brooks-Gunn & Furstenberg, 1989; Reppucci, 1987; Reppucci et al., 1983; Vincent & Trickett, 1983). On the one hand, sexuality is exploited flagrantly in the media; Americans are bombarded constantly by advertisements and entertainment that is designed to titillate and excite. On the other hand, adults and other authority figures disapprove of sexual activity for teenagers. An excellent example of this double bind comes from the three major television networks. Although sexual behavior is commonplace in many of today's shows, all three networks continue to reject advertisements from condom manufacturers and do not allow public service announcements that mention condoms unless the latter are linked directly to disease prevention rather than pregnancy prevention (Brooks-Gunn & Furstenberg, 1989). During the writing of this chapter, the Fox network put out a press release stating that they would begin to accept advertisements from condom manufacturers; however, these advertisements must be related to disease prevention rather than contraception (Melanie Gerig, Fox Network, personal communication, January 9, 1992).

These contradictory messages create conflicts about sexual morality and behavior. Reppucci (1987) states, however, that the guilt, fear, and confusion caused by the societally imposed moral dilemma is not intense enough to prevent adolescent sexual activity. Rather, according to Reppucci (1987), it prevents contraceptive use because it prevents adolescents from accepting their sexuality. Therefore, Reppucci (1987) calls for a societal focus for pregnancy prevention efforts. In particular, societal acceptance of sexuality is viewed as paramount to adolescent contraceptive use (Fox & Inazu, 1980; Reppucci et al., 1983). The idea is that societal acceptance of teenage sexuality, and the concomitant acceptance by community, family, parents and peer systems, will facilitate the communication and support necessary to encourage sexual responsibility.

Much to the chagrin of ecological preventionists, the position of societal acceptance of teenage sexuality has not been well received. Proposing sexual acceptance often is associated with permission or the encouragement of sexual activity (Jorgensen, 1991; Reppucci, 1987). This moral objection precludes many from even discussing the issue of teenage pregnancy, much less agreeing that sexual acceptance should be encouraged in schools or churches. Thus ecological preventionists have been frustrated in their attempts to have an impact on societal attitudes and values, and there continues to be tremendous controversy about the sexual behavior of teenagers. Much of this controversy seems to stem from societal ambivalence about teenage sexuality (Jorgensen, 1991). On the one hand, social policymakers have recognized the importance of the issue by providing federal and state initiatives to support research on the antecedents and consequences of teenage pregnancy. On the other hand, as Jorgensen (see Chapter 5) indicates, this research has yet to translate into a comprehensive framework for prevention services. Society is simply unwilling to acknowledge and accept teenage sexuality. A recent example of this is the 1991 decision made by Department of Health and Human Services Secretary Louis Sullivan in which he canceled federal funding for a national survey of teenage sexual behavior. Leukefeld and Haverkos (see Chapter 7) believe that the controversy regarding the sexuality of teenagers provided the impetus for this decision.

Despite continued controversy and ambivalence, advocates for societal acceptance of adolescent sexuality remain steadfast in their beliefs. Teenage pregnancy prevention committees have been established across the nation, sex education (and, in some cases, decision-making and relationship) classes have been instituted in many school systems, and the energies of key politicians have been marshaled to bring the message to the country. Society must remember that today's teenager is tomorrow's taxpayer, and by acknowledging and accepting their needs and issues, in the words of Thomas H. Kean (1989), governor of New Jersey, "The life you save may be your own" (p. 828).

NATURAL CAREGIVING

The concept of natural caregiving stems from the theory that many of today's problems can be prevented via social support and family networks (Gullotta, 1987; Heller & Swindle, 1983). One's own (i.e., natural) interpersonal resources can provide empowerment, emotional strength, and the ability to solve problems successfully (Gullotta & Adams, 1982). Although peer support or leadership can be considered a form of natural caregiving, pregnancy prevention efforts that incorporate a peer-based model have been interested primarily in skill enhancement (see the earlier section on competency). Research on the role of family involvement in promoting adolescent sexual responsibility is sorely lacking.

Of the few studies that have investigated the relationship between family involvement and contraceptive use, the conclusions drawn are quite promising. In a study of mother-daughter relationships, Kastner (1984), using a sample of 237 females (ages 15-19), found no correlation between increased communication and increased sexual activity, whereas increased communication did correlate highly with contraceptive use. In a more recent study, Casper (1990) obtained similar results. Using data from the 1982 National Survey of Family Growth, logistic regression procedures revealed that positive family interactions can be a beneficial influence for adolescent contraceptive use. These findings suggest that parental acceptance of teenagers' sexuality does enhance sexual responsibility, and many professionals contend that similar acceptance and openness in schools, churches, and communities may lead to impressive results. Unfortunately, there continues to be a dearth of research on the role of natural caregiving in promoting sexual responsibility.

CONCLUSIONS

Unfortunately, the current state of affairs for teenage pregnancy prevention initiatives is poor. Although two of prevention's tools (education and competency) have received some attention, the other two (community/systems intervention and natural caregiving) have yet to be developed, much less adequately researched. Unfortunately, one tool alone cannot build the bridge toward sexual responsibility. The assumption that increases in knowledge and changes in attitude will lead to desired behavior change (i.e., responsible sexual behavior) has been challenged, and the long-term impact of these types of prevention programs is questionable (Beck & Davies, 1987; Brooks-Gunn & Furstenberg, 1989; Herz et al., 1986). In addition, although there are a smattering of well-designed and effective programs, they barely scratch the surface of the problem. National statistics for the prevalence of teenage pregnancy, for example, have remained relatively constant (Furstenberg et al., 1989). In addition, program evaluation efforts are in their infancy, and there is widespread reluctance to attempt novel experimental and program ideas. How, therefore, can sexual responsibility be promoted unless all of prevention's tools are incorporated?

Societal reluctance to confront the moral issue of teenage pregnancy has created a fragmented system of preventive efforts with no cohesive or unifying framework. Whereas some communities support pregnancy prevention initiatives, others do not. In addition, although federal politicians pay lip service to the need for teenage pregnancy prevention, the national commitment is questionable, and there are yet to be large-scale efforts to affect teenage pregnancy.

Current research suggests that interventions designed to target such broad-based adolescent concerns as problem-solving ability and goal-directed behaviors hold merit in the attempt to reduce unwanted teen pregnancy. Researchers adhering to this approach contend that teens develop a greater sense of motivation and an increased ability to plan for the future, which in turn lead to more responsible sexual behavior. If one's goals, for example, are to lose weight, to make the track team, and to attend college, unwanted teenage pregnancy is an incompatible behavior.

What is becoming increasingly clear is that there is a tremendous need to develop a comprehensive and cohesive framework for teenage pregnancy prevention efforts. Morrison (1985) writes that the literature on adolescent pregnancy is large and diverse. Though this offers a program developer or researcher substantial information regarding the topic, this also has created a disjointed and disorganized body of information that serves to confuse the real issues. Studies often use different samples, different measurement techniques, different constructs, and different evaluation criteria. Therefore, few generalizations can be drawn. Thus, despite the millions of public and private dollars being spent to reduce the negative consequences of teenage pregnancy, there continue to be questions about what works, for whom, and under what circumstances.

Fortunately, there are recent efforts to rectify this problem. In an article sponsored by the Children's Defense Fund, Philliber (1989) reports on the development of a national network for teenage pregnancy prevention efforts. National/Net has been in operation since July 1989 and is managed by the California-based Social Research Applications. This nonprofit organization provides technical assistance on three levels. The first level is simply their no-cost willingness to examine any teenage pregnancy prevention program that is in the planning stage. National/Net will review the intervention model and research design, and can supply prototypes of data collection instruments. The second level of assistance is for a subgroup of specifically selected projects; these selected projects can receive, at no cost, a complete impact evaluation, including site visits and data analysis. Finally, on a limited basis, National/Net also will provide reviews of ongoing pregnancy prevention programs. Program developers wishing to receive more information about Social Research Applications can write to the organization at 170 State Street, Suite 280, Los Altos, CA 94022-2812, or call (415) 949-3282.

Of additional interest is that the first state-based network for the coordination of teenage pregnancy prevention programs has also been developed. Tex/Net began in June 1989 and is designed to standardize and assist with evaluation plans. This project operates in collaboration with the University of Texas School of Public Health in Houston and is also available to provide technical assistance to other states wishing to implement this type of system.

The standardization of program evaluation procedures is viewed as a crucial step toward the development of a national policy regarding teenage pregnancy prevention initiatives (Card, Reagan, &

Ritter, 1988; Hayes, 1987; Kirby, 1984; Philliber, 1989; Zabin & Hirsch, 1988). Philliber (1989) discusses three critical areas of program evaluation, the first of which is the needs assessment. Detailing a population at risk or identifying specific target issues (e.g., dropouts caused by teenage pregnancy) will provide guidance for the development of prevention efforts. More specifically, the needs assessment will articulate what a program should be designed to do, and answering this question will assist in the development of intervention procedures. A thorough needs assessment can also provide information regarding clients' accessibility to a program and potential program formats.

The second critical area is process evaluation. Once a decision is made regarding target population and preventive intervention, this evaluation serves to determine if the program is being implemented appropriately. Is the curriculum being followed? Are participants attending? Are the procedures being implemented correctly? These questions must be answered if projects are to be standardized and replicated.

Third, outcome data must be analyzed to determine the preventive impact of the intervention. The data used to evaluate program effectiveness should be guided by the goals and objectives of the project. As was discussed previously, most programs evaluate changes in knowledge or attitudes. Changes connected to the goals are believed to reduce unwanted teenage pregnancy. Given the equivocal findings, however, future programs must expand the scope of outcome research. In particular, direct questions and observations must be used to determine if the program changed the age of first intercourse or the frequency of intercourse. Did the program increase contraceptive use and, if so, for how long? Did the program improve emotional functioning or decision-making ability? Did the program alter the rates of teenage pregnancy? Answers to these questions will provide information about which types of programs are maximally effective for which type of population and provide the foundation and impetus to develop a national agenda for the prevention of teenage pregnancy. Finally, hit-or-miss prevention programs have been shown repeatedly to have poor long-term outcomes. A comprehensive approach that incorporates all of prevention's tools is clearly needed.

REFERENCES

Alan Guttmacher Institute. (1981). *Teenage pregnancy: The problem that hasn't gone away.* New York: Author.

Allen, J. P., Philliber, S., & Hoggson, N. (1990). School-based prevention of teenage pregnancy and school dropout: Process evaluation of the national replication of the Teen Outreach Program. *American Journal of Community Psychology, 18*(4), 505-525.

Beck, J. G., & Davies, D. K. (1987). Teen contraception: A review of perspectives on compliance. *Archives of Sexual Behavior, 16*(4), 337-368.

Brooks-Gunn, J., & Furstenberg, F. F. (1989). Adolescent sexual behavior. *American Psychologist, 44*(2), 249-257.

Burt, M. R. (1986). Estimating the public costs of teenage childbearing. *Family Planning Perspectives, 18,* 221-226.

Campbell, A. A. (1968). The role of family planning in the reduction of poverty. *Journal of Marriage and the Family, 30*(2), 236-245.

Card, J. J., Reagan, R. T., & Ritter, P. E. (1988). *Sourcebook of comparison data for evaluating adolescent pregnancy and parenting programs.* Los Altos, CA: Sociometrics.

Casper, L. M. (1990). Does family interaction prevent adolescent pregnancy? *Family Planning Perspectives, 22*(3), 109-114.

Cates, W., Jr., & Rauh, J. L. (1985). Adolescents and sexually transmitted diseases: An expanding problem. *Journal of Adolescent Health Care, 6,* 1-5.

Christopher, F., & Roosa, M. (1990). An evaluation of an adolescent pregnancy prevention program: Is "just say no" enough? *Family Relations, 39,* 68-72.

Curran, J. W., Jaffe, H. W., Hardy, A. M., Morgan, W. M., Selik, R. M., & Dondero, T. J. (1988). Epidemiology of HIV infection and AIDS in the United States. *Science, 239,* 610-616.

Cvetkovich, G., & Grote, B. (1983). Adolescent development and teenage fertility. In D. Byrne & W. A. Fisher (Eds.), *Adolescents, sex and contraception.* Hillsdale, NJ: Lawrence Erlbaum.

Danish, S. J. (1991, June). *Go for the goal: A school-based prevention program.* Institute presented at the Biennial Hartman Conference on Children and their Families, New London, CT.

Danish, S. J., Howard, C. W., & Farrell, A. D. (1991). *Going for the Goal projects.* Richmond:Virginia Commonwealth University.

DeAmicus, L. A., Klorman, R., Hess, D. W., & McAnarney, E. R. (1981). A comparison of unwed pregnant teenagers and nulligravid sexually active adolescents seeking contraception. *Adolescence, 16,* 11-20.

DePietro, R., & Allen, R. (1984). Adolescents' communication styles and learning about birth control. *Adolescence, 19,* 827-839.

Dryfoos, J. (1985). School-based clinics: A new approach to preventing adolescent pregnancy. *Family Planning Perspectives, 17,* 70-75.

Durlak, J. (1983). Social problem-solving as a primary prevention strategy. In R. D. Felner, L. A. Jason, J. N. Moritsugu, & S. Farber (Eds.), *Preventive psychology: Theory, research, and practice.* Elmsford, NY: Pergamon.

Edwards, L., Steinman, M., Arnold, K., & Hakanson, E. (1980). Adolescent pregnancy prevention services in high school clinics. *Family Planning Perspectives, 12,* 6-14.

Evans, J. R., Selstad, G., & Welcher, W. H. (1976). Teenagers: Fertility control behavior and attitudes before and after abortion, childbearing or negative pregnancy test. *Family Planning Perspectives, 8,* 192-200.

Felner, R. D., Jason, L. A., Moritsugu, J. N., & Farber, S. (1983). *Preventive psychology: Theory, research and treatment.* Elmsford, NY: Pergamon.

Fielding, J. E. (1978). Adolescent pregnancy revisited. *New England Journal of Medicine, 299,* 893-896.

Flora, J. A., & Thoresen, C. E. (1988). Reducing the risk of AIDS in adolescents. *American Psychologist, 11,* 965-970.

Fox, G. L., & Inazu, J. K. (1980). Patterns and outcomes of mother-daughter communication about sexuality. *Journal of Social Issues, 36*(1), 17-30.

Freeman, E. W., Rickels, K., Mudd, E. B. H., & Huggins, G. R. (1982). Never-pregnant adolescents and family planning programs: Contraception, continuation and pregnancy risk. *American Journal of Public Health, 70,* 790-797.

Furstenberg, F. F. (1991). As the pendulum swings: Teenage childbearing and social concern. *Family Relations, 40,* 127-138.

Furstenberg, F. F., Brooks-Gunn, J., & Chase-Lansdale, L. (1989). Teenaged pregnancy and childbearing. *American Psychologist, 44*(2), 313-320.

Furstenberg, F. F., Moore, K. A., & Peterson, J. L. (1986). Sex education and sexual experience among adolescents. *American Journal of Public Health, 75,* 1221-1222.

Furstenberg, F. F., Shea, J., Allison, P., Herceg-Bacon, R., & Webb, D. (1983). Contraceptive continuation among adolescents attending family planning clinics. *Family Planning Perspectives, 15,* 211-217.

Gilchrist, L. D., & Schinke, S. P. (1983). Coping with contraception: Cognitive behavioral methods with adolescents. *Cognitive Therapy Research, 7,* 379-391.

Gordon, D. E. (1990). Formal operational thinking: The role of cognitive developmental processes in adolescent decision-making about pregnancy and contraception. *American Journal of Orthopsychiatry, 60*(3), 346-356.

Gordon, S. (1983). Politics of prevention and sex education. In G. Albee, S. Gordon, & H. Leitenberg (Eds.), *Promoting sexual responsibility and preventing sexual problems.* London: University Press of New England.

Gullotta, T. P. (1987). Prevention's technology. *Journal of Primary Prevention, 8*(1-2), 4-24.

Gullotta, T. P., & Adams, G. R. (1982). Substance abuse minimization: Conceptualizing prevention in adolescent and youth programs. *Journal of Youth and Adolescence, 11*(5), 409-424.

Hardy, J. B. (1987, July). Preventing adolescent pregnancy: Counseling teens and their parents. *Medical Aspects of Human Sexuality,* 32-46.

Hayes C. D. (1987). *Risking the future* (Vol. 1). Washington, DC: National Academy Press.

Heller, K., & Swindle, R. W. (1983). Social networks, perceived social support, and coping with stress. In R. D. Felner, L. A. Jason, J. N. Moritsugu, & S. Farber (Eds.), *Preventive psychology: Theory, research and treatment.* Elmsford, NY: Pergamon.

Herz, E. J., Reis, J. S., & Barbera-Stein, L. (1986). Family life education for young teens: An assessment of three interventions. *Health Education Quarterly, 13*(3), 201-221.

Jay, M. S., DuRant, R. H., Shoffitt, T., Linder, C. W., & Litt, I. F. (1984). Effect of peer counselors on adolescent compliance in use of oral contraceptives. *Pediatrics, 73,* 126-131.

Jones, E. F., Forrest, J. D., Goldman, N., Henshaw, S. K., Lincoln, R., Rosoff, J. I., Westoff, C. F., & Wulf, D. (1985). Teenage pregnancy in developed countries: Determinants and policy implications. *Family Planning Perspectives, 17*(2), 53-63.

Jorgensen, S. (1991). Project Taking Charge: An evaluation of an adolescent pregnancy prevention program. *Family Relations, 40.*

Kastner, L. S. (1984). Ecological factors predicting adolescent contraceptive use: Implications for intervention. *Journal of Adolescent Health Care, 5*(2), 79-86.

Kean, T. H. (1989). The life you save may be your own. *American Psychologist, 44*(5), 828-830.

Kirby, D. (1984). *Sex education: An evaluation of programs and their effectiveness.* Santa Cruz, CA: Network.

Lieberman, J. J. (1981). Locus of control as related to birth control knowledge, attitudes, and practices. *Adolescence, 16,* 1-10.

Miller, W. B. (1976). Sexual and contraceptive behavior in young, unmarried women. *Primary Care, 3,* 427-453.

Morrison, D. (1985). Adolescent contraceptive behavior: A review. *Psychological Bulletin, 98*(3), 538-568.

Nadeson, C. C., Notman, M. T., & Gillon, J. W. (1980). Sexual knowledge and attitude of adolescents: Relationship to contraceptive use. *Obstetrics and Gynecology, 5,* 340-345.

Onyehalu, A. S. (1983). Inadequacy of sex knowledge of adolescents: Implications for counselling and sex education. *Adolescence, 18,* 627-630.

Orr, M. (1982). Sex education and contraceptive education in United States public high schools. *Family Planning Perspectives, 14,* 304-313.

Oskamp, S., & Mindick, B. (1983). Personality and attitudinal barriers to contraception. In D. Byrne & W. A. Fisher (Eds.), *Adolescents, sex and contraception.* Hillsdale, NJ: Lawrence Erlbaum.

Philliber, S. (1989). *Evaluating your adolescent pregnancy program: How to get started.* Washington, DC: Children's Defense Fund.

Proctor, S. E. (1986). A developmental approach to pregnancy prevention with early adolescent females. *Journal of School Health, 56*(8), 313-316.

Reppucci, N. D. (1987). Prevention and ecology: Teenage pregnancy, child sexual abuse, and organized youth sports. *American Journal of Community Psychology, 15*(1), 1-22.

Reppucci, N. D., Mulvey, E. P., & Kastner, L. (1983). Prevention and interdisciplinary perspectives: A framework and case analysis. In R. D. Felner, L. A. Jason, J. N. Moritsugu, & S. Farber (Eds.), *Preventive psychology: Theory, research and treatment.* Elmsford, NY: Pergamon.

Romig, C. A., & Bakken, L. (1990). Teens at risk for pregnancy: The role of ego development and family processes. *Journal of Adolescence, 13,* 195-199.

Schinke, S. P. (1984). Preventing teenage pregnancy. *Programs of Behavior Modification, 16,* 31-64.

Schinke, S. P., Blythe, B. J., Gilchrist, L. D., & Burt, G. A. (1981). Primary prevention and adolescent pregnancy. *Social Work Groups, 4,* 121-135.

Spivack, G., & Shure, M. (1979). *The social adjustment of young children.* San Francisco: Jossey-Bass.

Stanford Research Institute International. (1979). *An analysis of government expenditures consequent on teenage childbirth.* Prepared for Population Resource Center, New York.

Vincent, T. A., & Trickett, E. J. (1983). Preventive interventions and the human context: Ecological approaches to environmental assessment. In R. D. Felner, L. A. Jason, J. N. Moritsugu, & S. Farber (Eds.), *Preventive psychology: Theory, research, and practice.* Elmsford, NY: Pergamon.

Vinovskis, M. (1988). *An "epidemic" of adolescent pregnancy? Some historical and policy considerations.* New York: Oxford University Press.

Watson, F. I., & Kelly, M. J. (1989). Targeting the at-risk male: A strategy for adolescent pregnancy prevention. *Journal of the National Medical Association, 81*(4), 453-456.

Weissberg, R. P., & Elias, M. (1991, June). *Two innovative social competency promotion programs for elementary-school and middle-school students.* Institute presented at the Biennial Hartman Conference on Children and their Families, New London, CT.

Westoff, C. F., Calot, G., & Foster, A. D. (1983). Teenage fertility in developed countries. *Family Planning Perspectives, 15,* 105-110.

Wilson, P., & Kirby, D. (1984). *Sexuality education: A curriculum for adolescents.* Santa Cruz, CA: Network.

Zabin, L. S., & Hirsch, M. B. (1988). *Evaluation of pregnancy programs in the school context.* Lexington, MA: Lexington Books.

Zabin, L. S., Hirsch, M. B., Smith, E. A., Streett, R., & Hardy, J. B. (1986). Adolescent pregnancy-prevention programs: A model for research and evaluation. *Journal of Adolescent Health Care, 7,* 77-87.

Zabin, L. S., Kantner, J., & Zelnik, M. (1979). The risk of adolescent pregnancy in the first six months of intercourse. *Family Planning Perspectives, 11,* 215-222.

Zelnik, M., & Kantner, J. F. (1977). Sexual and contraceptive experience of young unmarried women in the United States 1976 and 1971. *Family Planning Perspectives, 9,* 55-71.

Zelnik, M., & Kim, Y. J. (1982). Sex education and its association with teenage sexual activity, pregnancy and contraceptive use. *Family Planning Perspectives, 14*(3), 117-126.

Author Index

205

Subject Index

About the Editors

Thomas P. Gullotta is CEO of the Child and Family Agency in Connecticut. He currently is the editor of the *Journal of Primary Prevention*, serves as a general series book editor for *Advances in Adolescent Development*, and is the senior book series editor for *Issues in Children's and Families' Lives*. In addition, he serves on the editorial boards of the *Journal of Early Adolescence* and *Adolescence*, and is an adjunct faculty member in the psychology department of Eastern Connecticut State University. His 59 published works include 2 textbooks, 6 edited books, and numerous articles focusing on primary prevention and youth.

Gerald R. Adams is a Professor in the Department of Family Studies at the University of Guelph. He is a Fellow of the American Psychological Association and has been awarded the James D. Moran Research Award from the American Home Economics Association. Currently he has editorial assignments with the *Journal of Adolescence, Journal of Primary Prevention, Journal of Early Adolescence,* and *Social Psychology Quarterly*.

Raymond Montemayor is Associate Professor of Psychology at The Ohio State University. His research interests include parent-adolescent relations, conduct disorders, behavioral approaches to the study of adolescence, peer relations during adolescence, and adolescent substance abuse. He is Associate Editor for the *Journal of Early Adolescence* and is an editorial board member for the *Journal of Adolescent Research*.

About the Contributors

Gary M. Blau (Ph.D., clinical psychology) is currently the Director of Clinical Services at the Child and Family Agency of Southeastern Connecticut. Since receiving his degree in 1988, he has worked in children's mental health with a primary emphasis on victimized children, child custody and permanency planning, and emotional trauma. He joined the Child and Family Agency's staff as director of clinical services in 1990. He serves on the editorial board of the *Journal of Primary Prevention* and has published and presented in the areas of primary prevention, child custody, and family violence. He is also writing a chapter on clinical interventions for violent families.

Cynthia R. Christopherson is a Ph.D. candidate in the Department of Family and Human Development at Utah State University, where she received her M.S. degree in 1990. She is an active member of the National Council on Family Relations. Her interests include adolescent pregnancy issues and parent-child communication.

A. Chris Downs was Professor of Psychology at the University of Houston—Clear Lake. He received his bachelor's degree in psychology in 1973 from Indiana University at South Bend and his Ph.D. in 1978 from The University of Texas at Austin. Winner of many teaching awards and designated "Master Teacher" by the University of Houston, he has published extensively in the areas of physical attractiveness and sex-typed roles. A contributor to Volume 3 of this book series, he continues to write and publish in social and developmental psychology and currently works in the private sector.

Patricia Hyjer Dyk received her Ph.D. in family and human development from Utah State University. Currently, she is Assistant Professor of Sociology at the University of Kentucky with a research appointment in the Agricultural Experiment Station. She has published in *Journal of Youth and Adolescence, Journal of Adolescent Research, Journal of Family Issues,* and *Family Relations,* and has coauthored several book chapters on adolescent sexuality. Her research interests focus on adolescent development in the family and community context particularly with respect to sexuality, identity, and gender role socialization.

Harry W. Haverkos is a board-certified physician in internal medicine and is trained in infectious diseases and epidemiology. He has been researching AIDS since 1981. In 1988, he was awarded the Public Health Service (PHS) Commendation Medal for effective leadership in AIDS research associated with intravenous drug abuse. He is currently the Acting Director, Division of Clinical Research, and Associate Director for AIDS at National Institute on Drug Abuse (NIDA). He is also a consultant for the Division of Infectious Diseases at the Walter Reed Army Medical Center.

Marie C. Hendren is a graduate student at Wayne State University with a specialization in adolescent and family interventions. She is a student member of the American Psychological Association and the Society for Community Research and Action, and is a research assistant with the Detroit Teen Parent Project.

Lisa Scarborough Hillje holds a bachelor's degree in psychology from the University of Houston at Clear Lake. She served as chief supervisor of the university's Human Experimental Psychology laboratory from 1989 to 1991. She is currently engaged in graduate-level studies and in clinical psychology supervision in a drug and chemical abuse rehabilitation center. Upon completion of her graduate work, she plans to work as a clinician, primarily with adolescents. A parent of two daughters, she continues to focus her research interests on developmental competency issues among children and adolescents.

Stephen R. Jorgensen is Professor of Human Development and Family Studies at Texas Tech University in Lubbock. He holds a Ph.D. degree in family sociology granted by the University of Minnesota. His research interests focus on fertility-related behavior of those at risk of unintended or unwanted pregnancy, such as adolescents and economically depressed groups. He currently serves as an independent evaluation researcher for an adolescent pregnancy prevention program sponsored by the U.S. Office of Adolescent Pregnancy Programs.

Pamela K. King is a master's candidate at Utah State University. She received her B.S. in Theater Arts/Speech Communication with minors in Psychology and Spanish. Her current research interests are adolescent risk behaviors, including sexual behavior and motivations in relation to identity status. She plans to pursue a career in college teaching, and interventive and preventive programs working with youth and families.

Carl G. Leukefeld is Director of the Drug and Alcohol Abuse Research Center at the University of Kentucky. He received his doctorate at the Catholic University of America in 1975 and his master's degree at the University of Michigan. His current research interests include the use of judicial sanctions, drug abuse treatment, and the impact of HIV on the drug abuser. He has coedited eight books and is currently working on three: *Improving Drug Abuse Treatment, Treatment in Jails and Prisons* and *Frontiers of Cocaine Treatment.* He is an editor or consulting editor for four professional journals and has served as a consultant to various organizations, including the Council on Europe, World Health Organization, several European countries, U.S. Customs, U.S. Army, U.S. Navy, National Institute of Justice, National Institute of Corrections, and American Probation and Parole Association, as well as state and local agencies. He is the former Chief Health Services Officer of the United States Public Health Service and resides in Lexington, Kentucky, with his wife and three children.

Brent C. Miller is a Professor in the Department of Family and Human Development at Utah State University. He received his Ph.D. in Family Sociology from the University of Minnesota in 1975. He has been a member and chair of several national peer review and advisory panels for the National Institute of Child Health and Human Development and for the Office of Adolescent Pregnancy Programs. He has been the Publications Vice President and Program Chair for the National Council on Family Relations (NCFR), and in 1991-1992 he became President of NCFR. He publishes widely about marriage and family topics, and about adolescent pregnancy-related issues. His most recent coedited book is *Preventing Adolescent Pregnancy: Model Programs and Evaluations*.

Annette U. Rickel is Professor and Director of the Community Psychology Program at Wayne State University. She received her Ph.D. from the University of Michigan and is a fellow and past president of the American Psychological Association's Society for Community Research and Action. A recent American Council on Education fellow, she has published 3 books and more than 45 articles and chapters.

Richard G. Rodriguez is a doctoral student in clinical psychology at the University of Massachusetts, Amherst. His research interests include social stigma and self-devaluing processes, health psychology among social and ethnic minorities, and research in psychotherapy. He is currently working at the Gay and Lesbian Community Services Center in Los Angeles and is an intern in the counseling department.

Ritch C. Savin-Williams is Professor of Clinical Psychology and Human Development at Cornell University. He teaches courses on developmental and clinical issues among sexual minorities. His writings include two books, *Adolescence: An Ethological Perspective* and *Gay and Lesbian Youth: Expressions of Identity*, and numerous articles and book chapters. Most recently, his research focus has been on identity development among gay and bisexual male youths. He is currently writing two books: *First I Slept With a Girl, or Was It a Boy?* and, with Kenneth M. Cohen, *Our Silence Is Deadly: Clinical, Development, and Policy Issues Facing Lesbians, Gay Males, and Bisexuals*.